GLACIER

ON

KILIMANJARO

Studio of Books LLC
5900 Balcones Drive Suite 100
Austin, Texas 78731
www.studioofbooks.org
Hotline: (254) 800-1183

Ordering Information:
Special discounts are available on quantity purchases by corporations, associations, and others. For details, contact the publisher at the address above.

Printed in the United States of America.

ISBN-13: Softcover   978-1-964864-65-5
               Ebook   978-1-964864-66-2

Library of Congress Control Number: 2024919422

GLACIER
ON
KILIMANJARO

Memories

a circumnavigation of Africa
with the mission to reform
German East Africa
in a threatened pre-war world.

Prologue

WHY?

It is January 13 2024 and the world has learned nothing during the last 120 years:

Nothing from two world wars, countless regional wars, energy wars, resource wars. Nothing learned from countless treaties and agreements that were being signed, ignored, or superseded by new conflicts, by trade unions; European, Asia Pacific, North American and others. Agreements were made by superpowers, and kingdoms, the United Nations was formed and NGOs acted to aid during humanitarian crisies, as did doctors without borders.

Countries are still being experimented with: Nationalism, Socialism, Fascism, Dictatorships Autocracies, Communism, Globalism, and Democracies. Division by arbitrary boundaries, ignoring historical, ethnical, and religious borders and districts. Victors became dictators. Religious dictatorships and Theocracies became energized as terrorist organizations and ethnic minorities were ignored or suppressed.

It is the heritage of colonialism at the time monarchies and empires were beginning to crumble.

International influence was purchased and supported with arms deliveries granting dangerous minorities control over unarmed majorities, creating puppet regimes for resource control.

The result? Over one hundred million refugees are flooding the world, escaping wars, oppression, political, religious, economic, and natural disasters such as climate change. Destabilizing functioning communities.

On the other hand, we have solved all the problems and, given policy changes to support the interests of ordinary humans, could end hunger, build sustainable off-grid housing, end the use of fossil fuels, use hemp for fiber and resins to save biodiversity, forests, water, and wildlife. We can grow gardens instead of toxic lawns, fruit trees instead of ornamentals and graze sheep beneath community solar farms, we can put solar covers over open irrigation trenches to stop evaporation, plant bee gardens and support pollinators on the margins of highways, distill drinking water and a myriad of other measures, to reverse climate change. We can defund wars and take assault weapons from the hands of civilians and reduce mass shootings. We could outlaw wars and grant a legal right to life to all humans and to nature. We have the means. Do we have the will?

This book examines possibilities and differences and seeks answers to questions about the human existence on this planet.

Glacier on Kilimanjaro seeks answers and hope where choices can be made for the betterment of all of mankind. To give life in dignity to everyone and to turn despair into hope by removing humans from the human resource list, after distributing the wealth created by labor fairly, rather than moving 98 % of wealth to 2% of the population, failing communities, our elders and our children.

To take humans off the endangered species list and to save the planet is the reason, this book was written.

TABLE OF CONTENTS

Prologue WHY?. V

Chapter 1 The story tells the story 1

Chapter 2 Faith 7

Chapter 3 Escape 11

Chapter 4 Snow in Africa? 22

Chapter 5 Stefan's story 24

Chapter 6 Altitude 31

Chapter 7 First to ski a new line 33

Chapter 8 Gone missing 44

Chapter 9 The rescue 48

Chapter 11 Tell me more. 51

Chapter 12 Showdown 54

Chapter 13 The farm estate. 60

Chapter 14 Sailing 64

Chapter 15 Hope 73

Chapter 16 Waldeck estate 77

Chapter 17 Youth summit 83

Chapter 18 The pilot group 87

Chapter 19 Trust 91

Chapter 20 The Vision 94

Chapter 21 Facilitation 100

Chapter 22 Consensus 107

Chapter 23 Consent 114

Chapter 24 Closing the divide 116

Chapter 26 The assignment 128

Chapter 27 Good bye Germany,
hello World 134

Chapter 28 On board Stella Maris 138

Chapter 29 Stefan the other captain 146

Chapter 30 Towards Bordeaux 155

Chapter 31 God's pocket 161

Chapter 32 Life like "God in France" 166

Chapter 33 Casablanca 176

Chapter 34 Inside two storms 186

Chapter 35 Crossing the Mediterranean 196

Chapter 36 202

Chapter 37 World trade 212

Chapter 38 Civil war within a
national war within a religious war 223

Chapter 39 Twins 229

Chapter 40 Thessaloniki 239

Chapter 41 Melting Time 245

Chapter 42 Leaving Europe 253

Chapter 43 Land of Empires 267

Chapter 44 Chopping the world order 274

Chapter 45 Into the red sea 282

Chapter 46 Djibouti 286

Chapter 47 A new threat at sea 289

Chapter 49 After the attack 299

Chapter 50 Cyclone 310

Chapter 51 German East Africa 319

Chapter 52 Dar Es Salaam 323

Chapter 53 The dark side 335

Chapter 54 The search for social justice 344

Chapter 55 Dar Es Salaam to Dodoma 350

Chapter 56 Johann 356

Chapter 57 Dodoma 360

Chapter 58 Was this Africa? 364

Chapter 59 Stefan returns from the snow......372

Chapter 60 Hadza.......................378

Chapter 61 To Life.....................393

Chapter 62 Home.......................405

EPILOGUE.........................408

REACTIONARY FORCES
by Christian Vogel:....................410

Chapter 1

The story tells the story

"You said you are related to me? How?" She yelled into the telephone as if she were trying to make me hear her through the air. "Let me turn the news down so I can hear you."

I waited until I could hear her breathing again. Then I repeated: "I am the grandson of your sister Maria, son of your niece Sabine."

"Did you say you are one of Bienchen's boys?"

"Yes. I am the third child and the second son. I was hoping I could visit you to introduce myself. I am playing the French horn with the orchestra at the spa for the season."

"Do you need a place to stay?"

"No, but thank you. The orchestra set me up with a room."

"Are you the one who went to Africa? Remind me, what was your name again?

"Gottfried."

"What are you doing here in Germany, why did you come back?"
"That is a long story. I will tell it to you over tea. I called you to see if I could come to visit you."

"Of course, you can. When are you free?"

"Mondays and Wednesdays afternoons."

"Come on Wednesday at three. The Café does not open until five. We can have tea and talk. Gottfried, right?"

"Yes, aunt Joan, and I thank you. I see you Wednesday at three."

The house was located on a small rise overlooking a lake at the foothills of the Bavarian Alps. The s-curved gravel road was flanked by birch and beech trees in fresh brilliant green Spring foliage. It leads to the parking area of the Café and guest house Joan had been running with her husband Stefan.

Joan is the younger sister of Gottfried's grandmother Rose, who was very close to her as they grew up. For him, meeting Joan was very important and exciting. He was hoping for a chance, to learn about his grandmother Maria who had passed away seven years before he was born.

Her untimely death had left a void in everyone's life, that was impossible to fill.

"We lost our compass and anchor, when she left us," he was told.

In her diary Maria had written:

"I am spent, the vessel is empty, I gave all of myself and now I long to return to the spirit whence I came. "

Gottfried was excited to see 'wild Joan' again.

Two world wars, the loss of children and loved ones gave Joan a tough outer shell, that could be interpreted as impatience, abruptness, or lack of humor.

Life had taught her to never give in and to never give up.

Gottfried was eager to hear her tell him her story.

When he entered the house, the smell of coffee and pastries greeted him.

The lobby was welcoming with its muted colors of gold and brown, a small reception desk, complete with inkwell and brass bell, black telephone, writing pad with blotting paper in a leather-bound frame. Vases with branches and flowers were set on side tables next to large, comfortable leather chairs.

To the right was an open door into a large dining room, with picture windows allowing a view of the lake and the Alps beyond.

To the left was a hallway. Muted light came from an open door to a small den.

"Hello," Gottfried called out. The sound of a television set was coming from the den.

"Hello," he repeated, walking in the direction of the open door to the den. Curtains were drawn and brass floor lamps gave a warm light to this room.

A figure sitting in a dark brown leather chair picked up the remote control to mute the television.

This is the best button on this gadget," she said as she rose to greet him:

"Let me look at you. You are all grown up!" She exclaimed." Last I saw you, you were nine years old, playing a hunting signal for me on a horn, you had made from a garden hose and a kitchen funnel.

Come over here so I can see you."

She took him by the hand and led him into the bright light of the dining room.

She walked around him, brought both of her hands to his head, and kissed him on both cheeks. After a long look into his eyes, she said:

"I remember your smile. And your dark, curious eyes.

You look like Bienchen. We will get along fine.

Welcome to our home."

She left him to fetch coffee and pastries.

Returning with a loaded tray, she gestured with her head towards the hallway.

"Come into the den. We have a snack and talk.

It is comfortable there."

He followed her and sank deep into a large stuffed leather armchair.

His eyes adjusted to the soft light. Honey-colored wood paneling, beamed ceiling, and forest green draperies with a green red and gold oriental rug made him feel cozy and warm.

A coffee table was holding the television.

It was flanked by two low stools which he soon recognized to be made from feet of Elephants. Other artifacts made of ebony and teak reminded him of artwork he had seen in Africa.

After pouring coffee, Joan placed a plate with pastries before him. What caught his eye, was a tart with berries and streusel, soaked in her secret sauce. She was famous for this creation.

In a soft voice she said:

"I am worried about Bienchen. She works too hard without any real help, just like her mother Rose."

"We were worried also. She had pneumonia recently.

Papa is a doctor who thinks his own family stays well, because he orders it so.

Doctor's orders."

He chuckled.

"I am glad you are here, darling."

She got up and kissed him again on both cheeks and squeezed his hands. She was more affectionate than Bienchen. Both had a toughness about them, that he took as the result of a hard an unforgiving life.

Her affection surprised him. It made him feel good.

Her face was beautiful. Penetrating, inquisitive gray eyes, and a surprisingly smooth skin. Crow's foot wrinkles from smiling were making her eyes even more attractive.

She wore her hair in a messy bun.

"Tell me about grandmother. All I know about her are the celebrations she gave us: Table-and night time prayers, Solstice, Christmas, Easter, and St. Martin celebrations.

I think it was because of her, that the doors of our house were always open to visitors and to the occasional wanderer, who stopped by to ask for help, shelter, or food."

Joan closed her eyes and after some moments had passed, she spoke:

"Maria liked to quote this:

"When we step before our maker, we are not judged by what we believe, but by what we have done."

That was our Maria. The runaway Catholic.

It was this quote, which made her break with the church, after she discovered the stories about the holy Grail and the Round Table of King Arthur.

Reading this, gave her the spiritual tolerance, she became famous for."

Joan opened her eyes, then took another sip from her cup, holding it with both hands like a challis. She offered it to an imaginary person coming in from the hallway, as if it was Maria.

"I loved my big sister. I drove her crazy with my frivolous jokes and my disrespectful behavior, always taking risks, always climbing out to the end of every limb, until it began to break. It was me, she always had to rescue. It was her who always made me feel safe."

She put down her cup, paused for a long time and hugged herself across her chest with both arms. Then she took a deep breath and continued:

"When it came to the bottom line, she knew that I would never abandon her.

Her confidences were safer with me then with any priest. Maria stopped going to confession. She no longer partook in the holy sacrament."

"What happened, did she stop going to church?"

Both hands forward, palms up, Joan said:

"Oh no. Our family went to church every Sunday.

Not going to worship was not an option. We got all dressed up for mother's most important event of the week."

Chapter 2

◆

Faith

After gazing into the distance for a long time, she began:

Maria took with her a book that looked like a bible. After entering the church, she went to an area behind the altar, where the choir gathered for singers to put on robes. Instead of dressing up, she quietly slipped down a set of stairs to a crypt beneath the altar.

There, she held her own service. She could speak directly to God and say her prayers. This gave her solace. One Sunday, she opened the book she was holding: It contained ancient writings about the holy Grail. She found lessons, that changed her heart from being upset about priests and parents to being able to see, that God appears in different ways to different people.

This consoled her doubts about truth in the bible. She did not see how the words "God created man in his own image" could result in so many different looking people on Earth as she knew existed. It occurred to her, that man was the one who created God in his image. As many humans as there were, as many manifestations of God she now knew, existed.

This finally put to rest her concern about the fact, that many children in our town went to a Protestant school and worshipped in a different church than our family. She now saw, that God was neither Protestant nor Catholic. She began to understand, that God had many representatives on Earth, not just the Pope in Rome or Martin Luther in Wittenberg.

She realized that she did not have to choose between faiths. She now could tolerate all forms of religious practice.

And," Joan added with a little smile, "she no longer felt guilty for having a crush on one of the protestant boys, who teased her, but secretly adored her. She had found her heart to be responding with pounding. She shared this secret with me."

Joan took the empty cup from Gottfried's hand and put it back on the tray.

"Now, my dear, I must rest before my guests come. Will you come visit me for lunch at noon on Monday? I want to talk Africa."

Gottfried took a long walk along the shore of the lake, thinking about what Joan had told him. He thought about his family and how their religious life was influenced by grandmother's unique way of looking at spirituality. It explained, why he grew up free to attend any religious service.

He was learning things about his grandmother Maria and his family.

In his heart, Joan became his substitute grandmother.

Gottfried was eagerly waiting to hear her story about Africa.

The weather had turned to rain. The sound of raindrops created a staccato, loud enough to be a background sound to Gottfried's next visit. He saw only the foothills on the other side of the lake, like a black and white painting. The mountain peaks were shrouded in mist.

Joan led him to a table by the window overlooking the lake. She had laid out lunch for Gottfried and herself. He noticed that her mood seemed to match the rainy weather outside: Joan began:

"You probably did not know, that your uncle Stefan left this Earth last year."

She gazed over the lake, where heavy raindrops were jumping up as if the lake was snapping back at them.

After a while, she continued, her gray eyes looking dark and sad:

"I do not like to eat by myself any more. I miss him so." She said and paused.

"Too much loss for a lifetime."

"I am so sorry."

Gottfried took both her hands in his. Her grief made him shed tears. He felt her pain.

She murmured softly, as her left hand slowly swept the view:

" Who will cut the hole in the ice in the winter, so I can take my daily dip?

Who will eat my breakfast or my lunch?

Who will get mad at the foolish world?

Who will yell at the television when they break for commercials?

Who will tell me when politicians are lying?

Who will tell me what is opinion and what is fact?

Who will complain about today's youth?

Who will show me the first crocus in Spring?

Who will cut the roses for my table?"

She squared her shoulders, looking straight at Gottfried, she said:

"He had a difficult life. He suffered from Malaria ever since Africa. Terrible headaches, fever. He lost part of his toes to frost bite he suffered on the glacier."

She pointed at the food:

"This used to be his favorite lunch. Radishes chopped and salted, with sweet cream butter on freshly baked bread with soft brie cheese and slices of salami.

I always served it on a bed of lettuce with parsley and mint. I stopped making it for myself."

Looking again with her gray eyes at Gottfried she murmured.

"I am glad you came."

She poured more coffee into his mug.

Chapter 3

Escape

"Tell me about Afrika." Joan demanded. "How old are you now?"

"I am twenty. I was the 'thank God the war is over' baby."

This answer made her smile.

"Tell me more." She said, making herself comfortable, her eyes now gazing at the distant shore of the lake.

"I was eighteen when I went to join the symphony orchestra at Durban, South Africa.

I spoke almost no English. I had memorized three sentences: 'What do you call this? How do you pronounce that? And I need money.'

To learn English, I had a dictionary and a book: 'The Lost Tribe of the Kalahari' by South Africa's author Laurens Van Der Post. He had given me this copy of his book personally, during a book tour to Germany. I began by copying every word in long hand, thinking to teach my hand the mysterious spelling of English words. I left the book open on my desk to continue every chance I had. I wrote down every word and its translation, until I remembered them and my hand knew how to spell them, without my mind interfering. I asked people how to pronounce words. It became my conversation starter. Generously, people explained their language to me. Soon I began to understand more than just the translation of words. I began to get a feeling, for what they meant.

A girl in the front row of the concert hall, always occupying the same seat, got my attention. Our eyes met. After a while, I suspected that she kept coming to see me. Finally, I decided to approach her:

"I should introduce myself, so I do not look at you and you have a stranger greet you each time you come to listen to us. My name is Gottfried." I shook her hand. She smiled at me.

"I know who you are. My father's newspaper wrote a story about the new musicians in our orchestra. You were introduced with a picture as the youngest new musician. I am Julia."

"I am Gottfried" I repeated foolishly. "I did not know I was in the newspaper. Can you show it to me some time?"

We made an appointment for the following week at a cafe across the street from the concert hall. A lively conversation unfolded, consisting mostly of my asking, what everything was called and how to pronounce words I saw in print.

She was amused, happy to correct my attempts at speaking her language. We wanted to continue our conversation. Soon, she began taking me around town to meet her friends, go to cocktail parties, literary events, and gallery openings.

She was showing me off.

I tried my new words on her friends. Thanks to her help and my book The Lost Tribe of the Kalahari, my English made rapid progress. She made time for me, whenever I had a night off and on days, when there were no rehearsals.

She became my pronunciation coach and my social director. She was sweet and popular. Jokingly, she asked me:

"What would you pay, if I became your caretaker?"

"I would pay attention," I answered.

She even invited me to meet her family. Her father offered us his cream-colored Bentley, so I could take her on driving excursions down the coast.

She was very protective, warning me of many places I should never visit.

I had to conceal from her my discovery trips into areas, she had warned me about: Bantu, Zulu, Indian and Chinese markets and of course the harbor. All very dangerous for Whites in her mind.

I never told her about a Zulu dance competition, I had stumbled onto one day, walking along the shore.

It took place in the middle of a large field of beach grass near the ocean. I had been following a trail through the dunes, when I felt rhythms in the sandy soil underfoot. Approaching a clearing, I saw several dozens of Zulu dancers in full war attire, head dress, oval shields, spears, shin guards, adorned with white feathers and fluffy white fir.

The dancers moved in unison in beautiful, complicated, well-coordinated patterns.

I was spellbound. A chief saw me and waved me to come to sit with him. He explained, that this was a competition of Zulu war dances. They did not use their drums and their voices were muted, to avoid being detected.

I came away with admiration for their artistry, choreography, and talent.

I could not mention this to anyone. Especially not to Julia.

Earlier I had shocked her by buying a bicycle, to increase my range of discovery.

"A push- bike?!" She exclaimed. "Are you mad? Boys ride push-bikes."

I looked down on myself. "Last time I checked, I was a boy," I said. She did not think that was funny. I felt, that I had to choose what I could talk to her about and what not.

One early morning, I was mesmerized by the beautiful sound of singing from a multi voice chorus and drum rhythm, I could hear through my open hotel window.

Thinking, that this was an open-air music festival further uptown, I leaned out of my window to get a better look. I discovered, that this was a native road construction gang of about fourteen workers with pickaxes and shovels, digging a trench down the middle of Durban's main street.

They were singing harmony in twelve voices with a fore singer and chorus answering, progressing steadily, maintaining their rhythm with their pick axes and shovels, as the fore singer moved from last position to the front.

I admired their artistry and was sad, that I could not share this experience with anyone. Especially not with my friend Julia. This made me feel sad and lonely.

I appreciated seeing the world through Julia's eyes even though she was not impressed when I told her, that my African lift boy at the hotel spoke English, Afrikaans, Zulu, and Bantu fluently. People in the orchestra kept trying to convince me, that colored people were a genetically under-developed form of humans, closer to apes. They showed me as proof Bantustan, hillside developments of tiny huts, which their white masters had constructed for them, to keep them from living near whites.

This was also given as a reason why colored or mixed-race people could not be admitted to listen to our concerts, even though their own music, which I observed, was stunningly beautiful and performed in perfect harmony, pitch, and rhythm.

I was sad, that Julia and my difference of seeing the world had begun to slow the natural progression towards a more intimate relationship. I could not see the miracle needed, to bridge this gap. Instead, I was watching this divide grow.

Every attempt at explaining what I saw and how I felt about it, was frustrated, because of my lack of words and immediately blocked by her supremacist attitudes.

Her white South African views got in our way. She was a white princess, raised under Apartheid."

"That does not sound good what happened next?"

"This reached its climax, when I learned, that my esteemed colleagues from the orchestra found it perfectly sane, to go on safari to Namibia, with the expressed goal of hunting, shooting and murdering bushmen for sport. A very special safari, they called it.

"A camera-shoot?" I asked innocently.

"Oh no, we hunt and kill them with hunting rifles," was the casual reply from the very same people, I admired as musicians. They were talking about this very same amazing ancient tribe, featured, and described in the book on my desk, from which I was learning English. Curious about that tribe, I asked about the title of my book at the local library. Here I found out, that this book was banned, the author living in exile in London and possession of this book was punishable by imprisonment and expulsion from the Country.

My admiration for these amazing ancient humans in the Kalahari Desert coincided with my growing fondness for one of the daughters of this racist, murderous South African society."

"Did you get in trouble? You said you left your book open on your desk at your hotel."

"Fortunately, I did not. I knew now, that I was on the wrong side of the law. This could get me jailed or deported, if I were to be discovered by the authorities of Apartheid, who had hired me to play music for them. I quickly made book and all my notes disappear."

"What did you do?"

"I was beginning to have trouble breathing in the company of bushman murderers at my place of work. I did not want to play music or associate with them. I felt isolated and lonely. I needed to be cautious. I struggled not to give away my feelings. I began looking for a way out of Africa, because I knew, I could not stay there. "

"How did you get away?"

"I think my guardian Angel intervened. One day, a piano soloist from Brazil walked into my rehearsal studio at the town hall, where I was practicing the French horn sonata by Beethoven. After introducing himself as Jacques Klein, the soloist for the upcoming concert, he asked permission to play the piano part of the Sonata with me.

We enjoyed playing together. Then we talked. I mentioned, that I had relatives in his home town of Rio De Janeiro. He told me about his problem of getting vertigo when travelling on aircrafts. We met and played together a couple of times. I decided to offer him a solution for his upcoming ten country Europe concert tour:"

"What did you tell him?"

"I suggested that I could be his driver and assistant for his upcoming Europe concert tour, using my car in return for his paying part of my return flight back to Germany. This meant that he did not have to fly at all during his ten country Europe concert tour.

He liked my proposal and agreed to have my flight to Munich arranged by his impresario."

"They did not catch you?"

"Yes, they almost did. But I made a diversion."

"How did you do that?"

"One afternoon, we were going to a cafe with a group of musicians, in a mini-mall, next to the town hall. The travel agent, who was handling my flight, called out: "Mister Gottfried, could you come in for a moment?""

"Did they ask questions?"

"Oh yes. They asked and I told the truth, sort of."

"Sort of?"

"When they asked me, what the agent wanted, I told them that a ticket to Germany had been booked for me. Which was the truth. Then I improvised. I told them about mama's pneumonia and how we were concerned about her, being, that grandmother Maria had also died of pneumonia. I said, that a flight had been booked, so I could be with her one last time."

"How did the orchestra react?"

"They were very concerned and upset for me. The next morning, the town manager arranged a telephone call to Germany. I assumed, that the call would be recorded. I hoped, that I would reach mama personally, to avoid someone asking too many questions. As you know, mama is the master of subtext, after what happened to her family during the war."

"What do you mean?"

"Remember when the Nazis came and took grandfather's library right out of his parish house?"

"Yes, I remember. Did they not shut down his Christian Community church?"

"Yes, they did"

"How did this make her a master of subtext?"

"Mama and papa corresponded daily throughout the war. Not once did they mention the Nazi Regime. Everything was said in subtext, like "officials came to collect books from our library" rather than "the Nazis raided the sanctuary."

" I see. In Africa, did you reach her?"

"Yes. I was lucky, she picked up the phone herself. I went right for the pneumonia issue, how concerned we all were and how good she sounded. I asked her how she was feeling. "Better," she said. "The crisis is past and I am in recovery. You do not have to worry." I gave an exaggerated sigh of relief. "I do not have to come home?" I exclaimed. "We can cancel my flight?" "Yes, my child. It was very sweet of you and your brothers, but you can stay in Africa and continue with your orchestra."

I told her how much I loved her and how glad I was that the crisis was over. We hung up. Then I reported this to the orchestra. They applauded the good news."

"Then what happened?" Joan had moved to the edge of her chair.

"More luck was needed: The day before my departure and two days after this phone call, the orchestra was having a couple of days off. I moved with my belongings from my City Hotel to a small tourist hotel closer to the beach, where no one knew me.

There, I repacked and gave everything I could not take back with me, to the Boys, including my 'push' bike.

On the day of my departure, I took a taxi to the bus stop. I saw several of my colleagues standing there, waiting for someone. I suddenly could see my plan failing. I asked the cab driver to leave me off a block away.

I waited, until the airport bus pulled in. Passengers left the bus and were met by my fellow musicians. Everyone I knew, walked away. I was able to board the bus unnoticed.

Once on board the plane to Johannesburg, I began to breathe deeply. I had literally been holding my breath from the terminal to the plane. A fellow passenger looked at me and said:

"I hate flying too. Where are you headed?"

"Johannesburg." I answered and closed my eyes.

"Did you actually fly to Johannesburg?"

0"Yes. Before we flew to Europe, we were invited to spend the night at friends of Jaques Klein's at Johannesburg. They were living in a post war slab building. When they heard my story, they told us about their escape from Nazi Germany and how they had vowed, never to move again, once they found a place to live. Like me, they had been surprised by the Apartheid Regime in South Africa. The fact, that South Africa did not openly have Anti-Semitic sentiments, gave them some reassurance. They kept a very low profile where they lived, ever since: The apartment had a small ante-room with an exterior door. This was as far as anyone was permitted to enter, who wanted to deliver something or pick something up. A second entry door led into a hallway with an offset door to the living room. The view into this hallway did not give away the surprise that awaited us. We were led to the inner sanctum of this unassuming apartment.

Inside, we found the most exquisite collection of artifacts from all over the African Continent, gathered by our host, a trader, who had travelled extensively into every corner of Africa. We felt privileged, to be granted permission to see this awesome treasure. We never left the apartment until a car service picked us up for the airport the next day. We arrived twelve hours later in Lisbon, where we spent a couple of days sightseeing and eating amazingly delectable samples from the best chefs in the world. We then took planes in opposite directions, one to Rio de Janeiro in Brazil and one to München, Germany."

"Did you do the concert tour with Jacques Klein?"

"Yes. We did the ten-country tour later that year as planned. The pianist was so pleased with our road trip, that he offered to buy a Jaguar E-type for me to use, if I would reserve time to drive him on future concert tours. I had to decline. I had already signed on for the season with our orchestra here at Bad Wiessee."

"How did you feel about leaving Africa?"

"I was stunned and very sad. I punished myself for not investigating the regime of that country, before signing on. I had been given the normal tourist information and assurances by the conductor, who hired me, how 'European' and 'civilized' everything in South Africa was. He was right. It was European. More European than was good for Africa. More European and more civilized than what was good for me.

Walking away from the girl was hard, but there was a growing chasm, too wide to bridge."

"How did your French horn professor react?"

"I reported, that I had left Durban in protest. I told him, that for me, music was a gift to all of mankind and not an exclusive pleasure and amusement for white racists.

I told him, how worried I was about the future if my friends, who represent a mere two percent of the population in their country but try to control 99% of everything. I had left word with one of the new musicians, to tell the orchestra about the reason for my departure: My Protest against Apartheid and the killing of indiginous people for sport.

Chapter 4

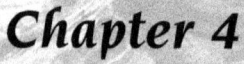

Snow in Africa?

The next time they met, Joan looked sad. She said to Gottfried with tears in her eyes:

"This is my favorite view of the Alps. It is why I wanted you to sit here with me today.

These snowcapped mountains remind me of my Stefan.

Right up to his last Winter with us, he gathered his little flock of skiers from the Alpine Club and headed up there, to teach Alpine skills and to enjoy racing down some of the steepest runs at breakneck speed, showing his students how it is done, besides telling them.

The competitive skier in him will live on in the stories he told. His eyes lit up whenever someone sat, to hear him tell of our Africa expedition."

A smile came through her tears as she rested her eyes on the reflection of the snow peaks in the lake.

"Snow? Snow in Africa?" Gottfried heard himself say.

"Yes, my darling, we found snow in Africa."

Joan and Gottfried saw each other throughout the Summer. He felt lucky, to spend many hours with her in conversation about her world, and about the way Joan, Maria and their friends wanted it to be. Joan talked about her concern about what was happening to the planet and Gottfried told her about his concern, regarding the job, his generation had to do, to set things right.

Joan was very animated, when she spoke about these early times. She went into great detail about her love for Stefan, for Gottfried's grandmother Maria and for their friends and partners Helena, Herbert and Wolf, who were part of this grand adventure into German East Africa.

"Tell me the story about snow in Africa." Gottfried begged.

Joan, gazing over the lake towards the Alps. She took a deep breath.

"When I first met Stefan, he was a sportsman and adventurer. He was all about competition, winning and record breaking, to show to himself and to the world that he was the best." Her thoughts drifted into her memory.

"I will recount his Kilimanjaro story in his words. As he told it to his skiing students countless times." She sat back and closed her eyes. Then she began to recall:

Chapter 5

Stefan's story

It was the end of the year 1912, when we arrived at Dodoma near the lake's region of Tanganyika. It was my second visit to German East Africa.

We were met by officials of the German East Africa Colonial Administration of Governor Albrecht von Rechenberg. They had orders to guide us on extensive tours of the region, assisted by interpreters, scientists and geologists, to explain, what we were seeing. We were free to choose anything we wanted to see.

Our task was to develop recommendations for reforms to the administration of the colony, to create a viable community and a commonwealth in a region, that was inhabited by a variety of people such as Jews, Muslims, Hindus, Christians, Atheists, and countless African tribes.

The German East Africa corporation had failed to produce expected profits, which forced Emperor, Kaiser Wilhelm the Second to take the Colony under a German protectorate. Governor Baron von Rechenberg, who served in this Colony from 1906 until 1912, was intrigued, when he heard of ideas, coming from our pilot group at the Waldeck estate Youth summit and ordered his development team to send us to East Africa, to show us the Colony in the hope, that taking a fresh look at possibilities and making suggestions for new policies, would be helpful in making the Colony successful this time.

As we approached the African Coast near Zanzibar and again, as we journeyed up into the plains-region towards Dodoma near Lake Tanganyika, we saw, sticking up from above the clouds, the peak of Mount Kilimanjaro. It was considered, to be the home of the Gods by many local tribes, a white cap, that could easily be mistaken to be lenticular clouds, or fog.

I knew, that the elongated summit of this enormous mountain was covered in snow.

We could not take our eyes off this wonder. We observed it from dawn to dusk in different light, until I had everyone convinced, that we were looking at a snow-covered mountain, right here, near the Equator in the East of Africa!

My first attempt to reach the summit with a survey team two years earlier had failed, due to inclement weather. I now had orders, to make a second attempt with our surveyors.

I had said nothing about my prior failed attempt to my companions, not to jinx my new summit bid. We talked about this mountain. We agreed that it was a Vulcanic mountain of gigantic proportions, that must have exploded at one point, leaving two separate peaks and a saddle in between. With extensive foothills surrounding its b

The geologist on our guide team was thinking, that this might be the highest free-standing mountain on Earth. It was now our job to explore and to survey Kilimanjaro.

I was once again to be part of that expedition. Our first attempt had been frustrated by dense fog. We had to retreat, after running out of supplies. Our porters refused to enter the mist zone and had run away.

To the knowledge of our guides, no African had ever climbed the summit. Those who tried, had not returned. People were telling each other tales about powerful spirits living on the mountain. They believed, that mountain gods did not like intruders. As far as we knew, no African alive knew what lay above the cloud zone.

This mountain was mine to scale and to explore, supported by a team of mountaineers and surveyors from Europe. The governor called on my friends, the surveyors from Bavaria. He told them to come back with the required supplies and gear. I had orders from the Colonial Administrator, to lead the expedition and to survey and map this mountain."

Gottfried interrupted Joan.

"Did you all go up with him?"

Joan glanced into the distance.

"I will tell you about my part in the expedition and then I will return to Stefan's story.

Stefan was tempted to run up fast, because the foothills and the rainforest are disguising the fact, that one gains altitude fast. The landscape at the base of Kilimanjaro looks almost like the foothills in our Alps.

Maria, Helena, Wolf, and Herbert decided not to join the climb.

They chose to begin venturing into the vast area we had come to observe, to get familiar with the land and its inhabitants. They agreed with me about the importance of this mountain for irrigation and wildlife habitat. We saw the need to know the mountain, that dominates the world we had just entered.

Three mountaineers and surveyors from Bavaria arrived and we began our expedition onto Mount Kilimanjaro. I was happy to accompany Stefan and his friends.

After two days of travel into the foothills, there were no more trails, other than those made by wildlife. With the help of porters, we set up camps, cut trails, removed obstacles, marked trees, and built piles of rocks as trail markers. We had a couple of dozen porters, who transported and stored supplies and gear in each camp as we picked our way up the mountain. Breaking trail and setting up tents required going up and down several times, carrying what each station needed for the way back and for emergencies.

Our porters worked for the Governor. They were a friendly, congenial lot. They kept to themselves during rest periods. They met their own needs, cooked for us and stored provisions in the pantry tents. They used machetes to clear circles in the vegetation, in the centers of which they built fires and slept under the sky by the ambers, rolled up in blankets and animal skins.

Once we reached the rain forest zone, we were able to convince them to sleep in the tents we had them shoulder all the way up here for this purpose. We consulted with their leader from station to station to be sure they were comfortable. We patched up their bare feet when they developed blisters.

Before the start of our trek, I thought I had become sick from something I had eaten.

I confided in Maria how I felt. After a long consultation, she suggested that I might have morning sickness. Maria was knowledgeable about these things. She was the nurse in our group. She had taken first aid courses in school and at the monastery and consulted often with Helena, the daughter of manufacturers of bandages and medical supplies, who also had a background in first aid. It had not escaped Maria's attention, that Stefan and I spent a lot of time together on the long boat journey and it was no secret how we felt about each other. Maria's caring and compassion were making me feel secure on this long journey. She said, after examining me:

"Joan, you must take care of yourself, as if you were with child. Soon, we will be sure. Promise, you will not strain yourself and pace yourself during this expedition.

Go nice and slow. Altitude is your enemy. Promise to return to lower altitude, whenever you feel sick."

I was more certain every day that Maria was right. I was sure, that I was pregnant. I began talking to the life, that was growing under my heart. I had not told Stefan or anyone else about this. I had asked Maria to keep it a secret for now.

Camps were set up about six-hour treks apart. After we had left the last settlement in the foothills. Game trails followed wild streams. Water would disappear in underground hollows and reappear further down the mountain, as wellsprings.

Our lead porter was an experienced tracker. He showed me tracks of Elephants, Giraffes, Gazelle, Elan, Warthogs and large Cats like Leopards and Lions and footprints of small mammals and birds in the silt next to streams. He pointed out treks of monkeys and small, nocturnal creatures. He could read the frequency of animal visits and was aware of their presence. There was a hush over the bush and inside the forest. I began to understand and to respect the fear, the population had about Spirits living on this mountain.

We did not feel threatened by the large animals, who were very shy and cautiously watching us from a safe distance.

I could observe jungle communication, reaching birds and monkeys, who were just as curious as I was. They seemed to be telling each other about our presence. Our head porter was great help in pointing out, what the different calls meant.

Each zone posted different challenges. The landscape looked as though at the time of formation, different forces were at work, from volcanic explosions raining down fractured rock to fine aggregate of pyroclastic flows, forming riverbeds and lava fields of glazed rocks with sharp edges, that made it difficult for our porters to find a trail on which to walk with their bare feet, while carrying heavy loads.

I never tired of the explanations given to me by our surveyor- mountaineers, about the geology of the planet and of this mountain.

Base Camp was established at the upper edge of the rain forest.

The vegetation had changed from ancient giants to smaller bushes and grasses. With some very tall, bizarre looking, free standing plants with umbrella tops like giant ferns. Clouds and thick fog shaded the vegetation. The temperature had dropped significantly.

This was now our base camp for the expedition to the Summit.

We had to proceed without porters from here, because they were afraid and refused to go up into the mist. Their stories were compelling, frightening and poetic at once.

We needed them to stay calm and not run away this time.

Progress had been slow. Impenetrable rain forest, waterfalls, streams and fallen trees had to be crossed. Rocks were covered in moss and rich tropical vegetation, making it necessary to poke with staffs for footing. Now and then, we followed game trails alongside streams. We insisted, that everyone take it slow to acclimate to the altitude.

I was in my own private zone with the idea, that I might be with child.

We soon left the mist and entered a desert zone. It featured a wide variety of rock formations. The plant cover consisted of many species of grasses and herbs that could survive this harsh climate on thin layers of soil covered rocks, moss filled spaces in between, bordering wet and dry stream beds.

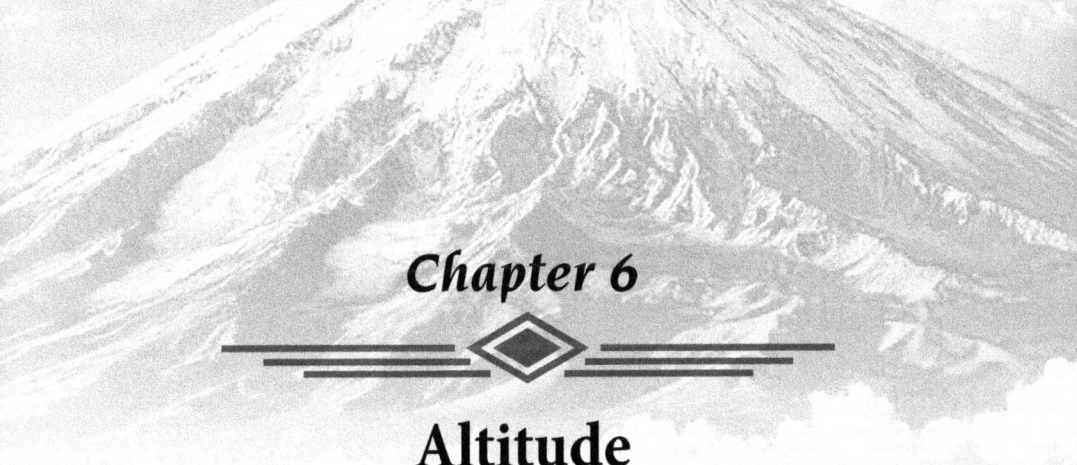

Chapter 6

Altitude

Visibility was now unobstructed. The view back down the mountain was covered in fog, this was the cloud zone we had seen from the ship and from the plain.

I was not sure, how much further up I could go. I found myself breathing hard.

Stefan asked me:

"Are you alight?" I replied:

"Climbing is difficult for me at this altitude."

Stefan stayed next to me and supported me. He and our climbing partners from Bavaria were used to high altitude, carrying large expedition packs into thin air.

Above us, we could see an elongated mountaintop, forming a saddle, from which two peaks were emerging: One to the south and one to the north.

The one to the right, south, appeared to be higher than the one to the left.

Now I too was sure: The top of Kilimanjaro is indeed covered with snow!

Beneath the snow cap is a zone, into which melt water flows, forming rivulets, nurturing swampy peat with richly vegetated chunks of humus, covered by a variety of high-altitude grasses and small bushes. A true alpine landscape. Missing were only our brown Alpine cows, with their bells. We yodeled to one another and to help those, who had gone down for more supplies, locate us further up. We finally made summit camp at the edge of the snow field.

I had to make the decision, not to climb further. I believed now, that I had in deed new life to protect. The altitude was beginning to wear on me.

We called this camp the Kilimanjaro Summit camp and prepared a special meal to celebrate the first time for Stefan and his partners to reach this altitude in Africa.

From here, the summit team would proceed to climb to the saddle, set up tents for the night to reach the summit in another day's climb, after an acclimation period.

I decided to return to base camp the following day.

The alpinists left before sunup. It was a hard decision for me, not to continue with them.

I was not comfortable up there and felt, that I needed more time to acclimate.

I was sure by now, that I was with child and I wanted to return to more comfortable quarters at base camp.

Chapter 7

First to ski a new line

I will now continue Stefan's story:

We were all excited about strapping on skis to be the first Europeans to ski in Africa.

The champagne powder was very light and slippery and hard to climb.

So far, we had not been able to see the plains below. Foothills, rainforest, cloud zone and the high moors, each had their own way of disguising our view.

When we finally reached the top of the clouds, they looked like a brightly lit fog, that swirled, moved by air currents.

We could feel and hear winds above and below from where we stood.

This mountain was making its own weather. We were enjoying an eagle's eye's view on a world unknown to most Africans and unexplored by Europeans.

I was excited to gain an unobstructed view of the ocean to the east and the plains, lakes, and rivers to the west from the saddle between the two peaks.

Soon Saddle Camp was set up and we took an extra day's rest to acclimate.

I was feeling lonely without Joan. I know, rule one for alpine survival is to go down immediately, when altitude becomes an issue. Joan was not comfortable yet in thin air. She had to go back down to basecamp to be safe.

Saddle camp looked just like any climber's camp in the alps: Small tents and gear for crossing glaciers and for climbing ice walls, small packs, to use for one day forays and to carry surveying gear.

We carried emergency medical supplies, bandages, and rations of high energy food.

Dehydration is a concern at altitudes nearing twenty thousand feet. We drank tea, made from melted snow, and ate rehydrated soup. We took with us our low temperature sleeping bags to bivouac on top.

We were wearing glacier eye protection with narrow slits to avoid snow blindness from the glare of bright sunlight on snow, face masks, covering nose and cheeks for frost protection. We had ice axes with long handles and spiked ends to steady our climb and to help with rock and ice. We used long ski poles with wrist straps and wide basket plates for support on the climb up. We wore mittens with silk liners and silk lined mohair socks, woolen long underwear under our trousers, layered over long silk underpants and undershirts to add a protective thermal layer. Warm woolen caps with ear muffs finished our frost protection, aided by wind proof hooded parkas.

We would have never expected to need alpine gear in Africa near the Equator, was it not for our last failed attempt.

We had left Africa in a vertical line into the sky, which transferred us as by magic into a world, as familiar to us, as the Alps. The difference was, that there were no trodden trails, no maps, no cairns, and no signs.

Everything was a first.

I appreciated Joan's supporting our expedition, even from the edge of the rain forest, where the porters were keeping house, cooking excellent meals for her.

The weather was stable. The temperature had dropped to well below freezing. We had begun the climb to the saddle in pitch black darkness. Our head lamps gave us light to set one foot in front of the other. Rob, Gustl, Joseph and I were skiing and climbing partners from back home. Now we took turns to lead, making first tracks into deep snow. Everyone seemed deep in thought and the quiet up here was interrupted only by the swishing of climbing furs under our skis and by steady breathing.

We were spread one rope length apart, connected for safety by climbing ropes. A couple of rock outcroppings required scrambling. We could imagine, that on the way down, we might be able to ski around them.

The idea of skiing in Africa, was a special thrill for us and being first to do so, was the icing on the cake, just like the snow on this enormous mountain was the icing on our Africa exploration.

At saddle camp we turned around. There, the African Continent laid spread out like a green and tan tablecloth to decorate our first meal with a view on the Continent to the West and the deep blue Pacific Ocean to the East. The haze towards the horizon was colored from light blue to purple on both sides to almost black at the horizon, making a straight dividing line between the land mass and the air under the biggest sky we had ever seen. The Indian Ocean and the African Continent were showing us how the power of the ocean and the power of this enormous land mass, caused different cloud formations to form. The curvature of Planet Earth was clearly visible from up here, in two magnificent arches.

We spend a couple of days resting and acclimating, before making the last push for the summit. Sunset and sunrise were taking our breath away. Glorious beyond description, in their rich palette of colors, ever changing and evolving. There are no words to properly describe what we saw, even to each other.

The two peaks were obstructing our view to the North and South. We had to redirect our orientation of the vast stellar canopy at night, with Orion being no longer the southern cross, as we know it from home, but the constellation appeared on top of the firmament. The milky-way in this pure air was so vibrant, that we felt, we could touch billions of stars, simply by reaching up.

There was no conversation. It felt like we had entered a gothic cathedral. The natives of Africa are right. This is a holy place. Here resides God.

We were transfixed by this natural wonder. We spoke only in whispers, not to disturb the universe in its magic cosmic order. I felt like I was standing before my creator.

On summit day, we once again left camp before sunrise to reach the peak by mid-morning. The honor of being first to stand on the peak of Kilimanjaro went to my climbing partners, by the flip of a coin. Heads- first to summit Mount Kilimanjaro, tails- first to make tracks on skis down the tallest mountain of the African Continent. I drew tails.

The three-hundred-and-sixty-degree view from the summit of Mount Kilimanjaro was breath-taking. We held each other in a long congratulatory group embrace, feeling giddy and laughing endlessly.

We spent a day with our instruments, surveying Mount Kilimanjaro.

The first descend on skis was mine. I could not wait to begin my glorious ride down.

The terrain did not look difficult to ski. The slippery powder snow invited giant slalom turns.

I decided to ski right back down to the edge of the snow to summit Camp, ahead of the others, who were finishing surveying, recording measurements and sketching.

I planned to have dinner prepared for them, when they caught up to me.

I choose a line to ski into a depression, the exit of which was hidden from view by a rock outcropping. I had a sense, that this would lead me back to the place, where we had entered the snow field. Here I was sure to find our tents and supplies.

Skiing by myself, made me feel invincible, like being a relative of an ancient deity, deserving to be revered and feared by mere humans, who consider this mountain to be inhabited by Spirits that do not let humans return.

"Those who wander into his cloud will never return," so the African legend goes.

I am by myself now. I feel the Spirit of the mountain. It is a spirit that needs to be appeased. I am not afraid. I am ready to embrace it, to become one with the mountain.

I make giant turns back and forth across my imaginary fall line, banking up to where the terrain is forming a wide chute. It is exhilarating.

I ran a wide sweeping turn, when suddenly the pressure under my skis disappeared. With a snapping sound, the ground under my skis gave way and the snow vanished.

I am in free fall.

The light fades until it is dark. No sound, except the occasional swish and drizzle of sliding snow.

I come to a halt when my skies start touching both walls of the crevasse. I can feel strain on my bindings and pressure under by boots. I am wedged between two vertical walls of ice.

I make a move to tap the wall before me with my ski pole, trying to get my bearings, when, with a sudden scraping sound, my skis slip further down.

At this moment, I realize, the gods are not pleased with my intrusion after all.

Trying to see, I push my facemask up to my forehead. I am trying to avoid slipping deeper into the abyss. Legs burning. Muscles vibrating. Desperately trying to stay motionless.

"Focus" I say to myself. "Breathe, breathe." Then, after what seems an eternity:

"Help me Joan, think of something," I whisper.

"Get off your feet" I hear Joan's voice.

"Wiggle your toes without shaking the skis."

"Do not go away. I need you now." I plead. "Use your intuition. Send help. Please Joan."

I am frozen with fear at this moment and the idea that Joan might lose me, terrifies me.

I can no longer sort out my feelings. I must obey Joan and get off my feet.

Breathing hard, I try to find a place to engage the tips of my ski poles in snow that had dropped into the crevasse with me.

I am now holding my breath.

Very, very slowly, without breathing, I lower myself into a crouching position, until my hands can reach the bindings of my skis.

"Stay focused!" I whisper. "Will my skis break under my weight?" I wonder.

Carefully, I release the clips, that tensions the springs behind my heals.

Next, I release the leather straps connecting the skis to my ankles above the boots.

Now, the only thing holding my boots to the skis, are the toe straps.

A pressure lock releases the toe straps once it snaps up. I am afraid of the motion this unsnapping can cause.

I see nothing.

I need to feel what I touch, but my gloves are in the way.

Taking them off, is as deadly, as keeping them on right now.

I hold one of my gloves between my teeth and use my left hand to carefully raise a clip. Success. One more. Done. I try to breathe.

My feet are now free and like an athlete on a balance beam, I pull first one toe out of the beartrap binding, then the other.

Slowly, I move one boot at a time on top of the toe straps.

I am now crouched over the top of my bindings with one glove between my teeth.

I know, I must put it back on my hand, before my next move.

Losing it, would be my undoing.

Success.

I am getting cold.

Exertion of climbing this mountain has taken its toll on my muscles.

Both hamstrings and calves are signaling me to remove my weight.

They are threatening to cramp.

I need to get my circulation back.

Hugging my knees, I slowly lower myself into a sitting position.

I pray that this shift of weight will not cause another slip deeper into the crevasse.

I know I would lose my skis in this event.

I am now sitting on a wooden bridge, jammed between two walls of ice.

No idea where I would land if I slipped again.

Fear and adrenaline helped to let me reach my sitting position.

I move first one leg, then the other.

Now I sit, straddling my skis.

I begin to breathe once again.

I arrange my poles to lean against the ice wall behind me.

I set the tips into the toe straps of my bindings.

This supports my arms and shoulders.

I do not dare reach for my back pack.

It also helps to insulate my back.

Cold is now rising from my toes up.

The crouching position has restricted blood flow to my legs.

I wonder about my toes inside my boots.

I can no longer feel them.

I am losing track of time.

How long has it been? I can no longer tell.

Long time… long… time.

I am slowing down mentally.

I hear Joanne's voice:

"Do not fall asleep.

Stay awake.

Wiggle those toes."

Joan interrupted Stefan's narrative and added her own part of the story:
"Waiting for the climbers to return, made time slow down for me.
In the eyes of our porters, the summit party had crossed a magic line.
I could see the worry in their eyes. I could hear them whisper.
I had gone up as far as my body could tolerate. I was disappointed.
Stefan did not know the reason why I had gone down. That could wait.

In my mind's eye, I saw them climb into the brilliant light above the clouds on pristine snow into a world, that has not been touched often by humans. Stefan would exclaim:

"We are the first ones. We are the champions of the highest mountain in Africa.

We are the kings of the mountain."

In my imagination, several hours of climbing at a snail's pace in thin air would follow. They argue about who will get the honor of stepping first on the peak and who will ski the first line down. I see them flipping a coin during their last rest stop before summit. They sip tea and eat biscuits, steeling themselves for their moment of glory:

A three-hundred-and-sixty-degree view from Africa's highest peak!
I can imagine the view from the summit. I am impatient. I scramble back to the edge of the snow. To Summit camp.

It makes me feel as close to God as I would ever be. I envy Maria.

She can find God anywhere. I found God up there.

That night, alone, I stuck my head out of the tent and saw the stars more clearly than I have ever seen them. The Southern Cross was over-head and I saw the big dipper on the northern horizon. To the south, new stars were visible. This took my breath away.

I fell asleep with a deep sense of gratitude, wishing I could share this view with Maria, my fellow star gazer.

I woke up early the next morning, made breakfast for my four hungry mountaineers.

My heart added a beat in happy anticipation. Soon I will hear the familiar yodel. I left the tent and stood up a little too fast; getting dizzy for a moment. Then I saw three figures appear. My heart dropped into my stomach. I attempted to comprehend what I was seeing. Only three? What might have happened? Rob or Stefan would have followed in the other's tracks.

I heard myself scream:

"Where is Stefan?"

My knees buckled. I dropped onto the ground. Light faded like someone had pulled the dimmer in the opera house. My poor heart was racing.

Words came from deep inside my throat:

"Where is Stefan?" I grunted. After a moment of silence, I whispered: "What did you do with Stefan?" Then I shouted at the top of my lungs:

"Stefan is still up there!"

I waited for Rob to say something. Nothing.

Gustl said in a matter-of-fact tone:

"Stefan is not here? Then we lost him. He went ahead of us. First tracks were his.

Rob, Joseph, and I were first to summit. We flipped coins.

You are joking, right?"

He looked inside the tent.

"He is not here?"

I knew yelling would not help. I did not dare move. I was about to faint.

Like an injured animal, I concentrated on breathing. Breath after short breath.

Now I whispered, my breath hissing:

"Do I look like someone who is joking? Stefan is not here!!!!"

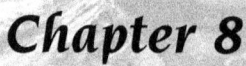

Chapter 8

Gone missing

A long silence followed.

Tears streaming down my face.

From deep in my belly, I hear myself plead:

"Where is he? Don't you think we have to do something?"

More silence.

Joseph, finally:

"Yes, Joan. Looks like we have a rescue on our hands. We expected him to be here long before us. Something must have happened. We will find him. We will go up to find his tracks. We did not follow him down. We made our own tracks. Now we must eat and drink.

Then we will take rescue gear and go back up to find him. We are too high in thin air to rush. We cannot make mistakes now. You know how he is. No one can stop Stefan."

Trying to regain my composure, I say:

"Tell me what I can do!"

"I now return to Stefan's story:"

"In the darkness of the crevasse I was getting cold. I began to feel sleepy.

I had no idea how long I had been here.

I began dreaming. In my dream I am in München at my parent's house. It is the Spring of 1909.

Father raises his hand to stop me, before I can run off to my tennis tournament.

"I want you to spend the Summer and meet new friends on this farm we talked about at breakfast this morning. "

"What farm?" I ask, pretending I cannot remember.

"Since when am I interested in farming?" I say impatiently.

"I need to get ready for a tennis match at the club.

"Hof Gut Waldeck," father repeats.

He sounds annoyed and as always when he gets impatient, he pulls out his large pocket watch and looks at the hands, indicating that it is time for me to pay attention to him.

"I just do not see myself belonging to that group." I whimper.

Father reminds me: "We talked about our concern over the divide of Catholics and Protestants."

"What does that have to do with me? Why is it helpful if I spend a vacation on a farm?

Why would anyone want me to be there? Don't you think I am old enough to make my own vacation plans?" I feel exasperated.

Mother takes a deep breath:

"Now, now," she says in her calmest voice. Her soft-spoken manner calms me. She looks fragile standing next to father. Like a drop of oil on rippled water, her voice brings the conversation back to a calm tone and we begin listening to each other.

Father explains:

"What this has to do with you, is the fact, that a social divide is growing between Protestants and Catholics. That will eventually get ugly. Political decisions by leaders of society must be informed by understanding each other. This does not happen by itself. It must be cultivated. This farm vacation is designed by families of Protestant and Catholic faith who believe that knowing one another will help close this divide and prevent further polarization. I would appreciate it, if you humor me and your mother and spend this summer at Hof Gut Waldeck where you will meet people your own age from Catholic families. "Do it for father," mother pleads softly.

"Do it for me." Mother looks at me over the rims of her eyeglasses. "We are a family with responsibilities. Looking outside of our own tennis courts and concert halls, is what we must do."

"Ok mother, we will talk about the summer later.

Now I must go and win a tennis match." With an air hit of a pretend tennis racket towards mother, I leave the room to change into my whites.

At this moment I heard a familiar voice. Just as I began feeling warm. Joan appeared to me, holding me in her arms. She whispered:"

Do not leave me. Fight. Fight. Fight. Feel the cold. Warm is bad. Cold is good.

Then I heard the first voice again:

"Stefan, can you hear me?"

I was not sure which voice was real.

I must have grunted something.

Next, someone dropped in beside me and began slinging lines around my chest and thighs. I still could not feel anything. I was in a mental fog.

I was being lifted off my skis, still in my sitting position.

I heard the clatter of my skis dropping into the abyss.

"That could have been me," I thought.

Again the voice.

"Wake up Stefan. We are getting you out.

We are bringing you up.

Relax. Do not fight us.

We are lifting you. Just breathe.

Look at me."

Now I recognize Robs voice. His lamp is blinding me.

Yes. It is Rob. Thank God.

Chapter 9

The rescue

I went in and out of consciousness.

Another eternity passed and I found myself laying in a sleeping bag on a toboggan my partners had improvised from two pairs of skis, with lines attached, to take me back to summit camp.

I think I saw Joan, but she kept slipping away.

I began fighting to keep her in front of me.

Now I knew I was inside a tent. In Joan's arms!

Then I passed out again.

Every time I woke up, Joan was there trying to give me sips of tea.

My frozen toes began to hurt more than a broken leg.

The rest of me was numb. I heard Rob announcing his plan: Make a seat to carry me. Others argue, that the scree is too dangerous for anyone to carry a body in a sitting position. It would be better to add extra cushioning to the toboggan and more cross braces, to hold things together, so they can slide me across the rubble, that covers Kilimanjaro's desert zone.

Josef said to me:

"We must get you down into the rain forest. Joan will stay right here beside you.

There are medical supplies at base camp."

My climbing partners took turns explaining things to me. Later they told me, that I kept asking the same questions over and over and over. Joan never left my side. I think I had Global amnesia. I had lost my short-term memory.

I went in and out of consciousness during the grinding sleigh ride. Once at base camp, it took a few days for me to recover from hypo-thermia. It took some time before I could eat a full meal. Soon, I regained enough strength, to be moved further down the mountain. Joan had given my heart the boost, that restored my will to live. My love for her was the first thing I could feel. Emotions began taking the place of frost in my veins. I knew, my frozen feet needed medical attention, I needed to be moved to a hospital. The pain in my toes was mind-numbing.

Once inside the forest, my partners crafted a pole-sled that was carried in front on the shoulders of two porters and dragged behind on the ground. I cannot remember details. I was happy to have Joan by my side.

I was proud of my friends and grateful for our porters.

We made it to the foothills and I was taken to a hospital.

The Glacier, I had fallen into, would later be named after me on the official map of Mount Kilimanjaro. The main summit was named after our Emperor:

Kaiser Wilhelm Spitze."

Joan rose from her seat, looked at Gottfried and said:

" This was Stefan's story."

Throughout the summer, Gottfried visited Joan as often as he could. He had so many questions!

"Tell me how this accident and his rescue affected Stefan," he asked.

Joan spoke in a soft, calm voice.

"Reaching the summit of Mt. Kilimanjaro and the fall into the crevasse with certain death inevitably approaching, followed by his rescue and the reunion with me, seemed to give his life new meaning. He realized, that life was a gift and that he had been given a second chance. He had achieved an important goal.

Now he could fully commit to the present."

"How did this affect your relationship?"

"Stefan became more attentive, his obsession with winning faded and he became more interested in living. Caring won over dominating. Our love became stronger. He saw new purpose and reason to be fully engaged in the mission we had come to East Africa to fulfill. He was over the moon when I told him that we were expecting a child. Gratitude was a new emotion for him. He did not recognize himself at first. For that he had me. I reminded him, that he was all he ever needed to be. We were just children then, really."

Gottfried wanted to look deeper:

"How did Stefan deal with the pain of his frozen toes and the consequences of the operations to save his feet?" Gottfried was sad now, to have missed Stefan.

said:

"If we do not win this war, we will not have a Colony and you will have nowhere to return to or to report about."

Chapter 11

Tell me more

The next time Joan and Gottfried met, she had set a table outside on a circular terrace, surrounded by perennial gardens, overlooking the lake. The weather was warm and pleasant, with almost completely still air. They could hear nesting activities of finches and the song of mockingbirds. The sound of tea pouring into cups seemed like an intrusion into this peaceful moment.

Gottfried had more questions:

"Tell me more about Grandmother and Grandfather. How did they meet?"

Joan gazed over the lake, took a sip from her tea, and began:

"Wolf and Maria met at a railroad station by the Eastern Shore. Maria and I were waiting for a carriage to take us to Gut Waldeck. Maria and Wolf took to each other like fire takes to dry grass.

Their eyes met and many little windows sprang open.

A conversation started at that moment, that would never end.

Only a few days later, Maria and Wolf created a cozy place by a bonfire, not too close and not too far from the flames, with a blanket underneath and a second blanket on top to give shelter from the heat of the fire and privacy for the heat that had begun to build between them.

Wolf had asked Maria to tell him how she and Joan came to be at this retreat.

He wanted to know everything.

Maria snuggled into his arms and began:

"It was a year and a half ago.

Easter anticipation was waking us early.

As always, Joan made fun of Easter, the ceremonies at Church, confession, and absolution. She says, she must make up sins, just to have something to confess.

Joan is a wild creature. Part of me admires her and part envies her. Behind her wild façade, there is loyalty, such as one rarely finds in this world.

I am different. Ceremonies and services of devotion fill me with a sense of awe.

It crossed my mind as a child, that one day I might take up the cloth and become a nun at a cloister, high up in the mountains.

Unfortunately, this conflicted with my desire to help people.

Instead, I took lessons in nursing and gardening, taught by sisters at a little cloister in the hills. I was drawn to help the poor and the disabled.

I felt bad, that other children did not have the same lovely home, as my family. I asked mama, if I could again bring Easter eggs to the children, who lived in the worker's row houses.

"After the service," mama said with a smile, "you can share as many eggs as you like. Have Gerda help you carry the baskets. Take Joan with you. It would be good for her to bring joy to these children."

Gerda, our cook, made sure that every year there were more eggs available to share, than the year before.

Mama loves poetry and memorizes many verses.

She likes to recite them to us on the way to church. It is no surprise, that we can recite poems to the sisters at the chapel on the hill.

I asked the sisters to teach me about first aid, the healing arts, care giving and midwifery.

My other passion is literature. I read everything I could get my hands on. Papa is old fashioned. He does not approve of girls reading books other than the bible. Poetry maybe. He would have preferred to see me doing sports, like Joan, or needlepoint, like mama.

Joan is a gymnast who can climb any tree and could outrun most of the boys in our neighborhood."

Maria began feeding Wolf grapes one by one.

She continued, after he had gently pulled her head down to his lips to give her a deep passionate kiss, which made her melt.

"Tell me more" Wolf urged her on.

Chapter 12

Showdown

"It was Easter 1908. Joan and I were giving a recital for dinner guests on holy Thursday.

I sang and Joan played the piano. We were performing Schubert's Winter's journey.

The first song is named Good Night. It tells of a lover, leaving his beloved girl, while she is asleep, because he feels a stranger in her world and does not want to overstay his welcome. He leaves a note by the door saying: "I will always be thinking of you."

Finding the note, breaks the girl's heart.

This story suddenly struck both of us in its tragedy and we broke out in tears.

We could not continue the recital. We had to flee to a quiet place to calm down, not sure, if we should be embarrassed, ashamed, or feel guilty, for having failed our parents and their guests.

Papa was irritated by this outbreak of emotion. He functions better in the calm center of the emotional range. Expressions of joy or grief make him uneasy. He now thought it best, to look for me, to calm me down. I saw him coming down the dark hallway, where I stood, trying to regain my composure. He took me by my hand and led me to the back door, opened it and said:

"Maria, dear, go outside and play for a while, until you have calmed down."

To me, this felt like someone had just asked me to step off a fast-moving train.

I was stunned by this dismissal. I felt my face getting hot and my hands forming fists.

I turned around, followed him back inside and before he could reach Joan's room, I said:

"No, Papa. I am not going to play outside. You will not send me away. You will stand and listen to me. It is time you hear, why this song has made us upset.

I know that you and mama want to give us a safe and wonderful world. We are not living in a castle in the clouds. We are living in the real world and notice, that things are not as simple as the fairy tale, we are being told."

Wolf took Maria in his arms as if to protect her. She leaned back into him. He took both of her hands, which were crossed over her chest.

"Go on ", he whispered into her ear. She continued:

"Papa said: "Now, now.""

I replied: No Papa, do not now-now me. Let me speak."

I fought back my tears. I continued:

"You know I love you and Mama more than anything in the world. But you must know, that we are not just an idea. We are real persons with feelings. We do not calm down by playing outside." I stepped closer to him. "We have friends. We see things."

Papa tried to put his hand on my shoulder. I took his hand. Holding it, I said:

"We are not little children anymore."

I took his hand into both of my hands, as if to plead with him.

" We cannot protect you from our lives and from things that happen to us."

Papa looked puzzled.

"What are you talking about?"

He did not know if he should step forward, towards me, or back, away from me.

He stayed put. I lowered my voice:

"We did not want to worry you, but last week, Joan was kidnapped at knife point and almost killed. If it had not been for some boys from our mine, acting immediately to follow, disarm and disable this monster, we might have never seen her again.

She would have vanished in the abandoned mine shaft, where they found them, where this man was trying to hide her. The boys knew, where to look."

Father pulled his hand from my grip and stepped back.

"You did not tell me? What were you thinking! Who helped you? Did you tell mama?"

In a whisper I replied:

"No. we did not want to worry either of you. We were afraid, she would tell you.

It does not matter who helped us. You would not know these boys, if you saw them in the street. I do not even know their names.

This is, what I am talking about. This perfect world we have here, is a cloud.

You, mama, the church, our school, the sisters at the cloister, you all act as if there were a perfect world into which you can send us to play, calm down, and be safe."

Now I wanted to have it all out, so I continued to face my stunned father:

"Why would you get irritated by my love for books? Why would you tell me to put them down? Why do you believe, that God made us all in his image and that we are all one happy family?"

Papa stood there like he had been struck by lightning. I went on:

"You do know, that we have been giving from our bounty at Christmas, Easter and on our Birthdays to children in the neighborhood. We were invited into their homes, even to visit, when they were sick."

Papa took a step towards me and took a breath as if to speak.

"No," I said, "do not interrupt me. Children on the street are calling us Catholic Church Rats. They worship a different God. One that is not Catholic but Protestant. They go to different schools. They worship at a different church. The boys who rescued Joan, are Protestants."

Papa tried to speak. I put my hand on his chest, so he remained silent.

"A few weeks ago, I posted a picture with a credo on my bedroom wall, that said in beautiful script:

'On the Day of Judgement,
we step before our Creator

*He will judge us not
by what we believe
He will judge us
by what we have done'*

I stepped even closer to papa and lowered my voice. In a whisper I said:

"Mama discovered my poster. She tore it off the wall and tossed it into the fire. When I protested, she slapped me in the face."

Now I began sobbing again.

"Mama …slapped me… over… that!"

Maria now began shedding tears over this memory.

Wolf tried to hold her close but she sat up straight, then took a deep breath and continued:

"I wrote this quote into an essay and handed it in, to see what my teacher would say.

He handed it to our religion instructor, who insulted me in front of everyone, in front of the entire class. He called this quote 'heretic'."

Papa tried to speak.

"No wait" I said, "I am not finished." In a hissing whisper I continued:

"I have not participated in Church services since that day. Instead, I hid in the crypt beneath the altar, where no one ever goes. There, I said my own prayers and spoke directly to God. I carried a book the size of my bible to avoid raising eyebrows on the way to the Cathedral. I started reading in it. It is about the Holy Grail. This opened to me a form of spirituality, that is not in conflict with different beliefs. Reading this book made it tolerable for me, to live with people, who think, that their faith is the only way to God.

It gave me a way to love you and Mama, even though I no longer believe, that the Catholic church and the Pope are the sole representatives of God on Earth, while the other half of the Christian world is Protestant and therefore doomed.

It made my relationship with the children from the protestant school easier.

The poor worker's children are all protestant. They blame everything, that is wrong or difficult in their lives on religion, and therefore on us."

I took papa's hand again and when he tried to step back. I followed him.

"I think it has to do with what people do to each other. What we do to them.

That makes me worry about suddenly becoming the enemy. We share so much of what we have. It should not have to be that way. I always bring extra eggs to a deformed girl in a wheelchair, who loves handing out Easter eggs. It makes her as happy as I am, when I do it."

I then took papa in my arms, kissed him, and whispered:

" Thank you, papa. I love you!"

Chapter 13

The farm estate

Maria fell silent. Wolf sat up and looked at her in the light of the fire. He took both of her hands and kissed her palms near the lifelines. He wanted to know everything.

"What happened next?"

He looked deep, into her dark brown eyes.

Maria took a deep breath.

"Papa was speechless. He held me in his embrace and said:

"Thank you, my child. Please look after your sister."

He left me, returned to our guests and I went to see Joan. We spent some time in Joan's room, holding each other. Her gray eyes seemed to have melted, they had turned red. This rekindled our emotions. We let our feelings have a free run. After some time, we calmed down enough to be able to join our parents and their guests. We performed more songs until dinner was served.

Our guests had met papa at a conference of leaders from coal and steel industries.

Dr. Scheffler was in the smelter industry and his wife Wilhelmine represented financial institutions. A concern, they spoke of, was the need to reconcile religious differences in the labor force. They agreed with papa, that collaboration was a matter of life and death to coal miners. The conference had agreed, that more social development was needed.

Papa had decided to invite missis and mister Scheffler to dinner. Mama liked extending the Easter Holiday with festive gatherings at our home. With our guests, we now moved after the main course to the parlor, for chocolate truffles and coffee. Joan and I were served hot chocolate with whipped cream.

Mrs. Scheffler brought up the religious divide again. She spoke about the need of introducing children from leading Catholic families to children from Protestant families to establish relationships with-, rather than opinions about the 'other half' of the population.

"Look at Karl and me," she said. "We have broken all the rules. Our courtship could have disinherited us, Karl being Catholic and me being Protestant. What saved us were those, shouting: "Think big, go far, break boundaries, build universities, build medical schools, teach science!"

She added:

"The house of Hannover invited an educator from Wuerttemberg, named Christian von Dillman, to promote science education. I was one of the first female students to graduate with science in my final exam. It brought Karl and me together. There is no religious divide in science. There certainly is religious divide in governance. Protestant families are often forced to move to regions governed by Protestant regents.

Emperor Frederick has softened the line by declaring:

"People should be free to choose their own way to God and eternal happiness."

It is my impression, that this divide is more deeply embedded with those, who are victimized by it."

Doctor Scheffler added: "Wilhelmine has made plans with a friend of her family, Anna Von Bülow, a relative of Chancellor von Bülow, who owns a large estate at the Baltic Sea, to make her estate available for a Summer, to host young adults from both faiths. To meet and to get to know each other." Turning to Joan and me: "I think you girls would enjoy participating in this event."

Papa replied:

"This sounds very interesting." He had not missed my glances to Joan that were saying: "Let's do this."

The next morning at breakfast, we brought up this farm idea again. I said:

"We would like to go to the farm if you let us. Mama, please?"

"Ask papa." Both of us turned to him:

"Can we papa? Please?"

"Since you both want to go, yes you can go."

Maria sank back into Wolf's arms.

"That is how we came to be here."

Wolf turned Maria in his arms and without thinking, he kissed her again deeply.

Maria returned his kiss. When she had recovered her breath, she said:

"Now you tell me a story. Tell me the story about our sailing trip."

"This will keep us up all night"

"Do you have something better to do?"

Maria snuggled into Wolf's arms and added:

"We have all the time in the world. I want to know every detail of the sailing adventure from where you saw it."

Knowing this would take time, Wolf made an even more comfortable nest with a boat cushion he found at the boat house. Glancing over Maria's shoulders, he could see faces of other participants in various groupings enjoying small bonfires and having quiet conversations, warmed by glowing ambers, faces lit by flickering flames.

Chapter 14

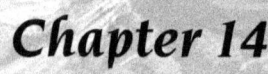

Sailing

Wolf took a deep breath and began:

"I saw a sailboat at the dock. It all happened very fast. Now we are here."

"This is it?" Maria said in disbelief.

"No. There is more. A lot more," Wolf replied, laughing.

Maria leaned into him. She made him feel things he had never felt before.

He felt as though she had taken possession of him. He liked it, even though part of him was still nervous and wanted to resist it. He felt a force greater than himself, compelling him to give himself to her. Most surprisingly he had no idea why, yet it felt right.

Destiny, he thought, had taken a hold of him. He was sure, that one day, he would find out the "why." For now, Maria had the power to melt him like butter in the sun.

Wolf liked it. He sealed her lips with a kiss.

Glancing beyond the bonfire in the direction of the Sea, he continued his story:

"I saw this sailboat at the dock from an upstairs window." He stopped and waited for her protest, and with a guttural burst of laughter, he continued:

"We all reacted to the sight the same way. There were voices saying:

"Do you know how to sail?"

"I love to sail, how about you?"

"I am on a racing team."

Everyone seemed to speak at once and we had a full crew in less than two minutes. Stefan and I went to see von Bülow to ask about the boat. She said: "If you have an experienced skipper and crew, you can take her out. Do not forget life vests."

"That is what I had said," interrupted Maria.

"Then you tell the story," Wolf laughed.

"I am sorry, please go on."

She put his hand over her mouth and kissed his palm.

"As I was saying, we inspected the sailing vessel and talked about who was going to do what. We agreed that Stefan would take the helm, I volunteered to do the foredeck. Joan wanted to trim the main sail, you agreed to trim the Genoa. Helena took the foresail and the task of keeping sheets on both sides of the mast, releasing, and taking up the slack during turns, then securing them, once the set was made.

Herbert would be our strategist. He was to raise and lower sails, keeping halyards organized below and passing up sails for sail changes, then repacking them.

We collected gear and made the ship ready, as if we were going to race her.

Soon we pushed off. It looked like a perfect afternoon for a sail.

Conversations were mostly about previous sailing experience and observations about this sailboat, its fine condition and the unusual design with its gaff rigged main sail and large cabin. We observed with a chuckle, that it would easily sleep all of us.

The air was balmy and the breeze was just enough to move us gently towards the horizon. We could see cumulus clouds, that looked like a skyline of snow-covered mountains in the Alps.

The updraft under these clouds promised a steady breeze to make our turns more exciting. I felt good about our team and my mind was already planning more extensive sailing excursions with this boat, when I noticed that the clouds had begun to move rapidly towards us.

The color of the sea beneath the clouds changed from gray to black. I called this to Stefan's attention and he told us to be prepared for things to get a little bit rough.

He loved it. I could tell he was aching for excitement and so was Joan.

A sudden lull emptied our sails and the surface of the water flattened out. The air became quiet and we were listening for signs of wind.

Eyes went up to the pennant on top of the mast and to the little tell-tale threads on the rigging. Everything had gone limp. It became eerily quiet.

Suddenly, we could hear, what sounded like a fast-moving train, coming out of nowhere.

The sea in front of our bow rose in a giant wave. We could see lines in the water, its color changing from blue-gray to white. Like curtains, we could see what looked like snow, heavy rain, or hail. Stefan looked up at the pennant, to check the change in wind direction. What I saw, was the wind jumping back and forth, forcing Stefan to hold the course steady, until some direction became dominant.

The wind now made the boat dance through the waves.

Stefan attempted to head the ship straight into the weather. He seemed determined to ride out this gale under full sail.

I was concerned about the rigging with as much sail as she was carrying now.

Visibility went down to nothing. We buttoned our jackets and tightened our life vests.

"Hang on!" Stefan yelled to no one in particular.

The roar and wind pressure increased so fast, there was no time to reef or to drop sails.

"This might de-mast us." Stefan yelled into a blizzard of big wet snow flakes, mixed with blinding hail and rain. Trying to point us into the wind, he steered to port.

The wind suddenly shifted. I could feel the pressure on the main sail build.

I could make out Joan struggling with the main sheet. I saw Joan hand Stefan the main sheet and Stefan handed her the tiller. I could not tell, why.

I was no longer able hear words over the roar of the wind and the angry sea, spraying foam and drops of salt water into my face. I saw you and Helena un-cleat the halyards from the mast to drop the fore sails and gather them up, before they could fill with wind again. Joan was struggling with the tiller.

Too late. The boat began leaning away from the wind, the boom was touching the water. Stefan, with the main sheet still in his hand, slipped. He grabbed the ship's rail with his right hand. With his left, he reached for the boom to brace himself. The boom was skimming turbulent water. I saw a big wave approaching Stefan's forward pointed legs. "This will wash him into the sea," I thought this frightening thought.

Stefan now raised his feet above the water, pushed himself off the boom and reached across his chest to grab the rail. At this moment, Joan pushed the tiller to steer the boat into the wind. The vessel righted herself. At the same instant, you tossed a line to Stefan, so he could grab a hold, as his boots were slipping again. For a moment it looked like you were trying to save Stefan and lose your own footing in the act.

I grabbed you and pinned you to the mast so we both would not slip.

As soon as the boat stood into the wind, air pressure and windspeed dropped. I took a deep breath. Like an ice dancer, Helena rushed to the ladder at the bottom of which she found Herbert. She went to see if the boat had taken on water and how Herbert was doing. They did not reemerge for a long time. The wind dropped as fast as it had built. Rain, snow, and hail had stopped. I could see land in the distance. One by one we resumed our positions, set sails for a downwind spinnaker run and headed back towards shore.

I called out: "Stefan eleven thirty, the dock."

The sky had now gone black over the manor house beyond the dock, just as it had gotten almost black over our boat, during the climax of the squall. This storm cell was moving fast. We were shaken by the unexpected violence of ocean, wind, hale, snow and rain.

What was bigger than this sudden event, was the impact it had on our sailing crew, inexperienced with such severe conditions as most of us were. We had barely met. Now it felt like there was a reason, why we found ourselves on a sailboat in a squall:

Fate put us on this vessel together and we have been taken through a test.

Everyone was deep in thought, as we approached the dock. Silently, we dropped sails, laid them out to dry and put things in order."

Wolf leaned back against the boat cushion.

"This is the end of my story. Sorry, nothing exciting, no shipwreck, just new relationships. Plus, a sailing team, that could bring a boat home through a violent storm."

Wolf put his hand under Maria's head, turned her face and looked deep into her dark brown eyes. He was having feelings he could not explain to himself. He had never felt like this before and was not sure what to say. After what felt like an eternity, he whispered:

"I think I am falling in love with you. I think fate has sent us here."

"I feel the same way" said Maria, snuggling into the cushion formed by his hands. She gazed at the stars and pointed to the big dipper and the North Star. She took his left hand and kissed the inside of his palm. This stirred up a new wave of feelings. Unlike the storm on the water, he did not want these feelings to stop. They left both Maria and Wolf breathless, just like the squall over the boat had done earlier.

The bonfire lasted all night. We were the only ones left. We moved closer to the fire as it burned down. Maria took charge of consolidating embers and I fed the fire with ever smaller pieces of wood. Maria took a guitar and began to play her favorite songs, which most of us knew. I knew all the words and we repeated each stanza, so the rest of us could fall in.

Our conversation turned to the reason we were at the farm. There were new fires beginning to flare up. Internal ones. Stefan, still the captain of the ship, began to speak:

"I did not want to be here. I have no interest in farming. I like sports. I ride horses. I ski. I play tennis. I sail boats. I like to win. What happened today, surprised me. I never thought I could care about people, other than beating them at sports. What happened on that boat today, has changed everything. You showed me something, I was not able to see before: Together, we brought the boat and each other home.

He took my hand. He held it and spread my fingers wide to match his palm to mine. My hand is much smaller than his. He was surprised by the attention he was getting from me. It confused and moved him.

After a long silence, during which I could see flames lighting the night, I could hear the snap of branches crack open in the heat.

Helena began to speak into the glow of the embers. Like a seer, who can tell the future. She said:

"I wanted to come here. I had to beg my parents to let me go.

It took both my begging and the support of Walter's parents, who are friends of my parents, to let me attend." She snuggled into Walter.

"Why?" asked Stephan.

Helena replied:

"My parents could not see any benefit from my coming here, to meet people from other faiths. They do not see, how it is possible to figure out, how humans on this planet can get along without killing each other over religious differences. They think history proves it. I disagree." Another long silence. Then Helena continued:

"I am afraid, making bandages for the wounded and injured, is a natural conflict of interest with peace and workplace safety."

Maria shoved another stick into the fire, lifted a couple of logs up to let air into the gap. New flames lit the group. Then she said:

"It is like this fire. We contain it, so it does not burn our blankets, we feed it, so it keeps us warm, we let air in, so it flares up, lighting the night and our faces." After a few more moments she continued: "Tonight, it is firewood. Before that, it was a tree. Before that, it was green. Before that, it was a sapling. Before that, it was a seed. Those, who only look at the seed, cannot not see this coming."

Stefan interrupted her:

"See what coming?"

Maria patiently, in a low voice:

"See the flames, see the light. It depends on how and from where you look.

We see different things from different angles. We are here to find out, what other people see and feel and to help them understand what we see. This afternoon on the boat Joan saw the boom in the water and Stefan's hand braced against it. Stefan saw the wave. Joan held the course until Stefan had pushed off to get both hands on the rail. Then she turned the boat to starboard. Into the wind. That righted the boat.

I saw Stefan needing a line to keep from slipping into the waves, while pulling himself back on board. I tossed him a jib sheet. Wolf saw the wind shift, called to Joan to change course. He pinned me to the mast, so I would not slip and fall. The capsize reversed and the boat righted itself. Stefan called out to warn about the boom that came swinging across. You all ducked just in time. Walter kept order below through all this, to be sure we could bring the boat home, once things on deck had calmed down."

Maria let her eyes scan the trees and flowers in the park, then she looked inside herself.

"That is what I mean: Different points of view saving the moment. This is how I see life. We are on this planet together for a reason:

In the face of that sudden storm, no one asked, what race we are, what religion or church we belong to, by what name we call God or which country our families came from. No one asked, what social system is best, or if some humans are chosen over others, to dominate them. All we cared for at that moment, was to stay alive and to bring the ship home with everyone still on board. We acted spontaneously, each of us seeing something different from where we happened to be. That is the reason, we are here tonight. In person. And not just as a memory."

A long silence followed. I could see flames following each hiss of gas from the core of heated logs in the fire, Maria had stirred. I could sense, how her words had lit a fire inside of all of us. Soon daylight was breaking in the eastern sky.

Finally, Wolf sat up and asked:

"Is there any more tea? I can use a night cup. We will have to continue this conversation. I think we are on to something."

Everyone agreed. The fire had burned down. After toasting to a great day and a good morning, we went to the big house to find our sleeping quarters."

Chapter 15

◆

Hope

"The stars began to fade and I saw a faint rose glow, that lit the eastern horizon.

Maria, Wolf, Stefan, and I went quietly up the stairs, lost in our musings.

Once on the upper landing, we said good night.

Helena and Herbert had gone off to bed. Wolf wrapped his blanket around himself and Maria. With a gentle kiss to her forehead, he said good night. Maria answered with a kiss to Wolf's fingertips.

Maria and I slipped into our room. One toss and one turn in the soft feather bed and Maria was fast asleep. I let the memory of this day pass in front of my inner eye, trying to let go of the image of Stefan almost getting washed into the sea. I finally fell into a deep, blissful sleep.

When I woke up, I confided my feelings for Stefan to Maria."
Jones gray eyes scanned the skyline of the alps. Then she continued: "We were so young then. Every day brought more unexpected and confusing events."
Gottfried was eager to learn more about these events: He said:
"I can see how your group was fused together by your sailing experience.
I am wondering how Wolf got to be there? Is there something in his

diaries?"

"Yes, there is. I found one of Wolf's journals Stefan had saved, tucked away in the attic." 1910.

The commencement ceremony at the Dillman Real Gyumnasium concluded with a performance of the last movement of the ninth symphony by Ludwig van Beethoven, performed by our school orchestra and the school choir.

My graduation was celebrated with a soiree at home.

Our guests included my uncle Christian von Dillmann, founder of the school. the mayor of Stuttgart, Berthold Stade and a number of dignitaries from the university of applied sciences and the medical school of the university of Tübingen. And my friends.

A small group of them surrounded me when the discussion turned to plans for the summer vacation. Helena, Herbert's girlfriend, spoke enthusiastically of a stay at the Waldeck estate on the Baltic Sea coast.

"Never heard of that place" Both Herbert and I replied. Helena explained: "Catholics and Protestants our age are invited to attend a farm holiday by the northern sea shore. It promises tennis, English, and Western horseback riding, driving teams of horses, swimming in the ocean, sailing, doing farm chores, working in gardens, the kitchen, the bakery and tending to a variety of livestock. No one will be leading discussions, except the participants themselves. It was conceived by a friend of the owner of the farm, Wilhelmine Scheffler, who is a mathematician, working in the new field of industrial finance and commerce. She believes, that without closing the growing divide between Catholics and Protestants, there will be a civil war before too long."

Our friend Herbert asked: "How will she prevent that?" Helena thought about it for a moment, then she replied:

"People must get to know each other, Sheffler says:" People will fall victim to rumors and conspiracy theories on both sides, speculating about the reasons for this growing tension, expressing what divides them, rather than what they have in common."

Ms. Scheffler stood up for this idea during a visioning conference of industry leaders, who agreed, that a first step in this direction would be for the children of leading families to get to know one another. She argued, that there is hope in familiarity and that out of knowing one another would come friendships and ideas for collaboration, leading into a peaceful future."

"You sound like a politician running for office," I told Helen. "The truth is, I am intrigued by the idea of such a conference."

I discussed my desire to participate in this retreat the next morning with my parents and suggested, that this might make a good graduation present.

People like to blame each other rather than a system. It is easier to believe than to know. Lies are easier spread than truth. Science is helpful, but can be misused and will be dismissed by people who believe, rather than study cause and effect.

I am concerned about losing sight of the divine by one-sided focus on the material and the misuse of science, by using its authority on believers, losing facts for sake of convenience. The visible, tangible side of things blocks us from noticing essence, vision and inspiration and from grasping the divine. We must reconcile science and divinity, to find truth. Churches on all sides are asking God for mercy and help. Threatening us with eternal damnation, while delegating all responsibility to a higher power. Very convenient."

Joan put the journal back into the box. With a sigh she relaxed. Then she said:

"This is what I found. I enjoy searching for the beginnings of our journey into a new world. It makes me sad, since I lost Stefan, but it brings him closer to me, because he is the reason, these documents still exist."

Chapter 16

Waldeck estate

The next time they met, Joan read a copy of a letter from Helena to her parents.

Gut Waldeck, July 15, 1910:

Dearest mother and father:

The journey to the north shore was beautiful, long but rather uneventful.

I felt safe in the company of Herbert.

People I met at the Waldeck Estate seem to have the same feeling of liberation, that we are experiencing, by walking into a conference without any religious leadership or agenda. No one has ever participated in a summer camp, that was not run by Catholic- or Protestant counsellors. No one has been at a summer camp, that did not have the purpose of advancing specific religious beliefs with instructions on how to become a leader in their respective belief system or way of life. There is curiosity about this unusual type of congregation in every participant. All seem to have resolved, that being friendly and open is a good place to start. Many brought musical instruments, books, and sports equipment. There is a willingness to share ideas, to listen and to get to know one another. I was hoping for this. And I thank you for humoring me and for letting me come here. The hostess of the Waldeck estate, Anastasia von Bülow, is part of Chancellor von Bülow's family. I am curious, what she will say to us, during her opening address tomorrow. Waldeck is a beautiful Manor house with elaborate stables, designed by Italian Architects, to serve as a seaside resort for equestrians, a market for breeders of fine horses and other livestock and a research facility for experimental, innovative agriculture. It is well run. We are going to be immersed in activities of our choice. Accommodations are comfortably appointed, ranging from single bedrooms to group quarters with sitting rooms and small libraries. Singles are sharing bathrooms and feature window benches in dormers, that lift the mansard roof like eyebrows to the Sea. Anastasia von Bülow told me, she was named in honor of her grandmother, who came from a long line of Prussian and Russian nobles. She is related to almost every family of nobility and power in Europe. She is highly regarded as owner-manager and excellent equestrian in breeding circles and as a trainer of dressage performers, hunters, and carriage horses. The fortitude she brings to the task of keeping her organization at the forefront of breeding and agricultural research stations, has earned her respect in all of Europe. She has a dry sense of humor and no tolerance for nonsense. Everyone can come to her for advice and guidance. I saw a ten-meter yacht, tied up to a dock at the little harbor, which I am sure she offers to guests who have credentials as sailors. I see Wolf arriving. I better post this letter and greet my friends.

Until soon
with love and gratitude,
Your Helena.

After Joan finished reading Helena's letter, she said:
"I want to read to you another few lines from Wolf's diary:"

"I met Stefan from Berlin and the sisters Maria and Joan from Essen at the railroad station. We introduced each other once we realized, that we were all waiting for the carriage to the Waldeck estate. We had come early to be able to choose good accommodations.

Everyone liked the charming dormers overlooking the ocean and the little harbor.

We noticed the sailboat. I could hear Joan chuckle irreverently: "I am the one who gets in trouble and Maria is the one who takes the blame. Yes. We both sail."

I could tell Stefan likes Joan. We both slid down the polished marble banister opposite the reception desk and exited with a forward roll from our hands to our backs and on to our feet. We stopped our forward movement with a smile and a bow.

"Ladies," Stefan said, "I am Captain Stefan." He reached out his hand. "I hope you are sailors." Both Joan and Maria answered at the same time:

"I am." I could see that Joan was taken by Stefan. She liked his open and uninhibited way of looking people straight in the eyes. Joan is a natural adventurer. She said:

"I wonder what we can do with the rest of this beautiful day? She looked at Stefan, glancing out towards the Sea. She could not wait to get her feet in salt water."

Stefan was interested. "Land or ship?" he asked. "I saw the sailboat"

Stefan turned to Maria: "How about you, Maria?" "I am not wild about sports. I can spend days with good books. But yes, I sail. My father thinks, I read too much. I like sports in moderation. How about you, Stefan? Do you race boats, do you compete?"

"Yes, and yes. My passion is tennis. Sailing is more of a technical challenge out in the elements. Most of all, I like mountaineering and skiing. How about you, Joan?"

"Six of us can get permission to take that boat for a turn."

"What are we waiting for. Wolf, are you in?" Joan said enthusiastically.

"Yes," I said. I stepped to a window facing the ocean and looked at the dock and the water. A sloop with polished teak trim and a tall mast with main sail flaked and tied around the boom was beckoning us. The sky revealed cumulus clouds in the distance, a dark gray bank of clouds appeared on the north-eastern horizon and a calm sea showed ripples, caused by a gentle breeze. The top of the mast sported a pennant, which had the wind coming from the west. Everyone was following my eyes.

Stefan pulled out a chair for me to sit across from him and Maria, who refilled my water glass and kept my coffee topped off. I really like her. And I think I like Stefan. He turned to me: "So, Wolf. You sound like a sailor." Then I heard Maria say:

"I would enjoy a breeze around my head after the long train ride."

I could hear Von Bülow saying, without looking up:

"You can take the boat. Stefan will be your skipper. Jan, our grounds man has jackets, boots, and life vests. I spoke with Stefan about my family, my graduation and about the unusual nature of this camp. We felt comfortable with each other. Stefan decided to take my luggage up to one of the 'eyebrow' rooms, to see if I liked it enough to share it with him. Our take on things is different enough for us to be compatible.

I think that nothing will tell you more about a person than to see them sail a boat.

That is our common ground.

I looked out of the 'eyebrow' window to study the cloud formation I had noticed earlier. From up here, I could not make out which way the weather was moving, so I said:

"We better check on our sailing partners and get going. My friend Herbert and his girlfriend Helena have arrived. I know they would be upset if we went on a boat trip without them.

They are sailors also."

When we went sliding down the curved railing, we almost ran over the girls who had come to look for us with the same thought in mind: Sail now, settle in later.

I spotted Herbert and Helena at the table. They had finished their meal.

They too were ready and eager to go sailing with us.

Helena jumped up and gave me a hug and a kiss on the cheek standing on her toes. Herbert and I shared a burst of laughter, as if we had just gotten away with robbing a bank. I showed them quarters, suggesting that Helena might want to join Maria and Joan to sleep at their suite, which had an extra bedroom. It took only a few minutes to get bedrooms sorted out, and after introductions were made, excitement about sailing became palatable. Maria asked again where they might find Jan, the groundskeeper.

Von Bülow pointed to a small boathouse near the dock. She told Maria, that she had sent word to Jan to expect us.

"Ship ahoy" Von Bülow said and looked in amusement at our motley sailing team, as we filed out through a side door to see Jan, who was waiting for us with gear.

Joan explained to Jan: "Stefan is our skipper, Wolf is first mate, doing foredeck.

Herbert is strategist in the pit, raising and dropping sails. The rest of us are the committee that tells them what to do and where to go."

Joan put the back of her right hand on her forehead, arched her back and said in a high-pitched voice: "Take me to Atlantis, please." A burst of laughter. "Use that vessel, if you must" she added, pointing to the dock. "Herbert will show us how to get there."

I began to like this high-spirited girl. So did Stefan.

Maria had taken my breath away from the first moment I laid eyes on her.

I saw a glimpse in her eyes that gave me hope, that she might feel the same about me."

Chapter 17

Youth summit

"Reading this, is exhausting to me now, as the event was invigorating me then," said Joan, smiling.

"I must rest now. Next time you come see me, I will tell you about the conversation that brought us to Africa."

When Gottfried saw Joan again, Spring had turned to Summer, reflections in the lake were like a mirror. The alpine skyline was now green except for some snow at the north sides up on the peaks.

Joan placed a sheet of paper on the table. She said:

"This is the transcript of the opening speech given by Annastasia von Bülow. She read:

"Dear participants of the first Waldeck youth Summit:

On behalf of our sponsors and our associates, I welcome you.
The days ahead will be as special for us as they will be for you.
It is my conviction, that spending time with us and with each other will be the opening of a new era for all of us.
This gathering was born from a concern, that many families have expressed.

It is the emerging divide between Catholics and Protestants. The concern is, that this polarization can lead to violence, threatening everything we have achieved.

The world is in a state of rapid change and development:

Only seventy years ago, it would have taken you between one and three weeks to travel by coach from where you live to where we are gathered today.

We are witnessing changes, made possible by people with vision. There are new and unexpected consequences we must face.

Power has begun shifting into new hands.

Established religious, socio-economic- and political arrangements are being questioned. Government is expanding; new parts of the world are being discovered and explored.

Development comes with risk.

Are we able to understand or to master these risks?

This new era has brought forth opposing forces in every part of society.

The question is, will we turn back or embrace this changed world? Consider that past and future are meeting right here, right now.

Are we willing to speak freely with each other without prejudice?

Can we make each other feel safe to do so?

Our vision for this event is this: To create an opportunity for getting to know each other.

We see this as a first step towards understanding and reconciliation of opposing forces.

To see how much society has in common instead of how we see differences.

We have invited members from different faiths to spend time together, get to know each other while we work together and play together. It is a chance to discover yourselves and each other, without guidance from counsellors.

We believe, that only acquaintance will preserve the peace in the long run.

I invite you, to choose activities, share ideas, ask questions, prepare meals, use our sports facilities. To work together, learn from each other, talk freely and get acquainted.

We trust that each of you brings ideas and knowledge to our conversation.

Learn to trust your inner compass, share ideas, ask, and answer questions about challenges we will face together tomorrow.

This is a safe environment. You will not be prejudged.

Activities are posted on the bulletin board in the order they happen from four o'clock in the morning to eight o'clock at night.

We invite you to sign your name next to activities that interest you.

After three days, we will convene after the evening meal.

Everyone will introduce themselves.

Following introductions, you will have an opportunity to share your thoughts and to ask questions.

You are invited to form pilot groups with other participants.

We suggest that these groups be no larger than six to ten participants.

At the end of the summit, during our final banquet, you will have an opportunity to share your take-away thoughts.

Pilot groups are invited to present summaries of your group's activities and conclusions.

With your help, we will have a good time during the next few weeks.

By order of prime minister Von Bülow, your participation will be noted on your academic record as a social study and public service event.

In the name of my staff and of our sponsors, I say welcome to Waldeck.

Meal times are six to eight o'clock for breakfast, noon to two o'clock for lunch, four to five o'clock for afternoon tea and seven to nine o'clock for dinner.

Please let us know of any allergies or food intolerances.

We ask, that you refrain from smoking and drinking alcoholic beverages during your stay.

Enjoy your time with us.

Welcome to Waldeck."

Chapter 18

The pilot group

Joan put down the typewritten transcript. She explained: "Maria, Helena, Stefan, Herbert, Wolf, and I decided to sit at different tables, to meet other people during meals. Of course, we also met a variety of other people doing chores and playing sports.

After dinner, we preferred to spend time together. Maria, Herbert, and Helena brought their guitars and Wolf tuned his violin. We talked about songs we knew and lyrics we could remember. Maria and I recited poetry and Wolf shared some poems of his own.

Nights were warm and the stars came out. A sharp sickle moon could be seen in the western sky in conjunction with Mars and Venus. Sirius was outshining other stars, looking like one of the planets. Maria, Wolf, Walter Helena, and Stefan shared my interest in constellations. The milky way was brilliantly displayed during these dark, clear nights.

We made music by the fire in the evenings. Other voices joined in our songs and everyone was surprised, how many tunes were known and how many were able to participate.

New songs were invented with repeating refrains, after the fore singer came up with new verses and the guitarists began using the bodies of their guitars as drums. The mood was buoyant. Everyone was included and seemed to be glad they had come."

"How did you go from getting acquainted to forging a plan to go to Africa?

How did you learn about German East Africa?" asked Gottfried, eagerly anticipating.

"During the day, we were the sailing team, that had formed the day we arrived.

We had bonded over this experience. However, we participated in different activities:

Wolf and Stefan were interested in working with horses. I saw Stefan ride dressage, Wolf was seen driving with horses from single carriage, to teams of eight, pulling a post wagon. Even pulling plows, harrows, and other farm equipment. He was a true horseman. I saw them sitting together after chores, shining their riding boots in deep conversation.

Maria was in gardens and greenhouses, inseparable from the woman in charge, a botanist and biologist, who answered her endless questions. Her night stand was soon stacked with books on gardening.

I was working in the kitchen, happy to see Maria walk in, where I was an eager apprentice. She was loaded with arms and baskets full of vegetables, she had harvested on the order of our chef.

Helena and Herbert were early risers. Helena was fascinated with poultry and water fowl. She also liked working with sheep and goats. Herbert was interested in dairy farming and processing milk. At the creamery, he learned to make butter and cheese.

A specialty of the farm was a soft goat cheese, which the chef used in many recipes.

Everyone liked his warm goat cheese salad. The early start gave them often a chance to trail Ana von Bülow. They soon assisted her with administrative tasks, curious about how this big operation could run so smoothly, without drama and seemingly without effort."

Gottfried was getting the picture.

"What was your favorite activity?

"I was fascinated by decorated pastries coming from the hands of their pastry chef.

I discovered the world between farm and table, that is unknown to most people.

At Waldeck, food preparation and food presentation were elevated to an artform.

I think, the secret of this enterprise, was the passion for excellence in everything they did.

Employees I observed in house and kitchen, were going about their work quietly and with purpose and one could get a sense of their satisfaction in doing things well.

They did not mind, sharing what they knew and how things worked.

I was drawn to the kitchen and the bakery. The pastry chef was a genius. He made edible art. The cooks liked the fact, that I am fast with knives, chopping piles of vegetables for them."

"What attracted you the most?"

"The art of seduction through the stomach. I learned baking bread, braiding loaves, and making crusty artisan breads, decorated with seeds and olives. I loved how food was presented at the table. Each dish a work of art.

Chapter 19

Trust

Gottfried moved to the front of his chair. He began to sense the real story coming.

"How did you attract Ana Von Bülow's attention, other than the sailing event?"

"Working in different activities of the estate, von Bülow and her staff had a chance to observe us. We never noticed, that we were being watched, until one evening, when our little sailing team approached her with the idea to form a pilot group:

The purpose being, to discuss the question, of what it was, the world needed from us, instead of trying to express, what we expected from the world.

We felt, that we had an obligation to look deeper, than to simply recite, what we were told. Von Bülow agreed that this was a good idea.

Maria wrote me this poetic note one evening:

"Sometimes it is chance that helps a seeking soul.
Even God's birds do not fall out of their nest.
In His presence, words can give solace,
to nurture the fledgling bird.
Words of a long-passed muse open his pages
to reveal the golden song of consolation."

Maria liked reading about the holy Grail. She had a sense of mission for her life, as a seeker. She was enthusiastic about the composition of our group."

"You and Maria have different reactions to the world. How did this affect your relationship, now that you were away from home?"

"Maria and I were very close.

The difference of what we saw and how we responded, made our bond stronger.

We were like hand in glove. We were very protective of each other and rarely engaged in sibling rivalry. Let me share with you another one of her notes, I found:

> *"When squares are crowding me*
> *I learn to float on wings like doves.*
> *The Living are rejecting me,*
> *while silent life of Spirit takes me in.*
> *Attracting me to join the inner circle,*
> *of those who drank the bitter potion.*
> *Those who in true heroic fashion*
> *keep courage and their faith untouched.*
> *No longer is there young or old,*
> *and rich or poor have lost their power.*
> *Where shepherds are elected king,*
> *to kneel upon the steps in prayer.*
> *To bring new light into the holy night,*
> *to shine into the depth of the abyss.*
> *So that the holy grail can nourish those,*
> *who are the guardians of the temple."*

That was my Maria." Joan waited for a reaction from Gottfried. He said, curious how these profound words were received in the group:

"How was her spirituality received by other participants and by those who were getting close to her?"

"Mariawascautiousaboutgettinginvolvedinconversations about religion or spirituality. When the subject came up, she listened carefully and would only speak, if she had a question about her understanding of what had been said to her.

We had resolved, that labels or church affiliation were not what we had come here to find. Getting to know people, while working with them morning to night was our goal.

Maria and I were getting closer and closer to Wolf and Stefan."

"Was there a change in your relationship with the other sailing team members?"

"The sailing team had grown close and like sailing a boat to a destination, our conversations began circling around the quest for things that needed to be done.

We felt secure in our group, to speak frankly and soon grew to trust each other.

We were able to explore ideas, without being judged, to speak about ideas for the future of a changing world, without being measured against traditions and patterns of traditional thought. We used one of the small living-room-libraries, to meet. We invited von Bülow to sit in, whenever she had time to do so. We were impressed with her

practical way of thinking and planning."

Chapter 20

The Vision

"Do you think your pilot group was a success?"

"Maria and I absolutely did. I found more of Wolf's journals. Let him tell us, how he saw things. We were intrigued by his ability, to reconcile scientific ideas with his search for a connection between physical and spiritual reality. He was not happy about the idea of separate worlds, like heaven, earth, and hell. Here is what he wrote:

"I find time to write late at night. I am discovering, that Maria and I are closer in our views about life's questions, than either of us thought possible.

We are discovering physical and spiritual attraction and stimulation, that is new to both of us. Even though this seems less of a mystery to her, than to me.

Maria is wise, soft spoken and gentle, while I tend to be more ridged.

Does it have something to do with my upbringing, or is there a difference between male and female? I think the creator had something special in mind about that.

I cannot stand to be without her. We linger at night, finding it difficult to say good night.

So much needs to be said. Our world is larger than most other people's worlds.

This was our first discovery: We both have a fear of running out of time.

Is that love growing from a seed, as she calls it?

Now the sailors have created a pilot group that meets every day from two to three thirty in the afternoon. We came together through the bond that was formed on our sailing adventure, when we first arrived.

Our group, with its diverse minds and talents lends itself to focused conversation. Together, we can make the transition from idealism and philosophy to practical applications. To me, the most important element is trust.

On the ship we learned, that we can trust each other with our lives. Now we are bringing this trust to the table with good results.

During our first few meetings, we agreed on principles to guide our conduct during our talks, starting with the mandate to reach consensus, whenever decisions must be made.

We take the risk of disagreeing. That is the freedom we grant each other.
We decided to give everyone a chance to explore their own unique point of view.
We made "point of view" the topic during one of our early meetings.
We decided that we needed a facilitator to be sure, everyone's voice was heard.
We agreed to ask Helena to be our facilitator, a role that comes naturally to her.

We agreed to identify the subject of our conversations.

We agreed to flush out sources of influence or information, to further clarify our own point of view.

This gives everyone a chance to share their background.

Each of us brings a lot to the table from family, upbringing and from the province in the country, we grew up in.

We come with education of ideas others have presented to us.
Now, there is no higher authority in the room, than our own minds.

Knowledge of time and space cannot be understood, without adding the element of living experience in the here and now.

I am not convinced, that there is a higher world beyond our grasp, that needs an interpreter or a representative, like clergy or the pope.

The fact, that we can speak on this level about our views about reality, is making me look forward to these conversations from day to day.

I have begun to trust, that we can even develop practical steps.

This is important to me. I feel, that we have become a true visioning team.

In Helena, we have a great facilitator, as we had Stefan as captain on the sailing ship.

Now our chosen topic is the destination.

The facilitator makes sure, we stay on course and no one is left behind, or goes overboard. I shared this poem with Maria and the group:

Born to see,
I was sent with vision
to view from my tower,
to notice the world.
To glance afar,
see what is near,
see moon and stars,
see trees and deer,
see in my mind eternal life
I like what I see,
am pleased with myself,
my vision to BE.
You, fortunate eyes,
become what you see,
be all that you are meant to be:
Look inside and out
see the beauty in me."

Joan now closed her eyes and took some time to gaze into her memory. Then she looked at Gottfried and, sensing that he wanted more, she said:

"These are Wolfs notes:
"Maria shared this poem with us:
My faith.
I believe the world
is created by a high and wise spirit.
I trust that deep devotion he deserves.
Do not know how I can praise him right,
cannot see, how dogma does him justice,
his highness can expect much more.
He has created us from dust,
not free of fault, but free to err
and when I step before him in the end

get face to face with my creator,
I will be judged, by what I did,
and not by my devoted faith.

Joan was pleased to see how Gottfried was clinging to her every word, actively listening. She beamed at him.

"This is what I have found so far.

There are more boxes with documents and notes.

My Stefan was the keeper of notes. He wanted to move forward in life with his daily activities. Like the captain of a ship, he always said:

"I keep the scraps for later, so the slate stays clean. This way I know, I do not lose the past.

Do not touch them or clean them out. One day, we might want to look back, to see how we have come to this place, or if we must find our way back home."

He always looked in front of him and treated each moment with the same energy and focus he brought to a tennis match, keeping his eyes on the ball, climbing a mountain, or during competitive skiing events.

Did I tell you, that every winter, he cut a hole into the ice of the frozen lake for me, next to our dock, to be sure I would not miss a day of taking a dip in the lake, which I like to do every morning, all year round, three hundred sixty-five days?"

Joan glanced over the lake, offered Gottfried more of her irresistible baked goods, then she said:

"Focus was my Stefan's strength. He kept us focused from the day we met, to the day he returned to the Lord. His voice is still in my heart. I always answer.

It keeps us close. My heart is where we met and it is here, we still connect."

She smiled through her tears.

Gottfried was deeply moved and felt privileged to share this moment with his great aunt Joan.

Chapter 21

Facilitation

The next time they met, Gottfried was still under the spell of what Joan had told him about Stefan.

"Tell me about Stefan's role in the pilot group. What did the captain do, when he was not at the helm?"

"At first, I was concerned about that. Then we chose Helena to be the facilitator.

I found that Stefan was meticulous about rules. In sports, as in his interactions with others, he was interested in establishing and following rules or in breaking rules, if they restricted him unnecessarily. It was his intention to widen the path for new and practical possibilities. That is how it worked for him. It balanced his competitiveness in the group.

He was the reality pole and the anchor. He would be irritated, when people went too far into theoretical or philosophical speculation of things, that were not experience based, or goal oriented. Then he would bring up the big "AND?" With this, he would reel us back into focus, bringing the conversation onto its intended purpose.

It was his impatience that would often lead us to good results. It made him take risks others were reluctant to take. He was surprisingly close to Wolf. They were partners in seeking practical goals. I saw them in deep conversation, when they thought no one was watching them."

Gottfried gave Joan a quizzical look.

"How did your group turn the conversation from the religious divide to action plans? What did you do to make your group effective at decision making?"

"Helena was a very good debater. Having her step back to be the facilitator, made her aware of possibilities, that came from differences in view, rather than trying to be right, defending her own arguments. She trusted in reaching consensus.

With Herbert by her side as the strategist, who could get a boat to its destination, they could steer a conversation from seemingly going nowhere, to definitely going somewhere. Herbert always asked, to verify our destination and Helena made sure, we understood and agreed, where and what that was."

Gottfried:

"How did she do that?"

"Helena had us agree on doing several exercises, beginning with our first agreement:

How the group should be seated, with or without tables, depending on the purpose of the meeting and what the theme of the session would be.

She reminded us of our conversation after the near capsize of the sailboat and how the worst did not happen, because everyone had a different point of view."

Gottfried: "Remind me of what agreements were, you made."

"There were several exercises, we agreed to do:

A point of view exercise:

One person sat in the center of a circle and each of us would describe in detail what they saw. We learned, that together we were able see the whole image, not just one side as was the view from each participant.

A listening exercise:

Everyone was seated in a circle. Using two tennis balls, the facilitator would hand the first ball to the speaker. Everyone without a ball would have to listen and wait, until the first speaker was finished, the second ball was handed to the person who wanted to respond.

Before this person was given the ball to speak, they had to repeat verbatim what the speaker had said. Then they had to explain what they took the meaning to be.

When that was confirmed, the speaking ball was handed over to the respondent and the reply was heard.

This taught us, that short statements are remembered better. That concentrating on what is being said is better than thinking of a reply, while the speaker is making their point.

A debating exercise:

Consecutive speakers would argue the opposite opinion, from what they really knew, or thought, still using the balls, to make sure, only one person spoke a time.

The facilitator paid attention to giving silent participants a chance to take the ball to speak, which helped to flush out all the ideas in the room.

This was an amusing exercise for all of us.

The most fun was the 'opinion vs. knowledge' exercise:

The speaker had to first confess to have no idea about the chosen subject.

The task then was, to sound profoundly convinced and knowledgeable, the way politicians do, when they are asked difficult questions by reporters, the public or by members of government. People with subject knowledge had to remain silent and stone faced. We shed tears laughing during this exercise.

Most important was practice in consensus building:

People could caucus in private with each other, the facilitator, or forge alliances.

No one could be excluded or silenced by a majority. The facilitator was to level the playing field, making sure that every voice was heard.

Discussions could end with the decision to table a discussion, until more information was available, or until after a consultant could be brought in, to weigh in with relevant information: Ethical, technical, or legal. We found, that good decisions could be made this way and lasting agreements could be reached, even when at the onset no common ground was visible to any of the participants.

Verry important and most popular, was to choose, which topic was of the most urgency and whether or not there was a chance to advance from philosophical or theoretical considerations to practical action plans."

Gottfried was fascinated.

"How did you get from theory to action?"

"We began with the discovery, of what we have in common:
We all wanted to do things, that made a difference in the world.

No one wanted to fit into precast molds.

There was the conflict of old versus new, tradition versus vision, religion versus science, the rule of law vs consensus, military or police power vs participatory rule making, mandate vs, choice.

We saw conflict between major religions as the most visible danger, with a potential of igniting violence, capable of incinerating everything that has been achieved to date by humanity.

To let an invisible authority sit in judgement on visible issues, turned out to be a power grab by people, claiming to represent the divine, the highest authority and the truth. Exclusive of anyone else. This could ignite conflict between knowledge and opinion, based on opposing belief systems and the insatiable hunger for power."

Joan fished another document from her box:

"Here is the 'Statement of Agreement' issued by our pilot group, that we submitted to the full assembly.

We agree that none of us can accept authority on principle, the delegation of

responsibility out of convenience or out of fear of the unknown.

We agree that science is the way to the future, provided, that it is used to unlock knowledge into the workings of living nature and the nature of substance, in service of all mankind, rather than for the benefit of a privileged few.

We agree that it would be effective to create new ideas and to try them in a real-life experimentation.

We reject to be frustrated by forces we found everywhere, that insist on stifling ideas and progress, based on precedence or conflicting interests.

We agree that there is a need to find a place, where such experiments can be held and created. We envision a world in which religious beliefs are respected, instead of being used to disenfranchise those with different traditions or different forms of worship.

We agree that we want to see a world, that does not discriminate based on gender, race, or nationality.

We agree that human rights are for all humans, no matter by which name they call their creator or where they were born.

We agree that the right to life needs to be granted to Nature, to provide a safe future for all living creatures.

We agree that air, water, soil, and oceans must be placed under commons protection, just like we do with public works like railroads, water systems, harbors, roadways, common pasture land and forests. Denying access to the commons is to deny the right to life.

We agree that war and military conflicts are a designed and are a planned violation against all of humanity. These actions are being accepted only because of lack of judgement, or bad information. Violence is glorified and supported by those, who benefit from the outcome and by a common belief, that wars break out like storms in Nature.

We agree that people feel pride and are compelled to serve their country and their rulers, who claim to have the God given divine authority, to call their subjects to arms and to threaten their citizens with incarceration or execution for treason, if they refuse to serve their cause and to take up arms on their command.

We observe that the world is being subdivided during international treaty conferences and that the population of regions in question is almost never part of these negotiations.

We observe that control over international trade and resources lies mainly with naval power and not with the will of

Nations. This has caused an arms race among superpowers on Europe's mainland and the British Isles. Construction of ever more powerful armored battleships has become the subject- and part of negotiations, over distribution and territorial control of colonies abroad.

Our concern is, that we are entering an era fraught with risk of armed conflict, reaching every part of life; religious, economic, social, political and territorial. This has become a global concern, as empires crumble and leave a vacuum to fight over.

The religious divide, that has brought us together here, is no longer the only cause for conflict. It can be used as a trigger to rouse emotions, hatred, and division, and is being used to rally nations to arms, from which no one can escape, because everyone and everything is now connected around the world.

We repeat: We agree that none of us is willing to accept authority on principle or to delegate responsibility out of convenience, or fear of the unknown. We believe that the most qualified deserve to serve in public office, representing common interests. Individuals, who love humanity and truth more than power, are best suited."

Joan took a deep breath and carefully placed the document back in the box.

"This is what we shared with everyone as takeaway of our pilot group."

Chapter 22

Consensus

Gottfried gently took this declaration out of the box and examined it.

"What did you do with this document?"

"We gave a copy of this statement of agreement to Anna von Bülow.

We had sent Helena and Herbert to invite her to our meetings whenever a view at the entire globe was needed. We trusted and hoped, that she would help us find a possible place for the creation of a social experiment, based on principles, contained in our agreement. We felt that Ana von Bülow could give us practical guidance. "

Gottfried placed the document back into the box, then asked Joan:

"Did you find issues, that you did not agree with? "

"Oh yes. We did not agree with those who believe, that emperors and kings are inheritors of power and authority, ordained by God.

We disagreed with those, who think royals, kings and emperors are free to trade, sell and privatize the world under their control, to people who see the world as a resource to be mined and stripped for profit, including natives and other humans.

We disagreed with private or corporate ownership of people, needed to run machines in factories or to dig minerals out of the ground, build infrastructure to support our way of life.

We disagreed that there is salvation in religious or scientific doctrines, because they tend to prevent real progress and cause irreconcilable conflicts in their rigidity.

We saw a problem with placing power into hands, other than those based upon qualification, not inheritance, blood line or industrial buying power, overriding the common good for the sole benefit of investors.

We had a problem with power, held in the name of God, like the Roman Catholic Church, the Protestant Church and any other form of rulership based upon the claim of divine providence, divine intervention, divine selection, divine bloodline, or divine dictate."

Gottfried was so excited now, he had to get up and walk back and forth. He asked:

"How did Von Bülow react to your ideas?"

"We were surprised by her enthusiasm and active participation. We presented our list of agreements. This set the stage for the next step:

A practical resolution that could lead to an action plan.

We were also surprised about how much she knew about us, who we were, who our families are and what potential we represent, the public engagement and social standing of our families, coming both from the Catholic and the Protestant side of society.

After listening to our presentation, she introduced herself as a person close to the prime minister.

She agreed to brainstorm with us about a possible location for a Social Experiment.

She suggested, that it would be possible to create a futuristic village in many places.

She became animated, when she told us about a colony the German Empire owned in East Africa.

Von Bülow said:

"As you can imagine, there are opposing forces at work there, just like here:

Some are the traditional empire builders, who want to use the military model of conquest and administration in newly acquired territories, acting as though they had no inhabitants or owners, when they were first discovered. They see territorial conquest as an opportunity to expand our Nation, extract wealth, treasure, and trade goods, with no regard to existing populations, traditions, or relationships.

On the other hand, we have Kiser Friedrich Wilhelm II, the new emperor of our Second Reich since 1888, who favors an approach, different from the violent British model of colonization, that has proven to be fraught with unrest, violence, and human rights abuses. Our colony is at risk of following in those footsteps.

Our emperor has asked his administration, to develop a more integrated model that includes local populations, uses their talents, their history, their culture and their existing trade and work experience, to benefit them, as well as the homeland that is now their owner and protector.

The Kaiser has ordered to raise the standard of living for natives, rather than to marginalize and squeeze them out. He does not believe in shooting those, who do not collaborate with colonial objectives. Instead, he wants to bring them into the fold of the Empire, by collaboration and the benefit of our experience in education and health care.

He is convinced, that no peace can be maintained and no sustainable wealth can be developed, by using traditional violent methods of colonization, which has caused perpetual conflict, uprisings, and destructive revolts.

The emperor has recently sent a new governor to German East Africa, named Albrecht von Rechenberg. Baron von Rechenberg is charged with developing infrastructure improvements, by advancing what the former East Africa Company has started.

His mandate includes research into existing social systems, the advancement of trade with our domestic market and to facilitate more trade with markets around the globe.

The emperor wants to bring wealth, stability, and steady development to the colony, appease warring tribes and improve the standard of living for everyone, the way different tribes here in Germany were brought under the umbrella of the second empire for the benefit of the entire federation of states. He asked for building education- health- and vocational training facilities, besides making infrastructure improvements.

He ordered, that research be done to find marketable crops and agricultural methods suitable for that climate, its soils, and the nutritional requirements for the people living in this region.

This should help planters, who are interested in a stable economy, support their cultivation and export of Coffee, Tee, Rubber, Hemp, Sisal and Cotton and to make their investment profitable.

We know of strong opposing forces here at home and in Africa, who believe in simply killing off unwanted "homeless herders" like the Massai and other tribes, who forage for a living, building fences and armed gates around their plantations to keep unwanted people and wildlife out."

Gottfried was beginning to feal a little nauseous, remembering his own Namibia- indigenous bushmen conflict in south Africa.

"Is this how Africa came into your conversation? How did she believe you were qualified to help the Governor or the Empire as individuals or as a group?"

Joan noticed his strong reaction and handed him a glass of water.

"We asked her about that. She said, that in her opinion, people with preset ideas, based upon history, or experience from East Prussia, Bavaria or from the industrial centers near the Ruhr and Rhine rivers, were not helpful in finding the right direction for the Africa colony, because too much of the social consequence of changes in Africa is not comparable to Germany, which caused the failure of the German East Africa Company in the first place.

Von Bülow looked a all of us and suggested:

"You have no preset ideas and your creative approach to problem solving will infuse something new into the conversation. There are people in our colonial administration who can see hope in that."

Gottfried, with eyes and ears wide open:

"Was that what made you think you could help?"

"We had several brain storming sessions with her on the merits of bringing consensus-based solution finding and -rulemaking to the Colony.

We agreed, that it was better to integrate agricultural, economic, religious, and ethnic traditions into a social system, designed to prepare these different social groups for a changing world, without insulting or disenfranchising them.

We agreed that colonial society had to move towards a merit-based leadership system, that represents everyone and moves away from traditional dictatorial governance.

We had witnessed the change, that took place in Europe, with the construction of railroads. We were personally affected by religious and economic strife.

After all, this was the reason, why we had come to this youth summit on her farm:

To learn what we have in common, rather than what divides us. This was no different here from places anywhere else in the world."

Joan was on a roll now.

"Once the summer event was over, Anna von Bülow used her influence to have the prime minister send emissaries to Waldeck, to spend a couple of days with us.

After listening to us, these officials began discussing a possible assignment.

They helped us to formulate proposals, created applications and consent documents for our families. They outlined a timeline and proposed we meet again at the department of foreign affairs in Berlin.

The governor of German East Africa was in Germany at the time.

He had come to facilitate financing for the completion of the railroad connecting Tanga to Moshi in the foothills of Mount Kilimanjaro and all the way to the lakes-region of Tanganyika, connecting railroads from Lake Tanganyika to Dar Es Salaam.

He looked at these proposals with interest and approved them with a stroke of his pen.

Like magic, levers were being pulled.

We were given the assignment, to study possibilities in GEA and to make recommendations for a more progressive and integrated colonial administration.

One that was not constantly threatened by revolts and strikes from an alienated population, that took the building of our Colony as an act of thievery of their inherited homeland and culture and as a violation of their indigenous rights.

We were being sent to East Africa to inspect the region, meet leaders of existing communities and to find ways to invite collaboration and to build trust.

What made this assignment intriguing to us was the fact, that there are many tribes, sects and religious groups, whose traditions were still widely unknown.

We liked the challenge and opportunity of trying consensus-based rule making and collaboration in harmony with Humans and with Nature.

We were told, that German East Africa is the gateway to the heart of Africa.

This promised possibilities of developing a liberal, social-economic commonwealth, that would not require natives to give up their identity, traditions, or faith, but to include them.

It would save the Colony from civil unrest and war and raise the standard of living for everyone involved.

We knew we had a lot to learn. This was a once in a lifetime opportunity for us."

Chapter 23

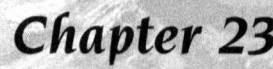

Consent

Gottfried: "How did your families react to this sudden switch in plans with such far reaching consequences?"

"All of us were raised in families with broad public responsibilities. Our families' concerns were about peace and justice across religious and economic dividing lines. We had this in common.

The use of people as labor force without offering them benefits from the wealth they help create, will sooner or later lead to conflict and civil uprising. We suspected, that if it was bad at home, it would be worse in the colonies.

Working on developing a better colony, was considered an essential service to our empire and an honor to our families.

It was like a call to arms and our families were ready to support it."

Joan got up and walked a few steps to stretch her neck, legs, and arms. Then she continued:

"Once prime minister von Bülow's relative was in our conversation, she could see that we were uniquely qualified. She sensed that we had grown up with conversations reaching far beyond our daily needs and that creative imagination and responsibility to the public, were nurtured in us since childhood. She liked, that we saw the need for connecting ideas with practical action plans. She knew we had a hunger for constructive solutions.

Looking back more than sixty years later, I can say, that she was very much like us and we were very much like her. There was immediate recognition. We did not need prompts from her. We were her kind of visionaries. She recognized this, after attending just a couple of our meetings.

Gottfried could not believe it, even though he himself had already seen several countries in Europe as a musician and had gone to South Africa before he was nineteen. He had to hear it one more time.

"Did your parents give their consent? You were all so very young."

"Our parents corresponded with each other. They convened a meeting of participating families with the Governor's team. We were surprised, how a call from the Kaiser to serve the nation, waylaid all our parent's concerns.

Consent agreements were signed, making us official investigators with authority to meet officials and African dignitaries, to ask questions and to present new ideas. We were given authority to view all relevant government documents.

We were expected to draft a report of our findings to Governor Albrecht von Rechenberg.

Chapter 24

Closing the divide

Gottfried was fascinated:

"Tell me about the pilot group one more time. How did you cope with all this as a group?"

"After this initial meeting, we were sent to Berlin for briefings, designed to help us understand what to expect and what was expected of us.

Logistics of travel arrangements, necessary equipment, financial requirements, and funding were planned and authorized by the administration.

Helena was now showing her strength as facilitator. We were in shock, thinking about the enormity of what had just happened.

Helena put things into perspective:

"This is not any bigger than our visit to Waldeck, which was motivated by our parent's concern over the religious divide. They trusted, that we would find a way to close the growing divide between our religions, through personal acquaintances and friendships.

It will be like this in Africa: We will divine what people have in common and chart a compass reading for our nation, as we did at Waldeck for each of us."

Herbert, always our strategist, said this:

"We are going to create an information stream. It will be our task to gather information and to sort opinion from reality, facts from wishful thinking, science from beliefs, public concerns from private interests. We will find economic and spiritual life, represented by leaders steeped in tradition. We will integrate their multiple views and use their influence to create a workable social and economic compact, that does not disenfranchise anyone.

I think the reason, we are in this conversation, is that we have demonstrated, that we can listen to more than one side."

Gottfried found himself engaged, as if he were one of the participants:

"What did Wolf have to say about all of this, is there anything in his diaries?"

Joan seemed to have anticipated this question.

She picked up one of his notebooks. She was beaming, she said:

"Wolf saw it this way: He wrote:"

"Africa is a multifaceted continent, that looks from the outside like a different planet and on the inside like a kaleidoscope of different tribes, fiefdoms, and kalifates.

The African Continent is so large, that many climate zones exist from deserts to tropical rain forests, to alpine heights, rivers, and lakes, each requiring different life skills.

Insiders and outsiders strive to connect to the world in a way, that benefits all the players. The most dangerous approach for Africa is to ignore any part of the whole."

"This was Wolfs take on things, "she said.

"How about Stefan?"

"Stefan was solid in his role as our captain. He looked for the next way marker. I was falling in love with him and Maria was my confidante. She was falling in love with Wolf. Maria was more spiritual and I am more practical.

Stefan's acquaintance with Wolf and Herbert was beginning to turn from a partnership into a lifelong friendship. They were quietly consulting with one another. They never excluded Maria, Helena, or me. They stepped up to authority, respectfully interacting with government officials, showing us off as a united front, not letting anyone take one of us aside.

"You are talking to all of us." They would remind everyone."

The next time Joan and Gottfried saw each other, Joan had found more papers:

"Here is another journal from Wolf:" Joan said, smiling.

"We are formulating things to do:

Our wide viewing angle on the Nation and the World is surprising even us.

We are illuminating for each other gray zones in the picture we have of our world.

My views on political and economic backroom dealings, often dismissed as conspiracy theories, are not taken by my friends as a distraction from the facts.

I see them for the first time verified by those, who know about decisions that are being quietly made, with far reaching consequences in this emerging new world order:

In my eyes, the fate of all of mankind is at stake. As a pilot group and as a team, we are taking a wholistic view on the entire planet, we see it all connected.

We agreed to see spirituality as being equal to physical reality. Religion as important as science. Individual existence connected to society and to humanity.

News information to the public is still in its infancy. Stories about the world are delivered in simple images, printed on postcards, displayed on posters with pretty pictures of things that will change the world very soon. Especially about Africa:

The public is intrigued by exhibits of exotic animals in zoos and humans from Africa in tribal costumes, exhibited in market places and carnivals, complete with face-painting and display of indiginous ceremonies. Popular are exhibits of preserved trophies of large animals from exotic places. They are stirring public interest and imagination, romanticizing the conquest. All are meant to appeal to people's emotions and to our national pride.

Two things happening:

First, I noticed the formation of associations of influential people, who could change the course of history, now numbering in the thousands.

Second, I see a coalition of large banks and wealthy individuals, who are financing infrastructure projects around the world, without public discussion, particularly the construction of large dams with power generators and armored battle ships, that can threaten or change the balance of power in oceans around the world.

I am concerned about a looming threat to world peace by an emerging arms race.

Regarding our Africa assignment:

As a group of advisors, we were made aware of opposing forces, fighting over control of the Colony of German East Africa: Policies, established for a region several times the size of the German homeland, were written by people who are either isolated in the African wildlands, or at home, listening to religious reformers and missionaries, or industrial interest groups in need of raw materials, markets, and investment opportunities.

None of these considerations include the needs of indigenous Africans.

We are to focus on things we can do or influence, to study the region in real time and to make recommendations for building a just and integrated world, that can go beyond well-established power structures and belief systems at home.

As I see it, the world is not just widening the divide between Catholics and Protestants. Hunger for resources and raw materials for industry and access to ports and shipping lanes, are becoming more important than the life of the population of the countries, where empires have laid their claims.

This is the real growing divide:

Humans vs. economic imperatives. Ownership vs. Partnership. Developed world vs. indiginous world.

European countries have taken possession without asking permission:

Ownership and control over colonies are negotiated, using incomplete maps of undiscovered areas, apportioning and subdividing "new" territories is done by people who have not even been to many of the regions of the planet, they have taken possession of. They are assigning each other parts of the world in treaties, that will have to be enforced by force of arms, following the model of the conquest of the Roman Empire.

The method used by the Roman Empire, was to invent inheritable, divine rights, which they granted to each other and enforced with the most powerful army of the day.

Now we are using the Roman law, with the power to dispatch chartered corporations, answerable only to investors. Just like Rome, we are ignoring the countries where we grant license to be active, according to the charters of such legal corporations.

The "right of the mighty", in my mind, is a recipe for war.

Science is conflicted and being misused to justify our global supremacy.

Observations by Darwin on the survival of the fittest were used, to justify our aggression towards nature, including people with different pigmentation, which are considered genetically flawed and therefore doomed to extinction.

Conveniently, anthropologists have begun using the term "race," to differentiate between humans, the way the Roman Catholic church and her "holy empires" defined humans by their conversion to Christianity and by whether or not they owned property.

"Heathens" were considered disposable, could be boiled, hung, tortured, and publicly displayed, to warn dissenters, who questioned the divine authority of the Holy Sea.

To include all humans under the definition 'Human Race,' was abandoned for the purpose of disenfranchising everyone on this planet, who is not a white Anglo-Saxon or Caucasian Christian. And in the case of The Holy Sea of Rome, excluding anyone who is not baptized or part of this man-made holy sea.

This is the heritage we are walking into Africa with.

We are being sent to appease conquerors and heathens.

To make ourselves feel better, we are proclaiming to be elevating heathens from their squalor and improving their lot, by forcibly appeasing them.

So called "science" has already determined, that they are doomed to become extinct.

It was omitted conveniently from Darwin's original text, that in nature, collaboration and mutual support are providing resiliency. Diversity is a source of health for all living organisms. We are led to ignore these truths.

Colonial Powers are negotiating among each other a division of the planet, forging coalitions, and making agreements, designed to suppress popular uprisings in colonized regions such as China, Asia, Africa, and South America, while at home, these rulers stir feelings of national pride, with the promise of a "place in the sun" for overcrowded conditions in the homelands under their control.

My fear is, that our religious divide is merely a distraction.

We are separating people by race and title to land and resources, which we grant ourselves exclusively.

I personally believe in one thing: No political system can function, unless these dividing barriers and 'God given' entitlements are first removed.

We find ourselves in the development stages of Systemic Injustice, based on the division of labor, management, ownership, and investors entitled to profits.

This system stands with both feet on the necks of Humans.

No right to justice, means no right to life.

Representation of the public by government is made impossible, because government is being directed by imperatives other than those of the public.

Industry requires educated individuals for engineering, research, and development.

Schools are repurposed, to teach science, like the Dillmann Gymnasium in Stuttgart, which I have graduated from. This high school has become a model for the nation. The divide I am beginning to see, is religious only in name and only on the surface.

Underneath lies the issue of Justice and the right to life for humans and nature.

I see conquerors subordinating conquered people, after taking away inherited social structures. Even Nobility, Kings and Emperors are losing their power to requirements of industry.

The race for military domination is vailed by propaganda about national pride.

I believe it serves only economic development and -progress but not the people.

This is a powder keg next to a pile of ordnance, about to be lit by an accidently dropped match. No one can control the explosion that will follow.

I studied the confiscation of Christianity by the Roman Empire. Roman emperors were unable to suppress Christians. They turned the Christian religion into a state religion. They called the world's population heathens, unless they were Christianized.

This is the naked truth as I see it:

Christianity has been bloodied by empire builders, who invented and imposed the law of the empire, enforced by armed mercenaries. They chose to include the entire planet. Those who were not committed Christians, lost their right to life.

Martin Luther, a former catholic monk, started the protestant movement in Germany. That began the endless conflict, we are now asked to resolve in a Colony, four times the size of Germany.

Christian Nations gave title of ownership to its own members, exclusive of all others.

To make room and to expand territory, it was convenient to exclude people of color, who could be temporarily tolerated as slaves and as workers in households, mines, or factories, providing, they are willing to be Christianized.

We are using religious differences to disguise the prevention of popular participation in the benefits, earned by labor of industry and large-scale industrialized plantations.

We ignore our ability to raise humans out of poverty and to create social justice for everyone, because our economic system can exploit the poor better in their squalor.

I see inventions of the war industry being turned against its own work force.

Tear gas and lethal weapons are deployed in the name of security and peace, protection of property and the public. Every time, demands for a place at the table are voiced, new so-called terrorists are born.

Industrial development is designed to advance science and technology, in service to the armaments industry, which is used to develop and conquer colonies, rich in natural resources. The promise of huge returns on investment was demonstrated by the British East India Company. This corporation is mostly owned by European Crowned Heads of State. It is a chartered corporation, licensed by its royal owners, to recruit and train forces abroad, to protect the corporation's investments, rights and interests against The demand of the population, to share in the benefit.

I see chartered corporations as raiders, acting against those, who were dismissed as owners, because they had no title to their property, that is recognized by the rulers of Empire. Former owners are now called terrorists, who are threatening the rights of the corporation and its investors. By consent of the colonizers, they must be suppressed or eliminated by armed force.

British colonies are military strongholds, governed by armies under martial law.

That is the new peace. Other empires are using the same model for their colonization.

The Hudson Bay company in North America is an example of a charter, granted without a clear understanding of the meaning of "the entire watershed draining into the Hudson Bay", which, as it turned out, to be almost twenty times larger than her investors had expected.

Countries are claiming treasure inside uncharted expanses of Central Africa, as well as the continents of China and Asia. These are examples of the oppression of indigenous people, unless they can provide markets for industry and provide labor, together with raw materials.

None of this is being explained to our public here at home.

We are asked, to make suggestions for rule making, different from British colonial governance, after studying conditions in German East Africa.

Our task is to make a commonwealth out of a war zone, rather than to establish more military reservations.

I must be careful to stay on topic and not bring into the conversation too many political issues, such as the fledgling social democratic labor movement, that is beginning to ask for a place at the table at home.

evelop new concepts, without harboring old ideas in our considerations. I agree. In my mind, it is unrealistic to use old ways, to achieve new outcomes. I am worried about the future of mankind."

Joan put Wolf's journal into the box and unfolded more papers. She said:

"Here is what Herbert wrote:"

"We are asked to create a model for colonial development, that up to now was a mirror image of our own country, with regional differences as diverse as the dialects, people speak. At home, we have begun the slow process of dismantling inherited kingdoms and turning them into states under an empire, uniting them as a federation.

A constitutional monarchy.

In the colonies, this idea seems impossible, because they have diverse groups and nations, living under different forms of leadership, religions gifted with a great variety of skills, in more diverse climates and with far greater distances physically.

From discussions in our pilot group, I am under the impression, that we are leaning towards developing a collaborative model, rather than the traditional colonial dictatorship, that must be enforced and protected by force of arms.

We are understanding our assignment to be to suggest, how to create a commonwealth in a colony under German control, that is sustainable and does not require constant military intervention. In fact, I believe, that we have a better chance of developing a social justice model with religious freedom in Africa than here at home."

Chapter 26

The assignment

It was now early summer and the garden was in full bloom. Joan and Gottfried met on the terrace, overlooking the lake, amid the sweet scent of blossoms and the buzzing of bees. Gottfried asked:

"Can you remember how your men were interacting in the group. How did the men treat you, Maria, and Helena?"

"All of us were very private in our personal lives. Maria was the kind of person I could take into my confidence.

Our men were amazingly gallant and respectful towards us. I do not remember them ever treating us with less than the greatest respect as equal partners.

That went into the style of our conversations as a group.

Helena, our facilitator by agreement, never abandoned her role.

Wolf could display biting sarcasm towards people, who expressed opinions as facts, to push an agenda. In our group, Wolf and Maria were moderating each other in their passion on issues of justice and spirituality. So did Helena and Herbert. Their contributions never originated from the two of them together, but always from their independent, individual point of view.

Privately, we women were inseparable from our loved men and very protective of each other."

Now Gottfried became eager to get on with the journey to the south.

"Once you had finished the briefings in Belin, how much time did you have before shipping out?

"The Governor wanted to send us on a new, armored, state of the art ship. It had been designed and was being built for the use of the German East Africa Colonial Government. We were included on the passenger list for the maiden voyage.

The ship was not ready in time.

We were expected to spend several years overseas, to establish field stations to do our research. We even had a motorcar made by Daimler Benz and a diesel tractor, that could navigate rough terrain.

I found a journal Maria had given me.

"Spring of 1912.

Once we were to set foot on the African Continent, we wanted to be sure of a process, to evaluate our findings. I felt lucky to be in such good company.

Today, Joan and I arrived in Bremen. We had returned home, after the instruction sessions in Berlin, during which we worked to have a large amount of administrative playroom, rather than to have administrators design every step for us. We take our mission very seriously. No one is to dictate, what information we are to find. We are determined to develop fresh ideas and not to be influenced by ideas, or concepts, of career administrators.

Wolf always says: "Only fools try the same failed thing over and over, hoping for a different outcome."

We reminded administrators of the fact, that our contribution could only be useful for the Colony, if we have the authority, to go about our investigation, the way we see fit.

Helena and Herbert turned out to be forceful administrators for our team. They stood tall on our behalf, as protectors of our mission.

Helena used her position with authority during discussions with the Ministry of Foreign Affairs.

Herbert excelled as diplomat, who delivered summaries of what we had taken away from each meeting. This helped to influence officials to follow our train of thought, rather than steering us towards their own ideas.

I was surprised, how friendly and elegant Herbert acknowledged everyone's authority, wisdom, and intent. Then he led them onto our path, without allowing obstacles to be raised. He made them see, that we all wanted to accomplish the same thing.

A Colony free of violent conflict, one that would be seen to benefit all parties.

Local native people, our Nation, the immigrant community, foreign participants, and investors at home.

International trade between Europe, India and other Nations around the world was important to us. He made them see, that we believe, that trade can be positively or negatively influenced by policies and treaties, made during negotiations in Europe.

As we have seen from the experience of the bankrupt German East Africa Corporation, if local conditions are unknown or ignored, we suffer regrettable outcomes and missed opportunities. Investments in infrastructure, such as railroads, schools and hospitals seem vital to the success of the Colony. That is our common ground.

Wolf and Stefan are well informed about the contest over dominance of oceans and harbors, as industry begins to grow and access to raw materials is of central importance to our nation. They know that it is not a good idea to be separating these interests from what the population at home is told.

Both have an issue with hidden agendas and the claim, that something is a matter of national pride, when the truth is, that imperatives are dictated by bankers, industrialists, and shipping concerns, without input from partnering populations abroad or at home or a mechanism to reward the public at home for public investments in the Colony.

Wolf had long conversations with Papa on issues of energy and trade, during our visit at home. The two soon began to trust one another.

We now must go to Bremer Haven, to ship out towards Africa on the vessel Stella Maris.

My relationship with Wolf has grown strong and committed. We want to have a family one day. It was important to me to introduce him to the family before our departure.

Papa is his usual practical self, seeing the duty to Country and the Future of the Nation as what he must support, the same way that mama sees her commitment to the Catholic faith as a guiding principle in her life. She had to bring some resolve to tolerating the fact, that Wolf is not a Catholic. His religious tolerance and knowledge helped her to like him in the end. We explained our mission in Africa and she came around to seeing that the world needed to work towards peace between people of different faiths and that dogma is not a way to bring people together.

When we left, we had the blessings of both our parents.

When we were about to depart, mama retired with her lacy kerchief and dried her tears, after kissing Joan and me on the forehead and on both cheeks, saying a blessing and a prayer to place us in the protection of several Saints.

She gave Joan and me each a talisman of three rosary beads, made from tiger eye stone, to add to our rosaries.

She walked out of the room, to seek refuge at the little altar in her study, where she keeps her bible, says her prayers, and sheds her tears.

Wolf and I are deeply in love. I have a strong sense, that fate has sent us to each other as protectors, friends, lovers, confidants, and advisors. We are a perfect match in many magical ways. We complement each other with our interest in religion, literature, mysticism, science, history, and philosophy. And Wolf likes my passion for books.

Wolf won my heart the moment I saw him the first time. I knew he was the one.

It felt like lightning had struck me. I was not surprised, when he turned out to be the first person in my life, who did not have a problem with my love of books and literature, one I could be with, without the need of constant small talk.

This makes me feel safe in his company.

Our shared sense of mission and purpose made up for our complete lack of experience with the other gender, limited to some childhood crushes.

No guidance available to teenagers, no explanations about birds and bees.

We took our clues from romantic literature and stories from the round table at the court of King Arthur.

The holy grail is an image that gives me endless material for comfort, thought, and wonderment.

Wolf and I have a sense of holy commitment to each other, with a free hand at experimentation in the world of the senses, for which neither our parents nor our churches had useful advice or guidance.

We are now about to leave Europe, to embark on a sea voyage, more than half way around the world, with no parental guidance or religious supervision. We are on our own. I am scared and a little giddy. I trust, that together with our friends, we will find our path and recognize our destiny.

With Joan, Stefan, Helena, Herbert, and Wolf by my side, I feel confident, that we will accomplish what we set out to do. We all feel that way. We are a team, ready to embark on a mission to make a difference in the world and I am proud to be part of the crew."

Chapter 27

◆

Good bye Germany, hello World

Joan seemed to catch travel fever the second time around. Reliving these days, animated her and made her seem young again.

She spurted out in an enthusiastic voice:

" I was excited. I could not wait to see Stefan again. Everyone went home before the big journey, to pack and to say good bye to our families and friends.

I think we were all in shock about this sudden development.

And yes, we were proud, to be given a chance, to serve our Country.

When we arrived at Bremer Haven, we stayed at a hotel near the harbor.

We were to meet some of the staff of the colonial administration, to receive our passports, currency for the countries we were expected to visit on the way and most importantly, to meet the captain of Stella Maris, Jacob Paulus.

His ship was one of the first diesel powered steel hulled trading vessels in the world.

Stella Maris was not the ship, the government had originally planned to send us out on, which would have gone directly from Germany to East Africa.

Stella Maris was a trading ship, that contracted freight deliveries from country to country, with only a general route of travel and the flexibility to react to requests and orders of cargo transport along the way.

Captain Jacob Paulus was a short, almost square looking man with penetrating blue eyes under bushy eyebrows, a square jaw, and a booming voice. Intimidating to us at first. He looked like a wrestler with his broad shoulders and his very trim, toned body.

A chuck of short cropped, dark blond hair, that showed the first signs of gray, was hidden under his navy-blue cap with a glossy black visor and an anchor in golden needle work stitched above the visor.

The hat band ended with a short black bow in back. It displayed the name of his ship:

Stella Maris on both sides.

He told us to refer to him- and address him always as "captain."

He explained, that we were assigned to his vessel by our government as his personal guests, residing in our own private quarters aboard Stella Maris.

Meals were to be served at the captain's table three times a day.

He cautioned us, not to engage, or fraternize, with the ship's crew.

Only his officers, the first mate, the cabin crew, and the captain himself were to be our contacts.

"This has to do with your safety and the importance of your assignment by the emperor," he explained.

"There is a strict hierarchy on ships. I am under orders, to deliver you and your belongings safely to your destination, without any incidents on board ship, or in ports of call. I will not be your personal guardian. I am your captain. You will obey my command like everyone else on this ship.

My contract is with our government.

Obedience is imperative for your safety and for the safety of my crew, the journey and for my reputation as your captain."

He pointed at his officers.

"Stuart Ed Haller is your quartermaster. Anything you need, you will request from him.

He is responsible for your comfort and well-being.

This is a freight ship, not a passenger steamer.

There is no need to for you to pay gratuity, your voyage has been paid for by our government.

The purser of Stella Maris was given extra funds you might need for harbor visits and for your expedition.

You will enter the wheelhouse only at my command, with my permission or after an appointment with my first mate Stan Nord.

Stan is my second in command.

He is acting with the same authority as your captain.

He is the go-to person for you, with questions or concerns regarding anything other than your quarters and your personal well-being.

Stuart Haller is a trained nurse. He will provide emergency medical services to you.

We have a well-stocked dispensary.

Any question Haller cannot answer, you direct to Stan Nord or to your captain."

With that, he turned around and walked off."

Joan was getting tired and promised more of her report during the following meetings.

When Joan and Gottfried saw each other again, they were both mentally in full travelling mode, anticipating the departure from the known world and venturing into the unknown.

Chapter 28

On board Stella Maris

"We moved from the hotel to the ship mid-morning.

Our gear had been delivered and stowed in a compartment on the ship, that would not be opened until the arrival at our destination.

We took to our quarters all our personal belongings and such items as we needed during the next weeks and months. We were excited, nervous, and glad to be on our way in good company. Each glad, there was a significant other to hold on to. We were not about to let go, until we would disembark at the far side of Africa.

Our families had said fair well and safe travel.

Fathers looked stern as mothers wiped tears of pride, mixed with tears of sorrow.

We had grown up suddenly and unexpectedly. Now it was our turn to look and act brave, to face the new reality, that looked straight into our faces.

There was no turning back.

We filed up the gang way.

Stefan in the lead, followed by myself, Helena, Herbert, Maria, and Wolf.

Porters delivered our travel luggage to our quarters, which were located several flights up, under the wheelhouse.

Service facilities and galley were located at the second level, our quarters above that and the captain's and officers' quarters up another flight of stairs, beneath the wheel house.

From there, the skipper could see most of the ship.

Stefan, our captain, pointed all this out, placing himself naturally between us and the ship's captain. Helena cautioned us, not ever to use the word 'captain' in reference to Stefan.

We were given six small rooms and a central lobby. Each room had two beds, private bath, and showers. The ship was new.

This was her maiden voyage. It even smelled new.

We could see ourselves living here for the duration.

According to captain Paulus, our journey could take six to sixteen weeks or more to reach our destination, depending on freight assignments to Stella Maris.

Stefan stayed close to the captain. We could tell that captain Paulus was pleased to see us pay close attention to every word he spoke. We knew right away that he was a deep well of knowledge and we had a lot to learn from him.

Wolf gravitated towards the second in command, Stan Nord, who patiently gave answers to all his questions.

Helena and Maria stayed close to Ed Haller, server and nurse, as both were interested in medical facilities.

Herbert was introduced by Ed Haller to a man in a little office, Emil Holt, the purser.

Holt, in charge of documents, currency, passports, entry and exit permits, wireless communication and cables to and from ship, was the administrator of Stella Maris.

I was drawn towards the kitchen. Haller introduced me to the head chef, Jean du Chalet, a lanky, tall fellow, with a big nose and a permanent smile.

Jean du Chalet handled knives like extensions of his fingers, with incredible speed and precision. I was eager to learn these skills from him.

Ed Haller pointed to his knife set and cautioned me:

"Best to stay on his good side. See what he will do to onions. He is a knife juggler, who also knows how to throw them. I have never seen him miss a target."

Maria and I were taken in by Jean's upbeat personality and frivolous sense of humor, good traits for someone, who depended on good relationships with food vendors all around the world. There was a glint in his eyes, telling us, that he never missed a thing. We knew it would be good to be his friend.

We settled in, had tea before dinner and began to get organized in our floating abode.

There is a strict social order on ships: We were cautioned by captain Paulus, Stan Nord and by Jan du Chalet not to mingle with the sailors: The rules where:

"Keep at a distance from the ship's crew, except the officers. Never leave the ship unaccompanied by officers."

Paulus explained:" The ship's crew work, when you see them and rest, when you do not. We want you to get acquainted with this vessel. We ask you to be escorted by one of our officers, whenever you go below and move around this ship. Life at sea is treacherous and unpredictable. I say this again: Never venture off the ship alone. Always be escorted by my officers. We are obligated to deliver you to your destination safely and in good health. That will not always be easy, out on the open ocean, or in foreign harbors.

When we make land-fall, we are entering countries with different cultures and laws.

Port cities are inherently dangerous. I suggest that you ladies respect dress codes of countries, that are not as liberal with garments, as we are in Europe. Consult with Stan Nord. There are also differences in greeting etiquette and it is advisable to know them and to respect them.

Stan Nord will tell you everything you must know.

We also ask you to be discreet and about all things concerning this ship, its cargo, operation, personnel, or its destination.

Being guests at my table, you will be hearing things and be privy to information, that has to be strictly guarded and must stay on board of this ship. I trust that you will respect my wishes in this regard, in return for our commitment to your safety."

We soon learned, that dining at the captain's table is a special privilege.

It gave us opportunity to learn about world events, ports of call, the past, presence and future of sea commerce and international trade.

Captain Paulus was pleased to have such interested guests at his table.

He generously shared his views, advice, and opinions with us.

Delectable dishes were prepared by chef Jean served banquet style: Five courses. Appetizers, salads, soups, main course du jour and de region plus his desserts.

This made it an epicurean journey half way around the world. He knew food.

Maria and I spent as much time in the kitchen as we could, learning from the best.

Maria and I were interested in plants from different countries and our chef was happy to share his vast wealth of knowledge with us.

Captain Paulus was not only a gourmet. He was also a connoisseur of all things containing alcohol. He kept an eclectic collection of liquors, whiskeys, champagne, red-, white-, and rose wines in bottles and in kegs in a temperature-controlled locker. He also had a collection of precious cigars and tobacco in what he called his humidor. Only the captain himself and his chef de cuisine had access to this treasure.

Stefan soon became the captain's favorite, by being interested in navigation and the operation of his ship. He followed the mapping and planning of each leg of the trip.

Herbert, the technical mind, was fascinated with the conversion of diesel fuel into power, transferred to the ship's propellers and the steering and navigation equipment.

Wolf was the observer of everything. He noticed canvas covered objects on deck, which he took to be cannon. He spoke to Maria about it. She suggested he ask the captain about the purpose for this weaponry. He decided to wait, until he had developed a better relationship with our captain and his first mate. We knew, Herbert, Wolf and Stefan had studied ballistics and the use of the newest weaponry at school. They wanted to know, how these cannons were designed, loaded, aimed, and fired. Wolf noticed the locking metal tracks on deck, leading to rotating bases next to the railing.

Maria the reader, was happy that she had brought with her plenty of books about our destination. She searched for historical records in Germany and found many interesting documents. She got the librarian in Berlin's library to be all excited and to go into a searching frenzy for her.

Wolf was supportive of her literary passion. This added to the intensity of their relationship. There was plenty of time for them to study these materials. Both were passionate about finding ways, to integrate this new colony into our young nation.

Wolf wanted to reconcile philosophy, history, and science, to become useful knowledge. He saw conflict between principles, that were introduced by special interest groups and the secrets of creation. Both Maria and Wolf shared deep religious devotion, without being allied to any organized religion."

"Did you know which route your steamer was going to take?"

"We learned, that Stella Maris was a tramp ship, that picks up and delivers freight from port to port. Our destination was the port of Dar Es Salaam, where she was to deliver us and her cargo for German East Africa. There, she would pick up goods from Africa, India, Thailand, and China.

Then she was to return to Europe, rounding the Cape of South Africa and touching ports in The Congo, Nigeria, Senegal, Morocco, Portugal, France and ultimately back to Bremerhaven. That was all subject to change, as new freight orders came in. Captain

Paulus explained it to us this way:

"Here are a few way points. Being a trader requires flexibility. We have ports of call in France, Portugal, Morocco,

Spain, Italy, Libya, Greece, Egypt, Arabia, Yemen, and Ethiopia. We pick up goods and fulfill shipping orders on our way. We know local markets. We are the diplomats of the high seas.

Nations can permit or deny our trade. Most ports are at the outlets of rivers, - trade routes to the interior of continents. Traders use barges and ships to take goods to market.

European naval powers negotiate control over ports, and thereby countries.

The need of raw materials drives the value and importance of harbor control.

Countries must enter into trade agreements with the owners of battle ships covering their ports. Often whole regions will be annexed, governed as Colonies, or turned into Protectorates, as France did with Algeria and Italy with Libya.

These decisions are negotiated at international trade conferences and treaties are signed. That determines the well-being of millions of people, as well as the economy of the countries controlling trade of the goods.

As middlemen, traders must know and understand this."

Paulus checked the large time piece he pulled out of his breast pocket by a heavy gold chain. Then he continued:

"Captains of international trading vessels find a way through this maze and must understand the present rules of each land.

Good personal connections and relationships are essential to success in this business. We must know who controls trade and under what conditions at any time.

This is always in flux.

Presently, the Balkans are at war with the Ottoman Empire, so we must stay away from Constantinople. The center of the Ottoman Empire was until recently an important trading port for Asian and Mid-Eastern goods.

Traders were bypassing the uncertainties and hazards of the ancient silk route."

Chapter 29

◆

Stefan the other captain

Joan pulled out another notebook with Stefan's hand writing: It read on the cover:

"Departure"

" My Captain Stefan kept records of everything, like a ship's log, "Joan said,

holding his notebook gently, as if she were holding Stefan's hand.

"Let me read it to you."

"It seems like a lifetime has passed in just a few moments.

I see the fog lift over the harbor across from the hotel. I am too excited to sleep.

I will remember last night, after everyone had finally left and just the six of us moved into a booth. Finally, the six of us were alone for the first time, since Berlin.

Walter gave a toast to our upcoming journey, to a world in a state of rapid change and to our engagement in German East Africa.

I like Walter and Helena's open mindedness and their commitment, to having each voice heard. They are our consensus builders.

I still feel an internal conflict, stemming from my upbringing during a time when each career track was part family tradition, part social mandate, with the need to maintain financial standing and influence in society.

My education was not a straight, well-trodden path, paved by academic tradition.

This made it hard for my family. I was given the best educators.

Unsuccessfully, they tried to make choices for me, following traditional patterns:

If not academia, then a military career, serving our emerging nation.

I volunteered for a year with the Bavarian field artillery-regiment. I studied philosophy at the university of Munich. With my fellow students, we did extensive soul searching about the future.

We were concerned, that our country is running out of space.

Railroads have caused an explosion of industry and trade. Distances from factories to markets have shrunk. Workers are moving into cities, following employment opportunities, even across borders.

This has caused food shortages, housing shortages, and land shortages.

We see no other solution than to find agricultural land elsewhere in the world.

Industry needs raw materials and energy.

Those, who have no land, go to the colonies, expanding our empire.

I worked with a group of surveyors mapping German East Africa.

My family tries to convince me, to pursue a career in art history.

That is my internal conflict.

I have not mentioned to anyone in our pilot group, that I have already been to this colony of German East Africa, as a surveyor.

I have an interest in horses and cannons. I could be an officer of the Schutztruppe in GEA. Wolf noticed that we have such things in common, besides our involvement with the two catholic girls. I represent the material world. He does well with spirituality, besides science. In our pilot group, we discovered other ways to solve conflict, besides force of arms and the right of the mighty.

Now we are about to leave on an assignment, that sets my preferences into a new light and brings my duty to the Nation forward.

Military solutions to nation building seem to be a road to perpetual conflict.

No peace can come from the use of military force. We are looking for new ways to reconcile opposing forces.

In myself, in the colonies and at home.

I will have to come clean with my friends. I do not want to sabotage the trust we have in each other. Maybe I can say, that I did not want to brag, or that I was not expecting for things to develop so fast in this direction. Perhaps I wanted to get to know everyone better, and to decide for myself, what I want to do with my life.

I did not expect to fall in love. I am surprised by my complex and confusing inner life.

During our voyage, I will have time to talk with Joan, to ask her what I should do.

. They can guide me. I am tired but too excited to find sleep.

Soon the engines will start, the horn will sound and a tug boat will tow us out of the harbor into open waters."

Joan pressed the journal to her chest and closed her eyes. After a while, she spoke, her gray eyes scanning the lake as though Stefan would emerge at any moment.

"We were tired from traveling to Bremerhaven, from saying good-bye to our families and from learning more about our assignment from Berlin. Once we returned to our quarters, we slipped into our beds, each following their own thoughts. We said our prayers.

We closed our eyes. I think we all failed to find sleep. I could see it in the faces the next day.

Everyone had a "morning after" expression and conversation was limited to "pass the butter" and "would you like cream?"

We caught a second wind after breakfast and the conversation turned to changing sleeping arrangements to be more pleasant to everyone and more logical to Eros.

By the time we had everything sorted and stowed, it was time for the first dinner at the captain's table.

It was getting dark, when Stella Maris was towed out of the harbor and into open water. Now she moved west under her own power and the steady hum of the engines began to move us towards a destination somewhere in France.

Dinner was a feast, far beyond our expectations.

Soon we crawled into our beds. This time, we were lulled to sleep by the vibration of the ship's engines and the gentle rocking motion the vessel.

The water was flat and Stefan became restless. He stepped outside. The full moon did not help, and I was not ready to fall asleep without him. I stepped out to join him on deck, where I found him gazing into the moonlit expanse of the sea. I approached him from behind and embraced him, feeling his muscles play, as he was holding on to the railing and leaning back into me.

"What's wrong?" I asked, "I missed you. Why can't you sleep?"

"I don't like it," he said. "It is too calm. This is the Atlantic and it is not the time of Year, when seas get this calm. We should be feeling ocean waves, not these little baby swells. These are tremors. They make me nervous."

"We are over-tired. Let the ship's crew worry about the ocean. We can look into each other's eyes, say our prayers, and feel the gentle sway as a blessing, instead of a threat," I whispered.

"You are right. I have a hard time being on a ship without being in charge. That makes me edgy, I guess."

He pulled my arms across his chest and held me tight, kissing me over his shoulder. I leaned into him even more to let there be no air between us. I liked the way this felt. It made me feel safe. I was in the closeness of my strong companion. I felt that there was more on his mind than ocean waves and I sensed, that it would be better to wait for him to say something, than for me to pry, since I did not know what I was looking for. I said:

"Let's go to bed and dream about the next destination. I believe it is Le Havre in France?"

"Yes, darling, that is our next stop. You are right. We might as well go to sleep."

I was lying awake, eyes closed, visualizing the map of Africa we had seen in Berlin, that showed, how the colonial powers had divided the entire continent into claims, most of which were larger than the entire territory of the claimants.

This was something that Maria and Wolf were concerned about. They had explained:

"People act, as if there is this huge continent, inhabited by wildlife and some wild humans with dark skin, none of whom can speak a civilized language and their world is laying there for the taking. Discovery, they call it. Conquest would be more accurate.

The Roman Empire marched heavily armed soldiers across Europe only a few centuries ago. They did the same thing to the tribes, that inhabited our world."

I fell into a restless sleep, that lasted until I could hear what sounded like a bell. I reached for Stefan's arm and whispered:

"What was that?"

"Why are you whispering? Did you dream we are at your parent's house? I hear nothing." He laughed.

"There it is again. This time I think there was wind."

"You are right, it is the wind and the sound you hear like a bell is the halyard, they raise the flag with, tapping on the flagpole. I think we are sailing into some weather.

I better check it out."

Before I could say any more, Stefan was up, slipping on pants, shirt and sailor's boots. He stepped outside. He saw a changed world from just a few hours ago.

I joined him. I saw the other travelers of our party standing close to Stefan, who was explaining, what this change in conditions might mean. I heard him say:

"We better get foul weather gear out and stow our belongings, so they don't slide around when things get rough."

I thought: "Our captain is speaking. I wonder what he has noticed that the rest of us did not."

Boom.

The bow of the ship had slowly risen and suddenly dropped into a deep void, where it landed with a loud bang on something that felt more like rock, than water.

A shower of ocean spray drenched us, reminding us, that it was water, our ship had landed on at the bottom of this valley. We could hear the ship's engines accelerate as the vessel was climbing up and out.

Stefan shouted:

"We must go inside and stow our stuff. Let us meet in the salon after, to ride this out.

This will be rough!"

His last words were drowned out by wind and the next impact of the bow in an even deeper valley on ever increasing seas.

We disappeared in our quarters, reaching out for hand holds, wherever possible.

Once inside, Stefan instructed me on the choice of clothes to wear.

We took out our life vests and fitted them.

Typical for Stefan, he made us get ready for worst-case.

He was throwing essential items into our waterproof duffel bags, when Walter and Wolf came in, also wearing life vests, looking like Martians, saying in chorus:

"Should we pack for evacuation? Looks like the answer is yes."

They disappeared.

Stefan said to no one in particular:

"This is the Atlantic. Known to go wild. I think we are on a good ship".

His voice was drowned out by another hard slam.

"Seaworthy," was the next word I could hear through the roar. Stella Maris was again climbing at a steep angle, making me worry, that she would simply slip backwards into a valley behind us, that would swallow us, life boats or no life boats.

Talking about a good ship was as reassuring to me as the story, they tell children about the chicken that had brooded and hatched duck eggs.

Now the hen ran back and forth along the water's edge, after the ducklings had begun to swim off, wondering, why their mom did not join them.

By the time we saw one of the ship's officers, we were huddled in the salon, wearing life vests, holding on to each other.

The ship dropped again and again towards the ocean floor, interrupting the Stuart in his reassurance speech.

We already began looking green, preparing for the worst.

A sudden drop of the vessel sent the sailor air born and landed him hard on the returning floor of the salon.

The look on his face was worth a million marks.

As soon as he was gone, we shed tears laughing from comic relief.

Seas began to run at unpredictable angles and the ship was being tossed around like a nutshell in the rapids of a wild river.

Faces began looking greener and I felt lucky, that none of us seemed to be getting seasick, even though all of us were getting very close to losing last night's dinner.

Chapter 30

Towards Bordeaux

The Stuart Haller now entered to announce that the ship's destination had been changed to avoid Le Havre and that the captain had ordered to sail directly to Bordeaux.

He explained, that the entrance to Le Havre was too dangerous under such storm conditions.

"The captain will take her further out to sea, to escape the currents, that make these waves so steep and dangerous."

Stefan understood, what he was talking about. The rest of us were just hoping, the ship would not capsize or slip backwards into the deep.

Once we had cleared the English Channel, the sea flattened out. It took a while to restore order in our quarters. The kitchen crew was able to cook again. Soon breakfast was served at the captain's table. The food tasted good enough to please any king of any country.

We were hungry from endless contractions our bodies had performed to counterbalance the wild movement of the ship. I was amazed how long it took for the sensation of the rocking ship to cease. Now level again, I felt in my interior continue the motion of the floor beneath my feet.

Maria and Helena felt the same sensation, which gave us reason to shed tears of laughter. Giddy from relief and over-tired, we crawled back into our bunks with our brave boys and slept most of the day.

We were now far out to sea. Occasionally, a feature would peek down at us, mostly in the form of clouds, tell-tale signs of land nearby, a welcome sight to us, even though we were not shipwrecked persons adrift.

In my dreams, I was back on the sailboat in Germany, where we had first bonded. The time that had passed since, seemed at once endless, like a distant memory and close, as though it had just happened a moment ago.

At the end of that day, the captain came to our salon, to invite us personally to his dinner table. We were pleased to find him in good spirits. The conversation at dinner revolved around shipwrecks of mostly wooden sailing vessels. He pointed out the merits of steel hulls, diesel engines, the evolution in ship design and how modern ships will accelerate international commerce, the same way railroads had changed life on land.

Captain Paulus was still surprised and pleased at the attention he received from us.

The part of the conversation that fascinated us the most, was about relationships of "old powers" with ancient countries like Ethiopia, Yemen, Egypt and Libya and the Baltic States.

Over time, these countries had been conquered and were annexed by expanding empires, often without changing their culture, their language, or their religion. They became foreign owned provinces, that paid taxes to the ruling empire, until these empires finally crumbled and the captives were hoping to become independent again.

This would be food for long discussions during hours of monotonous travel, when we had to lean over the railing of the ship to look back at our wake, to see evidence of forward motion.

Our captain did not get involved in politics. His job was to serve people as a trader, interested in ideology only, to understand the needs of his trading partners.

He was an old world-new world navigator.

We could sense, that he was uneasy about the possibility of getting into the crossfire of warring parties at sea.

Paulus told us:

"The way I do it is the same way I deal with the weather. I respond and react, stay flexible and do not take on powers that are greater than myself. It is the principle of survival of the smartest, not the fittest. I go like water in a rocky stream. Around the obstacles, not through them. Sometimes I must wear them down with time.

Information blended with good observation and common sense, are guiding me, when I navigate the turbulent waters of this changing world."

Paulus, looking around to see if we were listening, added:

"Mariners are a fraternity of the Seas. Each of us gathers information. We record it in the ship's log: Barometric readings, temperature of air and water, wind velocity and direction. Observations like the sighting of other vessels, the flag they are running under, their estimated course and speed. We interact in port and share our observations, without giving away details of our own cargo or destination.

Ships logs and -diaries end up in the archives of insurance companies like Lloyd of London, who insure our ships and our cargo. These ship logs are the geographical record, that contains better information than most countries have available at any moment. Sea maps were first developed by mariners and later used by governments around the world.

Sea captains are competitors, but more importantly, they support each other and share critical information about natural- and man-made risks and disasters.

Skippers like me, have no agenda, other than to deliver freight safely for their clients and to return their ships intact and well maintained. You will see our seamen constantly working to keep our vessel in ship-shape and I ask of you not to ask questions or interact with them. Be always in the company of an officer when you move around this ship.

We paid close attention to everything captain Paulus said and tried not to ask too many questions. We let Stefan ask questions and then explain to us everything that had once again gone over our heads.

Paulus was pleased to have a knowledgeable student and listener like my Stefan.

Meals at the captain's table were a classroom with a great teacher, who enjoyed good food and attentive students.

Stefan was our interpreter of seaman's terms, Herbert the technology translator and

Wolf was able to explain to us geographical, historical, and social issues."

Joan kept bringing out boxes and journals as her story unfolded. She was pleased:

"I am glad you give me reason, to bring all this out. I am the last survivor of our sailing team. To retrace our steps through time makes me feel the happiness, hope and what seemed like a tangible future back then.

Now it brings my Stefan close to me.

We had only faint hunches about what was in our future. We were focused on making the world a better place.

We discovered a world, consisting of nations fiercely competing for the realization of their hopes, dreams, interests, and control."

Joan glanced over the water's surface, following the ripples, a passing boat had made. Then, after the lake had flattened out again, she added:

"We were sailing into a world, suffering from confusion, depression, food shortages, loss of lives, through wars and illnesses, more so than what we had been told to expect."

Her gray eyes had turned darker, she was reflecting on the great picture and with a sad expression, she added almost in a breathless whisper:

"More experiences to live through, more heart break, for a person to suffer in one lifetime.

Religious freedom was now only a minor issue, considering what the world, we began to discover, had to grapple with: Imperialism, Colonialism, Nationalism all were beginning to rear their ugly heads.

Military violence and the use of modern weapons were gaining the upper hand and survival became universal and personal, making the world insecure and life perilous.

We were determined, to plant seeds in form of new ideas and to formulate questions that needed to be asked and answered. We were going to shed light on new forces, that would prepare mankind for a peaceful, sustainable future."

Joan repeated to bring her point home:

"I am the last survivor of our sailing team. "

After taking a few deep breaths, she sat up and squared her shoulders.

"Now, where was I? Ah yes. The voyage to Africa."

Chapter 31

God's pocket

Joan was gazing into the past, remaining silent for a long time.

Her eyes returned to Gottfried. She looked straight into his eyes. She spoke in a low voice, as if confessing something only for Gottfried's ears.

Almost in a whisper, spoken in confidence, she began:

"We were at the beginning of a journey into the world and into our lives.

We were thinking that ideas had to be tried and that those, who were too cautious, or afraid to try, would never know what the creator had in mind with his world.

I, Stefan, and the others had plenty of differences from our backgrounds to reconcile. We were so very young still, inexperienced, and not just a little bit frightened.

At the time, we could not yet finish each other's sentences. We did not understand the meaning of our feelings or the reasons, why we were drawn to each other.

Stefan the competitor, saw himself as the winner of everything and me, the daring tomboy, who thought, that everything that did not kill me, was worth a try.

I envied Maria, who was thoughtful and composed in everything she did, thought or spoke. She was my rock as a child and she was my rock now.

Time has melted away like snow in springtime.

I can now speak without having to worry about anyone's opinion or judgment.

Back then I was the risk taker, the wild one, who was attracted to reaching for the limits of everything.

My Maria was the nurse, who stood by, to dust me off and patch me up, when I had fallen.

I spent time with Maria privately. We explored our feelings for our partners, who were as different as two men can be.

Two men had fallen in love with two sisters, who were different enough from each other, that they were able to confide in each other the new puzzlement, wonderment, and excitement they were feeling.

Maria insisted, that our blissful experience was the creator's way to test the success of his creation.

Thereby validating our existence.

We both admired Helena, who seemed to be a sovereign partner to Herbert.

She was the grownup in our room.

I remember excuses we made, inventing reasons, why we had to spend nights with our men, excuses, that held as much water, as a spaghetti strainer.

Secretly, we were amused about pretend propriety, which was more like a dance between us, our partners, and social norms, we were in the process of leaving behind.

We came from parents, who grew up during a time, when the first person you kissed was going to be your future spouse.

We chuckled at the thought about our Victorian parents, who might have never seen each other in the nude, even in their nuptial bed.

Our way of speaking with our partners was less formal, more true, more real, and more honest, than our parents had ever dared to communicate.

They lived by externally imposed morals, customs, and rules, leading often to judgements, invented by moral terrorists in the name of God.

We were now sailing towards Bordeaux on the open Atlantic, after rounding the vast peninsula near Brest, that forms the opening of the English Channel to the Atlantic.

Stefan explained to us, that the coast of the Bretagne was now to the north, to port and that we were sailing past Nantes, towards the south-south east, towards New Rochelle, where the Charente Maritime and Cognac are located.

Cognac, our captain explained, is the home of the famous drink, named after the region, where it originated, about which captain Paulus had a lot to say in praise, and of which he owned a good store of precious bottles in his private vault.

This substance is not only very delicious and very precious, it can melt a lot of ice and facilitate positive outcomes in the most challenging and difficult negotiations with others.

Stefan spent much time observing the captain, watching him navigate, rounding the peninsula near Brest, entering the Atlantic, heading west into calmer waters.

Proximity to land was noticeable, by cloud formations, that did not pose a threat of more storms.

At night, I wanted to be close to Stefan and to hear him whisper in my ears, telling me everything he had learned during the day. I wanted him to myself for more than just fleeting moments, so we could follow the forces, pulling us together, forces, I did not know to exist, that even my wise Stefan was unable to explain."

Joan chuckled at the thought.

"This was not a competitive sport. This was Nature and the gravity of fate.

It could use some help. I decided, to act the damsel in distress, so I invented complaints, that made him want to take care of me.

I found myself under the covers, enjoying the gentle sway of the ship, like a rocking cradle. I asked him to join me, to make me well and to keep me warm.

This, I was sure, was the skill I learned from inventing sins for confession with my priest, so I could do penance and receive absolution." Another burst of laughter.

"The difference was, this time, these were not just impure thoughts. This time, it was pure joy. We managed to slowly remove all our clothes without making this a subject of conversation. We found ourselves in a state of bliss. A discovery began, that would keep us together for the rest of our lives." She was looking glad and sad at once.

"We kept reaffirming to each other, that we felt the power of destiny and that we could not possibly imagine the other to be any different, or more perfect, with all our funny quirks and faults. We discovered, that we had found the love of our life and that there was no one alive luckier than the two of us.

We were cozy in our bunk for many hours, until Maria came to check on us.

She just wanted to know, if we needed anything. "More time", was the answer.

She had plenty of that to give us. She had begun to use some of that herself.

The ocean had flattened out and the hum of the engines was soothing, together with a breeze from the forward motion of the ship, coming in through open windows.

We told Maria to bring us tea and water.

We never mentioned the storm, we had unleashed between the sheets, that neither of us had words for, or the desire to describe to anyone. We must have finally fallen into a deep sleep. We might even have missed a meal or two. Maria had given the others medical explanations for our time request.

What finally woke us, was the sound of our ship's horn, that communicated with another horn in the distance, announcing the arrival of the pilot and a tug boat from the Port of Bordeaux.

Stefan and I quickly dressed and joined the others at the rail, to observe the transfer of the pilot to our ship.

Stefan explained:

" Our captain will turn the helm over to a pilot from Bordeaux, who is familiar with local conditions and hidden hazards, sand bars and rocks or wrecks of ships that did not have the good fortune to be guided in.

Sand bars shift and new ones are built by flood waters from the river after storms.

Passable lanes are marked by red lane markers on the right coming in and green lane markers on the left going out.

Chapter 32

Life like "God in France"

We stood by the rail of the ship to observe. The landscape near Bordeaux consists of gently rolling dunes, shaped by dust storms, that once carried fine soil from the Sahara Desert, providing soil rich in nutrients for today's vineyards and fields, planted with a great variety of vegetables, fruit bearing bushes and trees, tended by farmers who are proud of their heirloom seeds.

"This region is very fertile," chef Jan du Chalet explained.

"The meals in and after Bordeaux will be a special treat. Your mouth will water for a long time, thinking about the bounty of our cuisine after we visit the ancient farmers market of Bordeaux."

We had not seen him this enthusiastic about a region or its food supply.

He told us, that even if we do not plan to purchase fruit or vegetables ourselves, his display will make our mouths water and get us ready for what he intended to create, after he returns to the ship with his treasure.

A friendship began between Maria, myself, and chef Jean du Chalet, that would last for the entire journey.

We were getting more excited, when the captain announced, that we would have two days of shore leave, while he was procuring a load of wine and spirits. He told us that he had made reservations for us to stay at the Hotel de Ville right in the center of town by the tree lined square, near the cathedral, where cafes and restaurants offered the finest cuisine anywhere in France.

Paulus, always inspired by life, always ready to celebrate:

"This is a good place for you to celebrate the beginning of your journey," he said.

"The next place we call on, will be as different from Europe as the North Pole is from the Amazon rain forest. Again, even here in Bordeaux, I ask you to be always in the company of one of my officers."

The minute we stepped on land, we knew what he meant. The ground still seemed to move beneath our feet from the constant motion of the ship.

Laughing, Herbert and Helena said, that a few glasses of Bordeaux's best red wine would level things out and calm down the cobble stone pavement.

One of the officers guided us to the Hotel de Ville and we found ourselves in a picture book setting of ancient buildings, adorned with sculpted sand stone bases, dormers, windows and doors with sculpted head stones, door frames and corners, decorated with an abundance of flowers in planters on the ground and on window sills. It looked like a feast was being celebrated.

Our guide told us that this is the way Bordeaux presents itself always.

The Hotel de Ville stood two stories taller than the surrounding buildings. The men showered us with roses, making us feel special.

After checking in, we went for a walk, to get our bearings. We found a comfortable outdoor café, across the plaza from our hotel and the feast began.

Herbert went inside to ask for service. Then he took his seat facing the traffic. He said:

"I had a dream about the six of us being stranded on a rocky outcropping out of sight of land. We were not wearing life vests. The life boat we had arrived on sank when it struck a sharp rock. Wolf wanted to dive down to retrieve a rope, to pull the wreck on shore. Stefan wanted to climb the rock, to see if there was land in sight.

Maria mentioned the stores of water. Joan wanted to save the food supplies and Helena reminded us, that only by working together, we could save boat, water, food and ultimately everyone's life.

We pulled up the life boat. We prepared a meal and dried our clothes on a fire we made in a protected grotto, using driftwood. We went to explore the Rock that was uninhabited except for birds. Stefan suggested, we watch the sky for tell-tale clouds, to see where land might be closest. Maria suggested, we look at the vegetation to tell us where we might be. Joan went to find edible plants. Wolf and I repaired the damage on the boat.

Helena built a fire with dry kindling and used wet seaweed to make smoke signals on top of the rock. In her hand, she held a flare, she found on the lifeboat, to light it, when we sight a passing ship after sunset. She asked Maria and Joan to make the smoke signals: Three short, three long, three short.

Stefan told us, that this meant SOS, understood by mariners. We were hopeful.

Then I woke up."

Herbert stood up and raised his glass

"My toast is to our journey. To the success of our mission. Together, we can meet every challenge, that presents itself. Here is to working together. Cheers."

We were treated to delectable samples of food, only Bordeaux can offer, followed by

a tour through vineyards, where we noticed rose bushes at the beginning and end of

every row of grape vines. It is for the bees, we were told.

The day ended with a wine tasting at the winery, where captain Paulus was ordering

a shipment of wine, to be delivered to Algiers in North Africa, followed by a six-course

meal, that gave meaning to the saying "we were living like God in France."

Just when we thought we had regained our land legs, we found the ground moving again. This time, it was a result of little sips of wine, from the tasting, even with little bits of cheese eaten between samples, served to cleanse our palette.

What finished us, was a sweet rose, lovely in taste and bouquet.

Our hosts had warned us, that this is a wine that does not tell you, that you had enough, until it is too late.

We held on to each other, as we walked back to the Hotel, trying not to get hit by the buildings and trees, we passed, that were moving like our ship during the storm in the English Channel.

I cannot remember waking up the next day, until it was time for dinner by invitation of the captain.

Little remarks were exchanged about the condition of our room, which matched the description I would have given to describe the room Stefan and I had slept in:

"A hurricane, mistral and tornado must have swept through this chamber."

The maid had said in admiration. I do not remember, what happened to this room. I know Stefan and I woke up cradled in each other's arms, knowing, that we love Bordeaux and that we love each other.

Images of this wonderful experience in France were locked into our minds.

The charm of the people matched the beauty of the architecture, the gardens, the vineyards, the markets, the restaurants, and the cafes we visited.

Our final meal was designed to impress us with the culinary art of France. The maître D'hôtel was impressed with the knowledge of the local cuisine our captain commanded. Our host was going to impress our captain by presenting food garnished artistically, a fusion of visual effects, scents, and flavors.

It was a formal affair, competitive to the point of being funny, intended to celebrate our departure from western Europe and our upcoming approach to the "wild and unknown"

African Continent.

Desserts were as sweet as they were beautiful from the show of flames on the crème Brule to the chocolate mints, little bits of cheese, to close the stomach, before a variety of digestifs were offered. Finally, the captain asked the men to retire to the smoking-lounge. Maria and Helena ordered espresso. I took my seat next to Stefan.

Paulus presented his most precious Cuban cigars to be ceremoniously cut, sniffed, licked, and lit with little puffs of smoke, rising like offerings to the Gods of good living.

I acted the brave, worldly woman I was yet to become and did, like I saw the men do, with the same flair, even downing shots of Pastis, that were served with a sweet, black, stiff espresso, chased with a glass of water.

When I found my voice again after the shot of liquor, I proposed a toast to my companions and to our captain Paulus in the name of the ladies in the lounge and our Africa Team, lowering my voice to sound more mature, praising this wonderful meal and the great sendoff, they had prepared so memorably, leaving us with a longing for home, to last the entire time, we were going to be abroad.

I called it a good omen for the success of our mission. Cheers.

I finished by saluting the Governor of the German East Africa Colony and Kaiser

Wilhelm, and our good relations with France and her Navy in the waters of the world.

All the while, there was in the background a singer, melting our hearts with sweet chansons, accompanied by a baby grand piano. In answer to my little speech, they played one line of Beethoven's Ode to Joy and one line of the

Marseillaise.

Everyone stood and saluted. When we finally retired to our quarters, I was once again the blushing teenager, come world traveler, hanging on to Stefan's arm to steady myself and for his protection from the big world, that had made me dizzy with wine, food, liquorand cigars. I now felt the way I had felt as a child, when I ventured out on a tree branch too high up and too far out and I needed Maria to come to my rescue.

This night, I asked to sleep in the room with Maria to calm down, to talk and to share my

feelings about this tumultuous fortnight, since we left home. I was afraid, I would otherwise find no sleep and miss the departure of Stella Maris.

The following day was foggy. We wandered in the company of our escort to the ship before sunrise. We were guided by one of the officers, who had been sent by captain

Paulus to be sure he would not lose us, before the journey had even begun.

A breakfast with strong coffee, hot milk, honey, croissants, confiture and cheeses of the region had been laid out, to let us ease our way into the new day, complete with water

and aspirin to meet headaches, resulting from last night's celebrations.

We barely noticed the activities of the tug boat and the pilot, who guided us out to sea. The fog was thick and other vessels in the harbor looked like ghost ships. Features of the landscape appeared like a soft aquarelle painting.

Sounds where muffled, prompting us to speak in very low voices. I remember thinking, that we were all far more nervous about leaving Europe, than we dared to admit.

Stefan was with the captain, observing the activities of navigation in almost zero visibility.

When we cleared the last harbor buoy, the fog began to lift, the pilot handed the helm to captain Paulus and Stefan came strolling into the room like it was nothing.

I remember a presentation the captain had prepared for us at the map room of Stella Maris. We were eager to learn as much as possible from what this world traveler knew.

Paulus laid his hand on his maps and began:

" Global freight shippers look at the world and see what one region has and what other regions need. By putting those two together we create value. We deliver goods as we promise. We are now carrying timber, loaded in Bordeaux."

I asked:

" Timber? I thought Bordeaux is a wine growing region. How did they become a timber exporter?"

Paulus pointed in the direction of the wine growing region.

" Wine growers of Bordeaux are expanding their vineyards to meet demand for Bordeaux Rouge. They clear cut acres of old growth maritime pine. I know this is a wood rich in resin, which is a perfect building material for dry climates.

We bring it to North Africa. We carry a load of cognac to fulfill orders. Also red wine."

Stefan looked down to the open loading hatches below.

" You do not just fill orders, but take freight you think has a market?"

" It is important, that we know about the needs of countries we visit. It gives us opportunities to serve larger communities and future orders will result. We give our trading partners what they need and the owners of our ship see a profit."

"Is there a difference for you, as a trader, in how countries are governed, can you tell us how well some types of governance work for traders compared to others?," Helena wanted to know.

Paulus looked at her approvingly.

"Very good question. We are sailing to Casablanca in Morocco. It is a French protectorate. We will deliver timber there. We will pick up spices, which is a commodity treasured around the world. Spices take little room. Like gun powder, we must keep them dry. Wine shipments create good relations and secure protection for us, by the French navy, who's commanders are stationed in north Africa. Our load of cognac will go to clients in Algiers by camel train. From there, we will receive a load of phosphate, which is used for agriculture in Italy."

Wolf was curious about north west Africa.

"Is there a difference between Algiers and Morocco? They are both under French control. Algiers was annexed by France and Morocco is a French protectorate. How does that affect you as a trader?"

Paulus clearly enjoyed this interview.

"Excellent question. Morocco features one important asset, which might have influenced France, to make it a protectorate, besides the fact, that Spanish Morocco is also a protectorate and not a colony. Morocco is the birthplace of one of the oldest universities anywhere in the world: Al Quarawiyyin in Fez, founded by a Muslim woman, named Fatima Al- Fihri. It is noteworthy, that this university is attended by Jews, Christians, and Arabic scholars as well as by Muslims. It has one of the region's most extensive libraries, which attracts scholars from around the world.

Today's European culture was greatly inspired and influenced by science and literary traditions originating in North Africa.

Spain, and France let Morocco retain its traditional government, customs, religion, and judiciary based on Islamic law.

Spain in Spanish Morocco, controls the region along the Mediterranean coast.

The French government offers Morocco protection in return for the right of French companies to do business in Morocco with immunity from local laws and taxes.

France found this arrangement less expensive than annexation. It does not require taking the region by military force like Algiers.

French Morocco polices itself and does it at its own expense. France can sell them weapons, instead of having to support a military government."

Chapter 33

Casablanca

Stefan unfolded another map, then he asked:
"Why are we staying at the Atlantic coast to land in Casablanca?

Are we not making a detour by going there first?"

"You are right, Stefan, it is a detour, that can cost us an extra day or two.

French Morocco is for us like staying in France. We trade French goods with French Traders, using French currency.

The phosphates, we are picking up, come from the plateau des phosphates, near Casablanca. The shipment we take on, is exported to Italy, landed in Genoa.

Good for Morocco, good for France and good for Italy, good for Genoa and therefore good for us.

This is the type of collaboration across borders, I am trying to show you, as an example of how everyone can benefit. Unlike in sports, international trade is competitive in other ways. We are looking to find win-win opportunities whenever we can."

Herbert had two questions:

"The population of Algiers and Morocco seem to be almost identical culturally and ethnically. Why treat them differently, colony one and protectorate the other?

And secondly, how come Morocco is divided in Spanish and French Morocco?"

Paulus was interested in this subject:

" Population-similarity is mostly on the surface. Algiers has a large contingent of Berbers, who are fiercely independent desert and mountain dwellers, who maintain trade routes across the Sahara, using camel trains, supplied, and supported by caravansaries for water and feed. The French government has employed them in the conquest against the Kalifate, paying them with the spoils of war and weaponry, similar to Napoleon in the war on Russia.

France gave Berbers certain leading positions in the military, that controls the annexed region.

The colony is always being contested by opposition nationalists, as well as by religious leaders, who wish to return to their own traditions. France also gave signals to the Spanish Crown, to stop expanding into Algiers from Spanish Morocco, which owns most of Morocco's Mediterranean coast."

Maria, always looking for the greater picture:

" As a trader, is doing business with colonies of France similar to trading with French ports in France and in protectorates? Are colonies becoming more French, with schools teaching children in French?

Paulus pushed his hat back.

"Yes and no. Yes, because we get paid in French currency and use French contracts, pay French tariffs and customs and use French banks to facilitate transactions.

No, because there is a level of administrative drag in a colony, that has to do with the fact, that colonial governors see themselves as fairly independent from the homeland and tend to make up their own rules. Fear of recurring insurrections drives many decisions and gives governors extra leeway with France.

This causes rule changes and personnel changes, affecting trade.

It causes delays, which raises our cost of trading with them.

I personally do not believe, that people should have to give up their identity or their culture. We are often approached by the "other side," which is a temptation to circumvent regulations and tariffs. We must remain neutral as international traders.

We never talk about that. Officially, we prefer constancy and consistency.

Colonies are more volatile than protectorates, where the marketplace is more richly stocked.

The less an occupying force imposes imported culture, the better for trade."

Wolf came around the plan table to look at Italy.

" How does this compare to trading with Italy's City states?"

Paulus unfolded a regional map of Genoa.

"A really good question. When we leave Casablanca, we will go through the Strait of Gibraltar and across the Mediterranean to reach Genoa.

Genoa is a city state, that has an elected government, like Venice or Hamburg.

Genoa maintains its own military security forces around the world, with fortresses and safe warehouses at strategic points.

Genoa also has her own banks, to facilitate international trade, builds her own ships and is a contender to any national government in trade- and naval power.

To Genoa, we deliver the most valuable vintages of wine from Bordeaux.

Phosphate, we expect to load in Casablanca, will go to Genoa. They sell it to Italy.

The benefit of trading with governments run by elected officials, is their competency and agility. They perform to remain in office. No inherited power is standing in the way of progress there."

Herbert looked puzzled.

"What do you mean by that?"

"Elected officials are savvy traders themselves. They know what their partners need.

The Doge of Genoa will help us with landing permits to Tripoli in Libya, which is a country, that has a long history with settlers from Italy, dating back to the Roman empire. Tripoli is an important trading port for that part of Afrika.

It also serves as a backdoor to Egypt during these uncertain times, especially with the decline the Ottoman empire, which is presently experiencing contests from Baltic states.

We find there is a difference in dealing with port authorities under elected governments of smaller scale. They are free and creative in their decision making. Their procedures are less cumbersome and more helpful than those, made by people who administrate affairs for inherited governments, owned by nobility, kings, emperors or even the Roman Catholic Church herself.

People in city states are better educated and usually better informed.

That is very important to us especially during times of constant change."

Stefan opening a plan page of the Mediterranean.

" Where will we go after Tripoli?"

Stefan's eyes had been roaming the horizon back and forth, as if he could wish the next destination to appear. He was goal oriented and competitive, more interested in the navigation part of the journey than in economics or the geo-politics of the day.

Captain Paulus followed Stefan's gaze at the horizon and noticed the change in Stefan's facial expression, which he acknowledged with a nod. Then he explained patiently:

"From Tripoli, we will sail to a port in Greece, Thessaloniki.

Thessaloniki is as close to the ancient silk road and the Balkan states, as you can get by sea. It has been the port of call for traders with Balkan States.

Today it is the eastern back door to the embattled Ottoman Empire."

Helena put both hands on the Greek part of the map and spread her fingers.

"What is the role of Greece in the Mediterranean and in the world of sea trade today?"

Paulus moved her hands to north west Africa and to Asia minor. Then he answered:

"Greeks ancient ocean traders with long established relationships in every known part of the world. These relationships have stood the test of time, through changing regimes, rising and falling empires and kingdoms. Greece regained her independence as a country in 1821.

Greeks have never accepted to be part or province to other empires, no matter who was officially in charge of that region. Greece had kings from as far away as Denmark

That is why Greeks have developed a high degree of adaptability as is documented in Greek dramas and legends, that are still read and performed around the world.

You all know Homer's work. Greek philosophers and scientists are still playing a fundamental role in literature, social order, medicine, and science."

Helena was curious:

"How does the history of this region play a role in our changing world?"

Paulus liked her questions.

"This is the region, where written history was born. History will be made here again.

Greece is the gateway between Europe, Asia minor and Africa. It is a melting pot of cultures, ethnic groups, and nationalities. It is a crossroads, where the known world and an emerging world of the future will meet.

Some consider Thessaloniki to be as important a seaport as Constantinople, Alexandria or Venice.

From here, one can embark to Africa, the Black Sea, Russia and through the Suez-canal, to east Africa, India, and Asia. As you will see, Thessaloniki is inhabited by a rich diversity of people, with different religious, ethnical, cultural, and national backgrounds.

Each has left their mark on her architecture. This is the home of open mindedness and tolerance. These qualities make this port important to world trade."

Stefan interrupted Helena's next question. He was getting ready to explode from impatience. It made all of us smile. We knew, he would rather be fighting an opponent in a tennis match or do a first ascent of a frozen mountain, than listen to these long elaborations, that did not even make the ship go faster.

Pushing the map of Africa into the center, he said looking to the horizon:

"Captain, I see a storm brewing on both sides of us, West from the Atlantic and East from the Strait of Gibraltar!"

Beaming, the captain acknowledged Stefan's observation for the second time.

Paulus liked Stefan, because he was a lot like him and he had begun to adopt him like a son. With a hand on Stefan's shoulder, he said in a calming voice as he stepped between Stefan and Helena, pointing towards the north-western corner of the African continent:

"Stefan is right. We will have to continue our discussion later.

As Stefan has just informed us correctly, there is serious weather coming our way from two sides and we must prepare. This will be a wallop of a storm.

We will be glad to have a steel ship, as modern as Stella Maris. The Atlantic storm was a cold weather storm. You will now witness a hot weather storm meeting a cold weather storm. They will energize each other, and you must go and get prepared.

That is an order.

If you excuse me, we must get our ship ready.

Go to your quarters and make sure, everything is buttoned down. Have supplies of water and food in your quarters for at least twenty-four hours, even though you might not be in the mood for eating during the next few days."

As soon as he had finished speaking, the ship did a little hop, like a duck over a wave in a pond. As we were crossing the opening of the strait of Gibraltar, where warm water from the Mediterranean makes a visible change in color from the warm, blue currents to steel gray cold waters of the Atlantic Ocean.

We were transfixed by this play of colors. Seconds later, we could see a red cloud forming in the east and a black cloud confronting us from the west.

Stefan spread his arms wide like an albatross and unapologetically he said:

"No time for sight-seeing today! Let me remind you of our storm experience in the Baltic Sea. It was a small boat and a small storm.

This, my friends, is the real thing.

It happens at both ends of the African continent. It will make this large steel ship feel like our little yacht before this double trouble. Sailors have written about it. Now we are getting a taste of it.

Let us check one more time the location of life boats, life vests and put on our gear. This weather can change our fate in just a few hours.

Look at our captain. He is getting ready to run a real storm.

His sailors are getting ready to see us to the other side of two storms."

With these words, Stefan ushered us back to our quarters, pointing at survival gear and finding life vests for us to put on.

The red storm from the east looked threatening, with discharge of lightning bolts.

It was filled with airborne fine, red dust from the Sahara Desert. Through our windows, the world had turned spooky. No visibility, no sound, but an enormous rolling cloud of solid red dust heading our way, lightning spiking down into the water like needles. It looked like it could bury and swallow anything in its path.

It made me cling to Stefan, I saw the others also holding on to each other. Everyone seemed to whisper, and the silence was breathtaking.

Stefan took me to the other side of the room to see, what the west had in store for us. We could see a black weather front approaching from the Atlantic.

Clouds touched the sea, suggesting heavy rainfall. The green-gray surface of the Atlantic was beginning to show a tremor of little wavelets, like water in an outgoing tsunami. It was retreating, leaving me curious about this change of events.

The calm was igniting terror in Stefan's eyes.

He began barking instructions at us, to secure loose objects and to suit up for a wild ride with the possibility of ending up in a lifeboat.

"Just like the last time, outside Le Havre," he said in his captain tone of voice.

"Trust me, this one will test the ship, the captain, the crew, and all of us.

This is a confrontation of anger and fury. Remember we must stay inside. There are hand runs along all the walls. Seas will wash over the rail and take us overboard, if we get caught outside. We have only ten minutes before these two storms will meet right on top of us."

At this moment, we could feel the boat turn with the bow towards the west, engines revving to full power. It made us think, that Paulus was attempting to outrun the Mistral to get back into the Atlantic, facing the cooler storm head-on.

At the same moment, the tremolo, we could see in the small waves, turned into a vibration, that went through the entire vessel. From a pianissimo of softly muffled sounds on the outside, a hum became audible, that was rich in low frequencies building a slow crescendo, to evolve into a roar, that one would expect from the throat of a lion. Spray of salt water was streaking across the windows.

At this moment, the bow of the ship rose up like a bucking bronco and we could see water stream by our windows on both sides of the room we were sheltered in. It suggested, that the bow must have cut straight into an enormous wave, as the ship rose at a steep angle, climbing what water it could not cut. We had to grasp anything that was bolted to the ship to avoid getting tossed around, when suddenly the bottom fell out and the ship pitched and shot straight down the other side of this huge wave. For a moment, the engines were whining as the propellers had nothing to push against.

Our senses were heightened from previous storm events. We had no way to imagine that waves could be this big.

Chapter 34

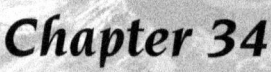

Inside two storms

Stefan was rarely speechless.

Today, he tried to breathe when the bow of Stella Maris slapped into the water, sending a wave of water and spray high over the entire ship. I could hear him count waves out loud. I remember him telling me, that waves came in sequences of seven, building up, building up, then beginning again from the bottom. I could hear everyone count waves now. Just audible over the roar of wind sounding like a freight train. The storm added a cacophony of sounds to the concert, playing on cables, halyards, flags, and corners of recessed doorways. The crescendo was still building. We began listening for sounds of items being torn from the ship, but could not hear anything of that nature.

We began to appreciate the skill of the navigators, driving our ship and I could see Stefan react to each shift in direction and power applied to the ship's screws with nods of approval. Then, the outside turned dark. The lights in our lounge began to flicker and finally turned off.

Outside, we could see emergency floodlights piercing red mist, rain and ocean spray washed over the structure we were sheltered in.

How glad I was, that none of us were getting sea sick!

Lights came back on, after what seemed like an eternity.

I could see white knuckles of everyone's hands, grasping something, that was welded or bolted to the ship.

Visibility had shrunk to nothing, a wall of a mounting red cloud of impenetrable density was overrunning us from behind and into another wall of black wet chaos from the storm ahead, which we were steaming straight into.

Atlas Meeting Poseidon. It was epic.

Had it not been so terrifying and shocking, we could have appreciated the beauty of this phenomenal display of violence, one made possible by red dust and sand from the Sahara Desert and another one made visible by torrents of water coming from everywhere at the same time with wind speeds exceeding hundred miles per hour.

The Sand storm that was chasing us, looked like a solid wall, rising straight out of the water, contrasting the blue of the flat ocean with its tremolo of waves in a sharp line of the maroon bottom of the wall with pillars of red and orange shapes rising to a cloud ceiling of magnificent cumulus formations, shaped like towers, lit by sunlight from above the clouds of the storm we were now in the center of.

The Atlantic side of the storm was rising out of gray-green water with white caps as big as ground fog, black at the base, white on top, displaying a black and grey wall, that was topped by a rolling wave of thick fog, pierced by beams of light and distant lightning bolts, that seemed to answer the lightning flashes of the red dust storm behind us.

Two storms merged in turbulence of opposing currents of water and air. The power of Nature could be felt, tearing at the structure of our ship.

Things were being swallowed up and we were sure, that one of those things could be our ship. It was a contest between cold, dense Atlantic air and hot, dust filled Sahara air, energized by the cold, dense Atlantic water, and warm, turbulent Mediterranean currents, trying not to mix, while taking out their frustration on Stella Maris.

She was once again dancing like a walnut shell in a waterfall.

All I could see, was the red of the Sahara storm entering and disappearing in the black of the torrents of rain water pouring out of Atlantic storm clouds. The sand storm was being absorbed by Atlantic rain and the gray-green of the Atlantic water was beginning to show red streaks.

The ship stayed the course until suddenly things became calm and breathless silence surrounded us, interrupted only by the hum of our engines. We could feel the ship turning back towards Morocco. Now we moved in the same direction as the Atlantic storm. Stefan, our captain explained:

"We are now following the heart of the storm right into Casablanca, where the Atlantic storm will make landfall.

What a clever captain we have. I knew he is an experienced sailor but I would have never guessed, he would be this good.

He might have just saved our lives, his ship, his cargo, and his crew."

Pretend as he might, Stefan was clearly shaken by this event. I could hear it in his voice and feel the place of pain on my arm where he had been holding on through the worst of the violence, that left all of us drained and exhausted, frightened, and relieved, yet thankful to be alive.

"How about some tea?" I heard myself say and we all broke out into torrents of laughter, that brought us to tears and did not want to stop, the more we wanted to suppress it, the more we burst out again, until our stomachs hurt.

The captain opened the door to check in on us and only nodded, seeing that we were laughing already. Then he disappeared. We did not see him again until Stella Maris was taking a pilot on board, to lead us into port.

Free from his duty, captain Paulus now came to see us again and invited us to join him for dinner.

"We are making landfall, while we are in the eye of a hurricane," he began.

" As you can imagine, the Mistral tore through the region dumping dust everywhere. Then the hurricane made land fall. Casablanca will need a day or two to recover. The harbor will be up and running, before the rest of the town. We will be delayed for a day. This will give you an opportunity to do a little exploration, as long, as you have one of my officers with you and always stay together." He raised his glass.

"Welcome to Morocco." Then he began to dive into his meal with the gusto of someone who was glad to be here and not at the bottom of the sea. He looked at us for a long moment, one at a time. Then he said to no one in particular:

"Did you enjoy the show? This was about as bad a storm as you will ever see and probably the worst on this journey. This is where the Atlantic meets Africa. We will celebrate your first steps onto the land, where our ancestors came from."

He gave a burst of laughter.

"You kids know how to make your first appearance with a splash."

We finished another one of the captain's opulent meals, with lots of toasts to the success of our mission and smooth sailing across the Mediterranean Sea.

We were very tired by the time the ship docked. The harbor was red from dust. We were minutes away from getting doused with more water from the other side of the hurricane.

Stefan drew us a map of the advancing storm, showing rotation reversal of wind direction. We watched the crew add extra spring lines and fenders, expecting the next incoming tide to be extra high.

On the positive side, rain from this storm washed away the dust from our ship and from streets and buildings. We were staying on board. After prayers, Maria and I kissed our mother's tiger eye beads on our rosaries. One moment later, we were fast asleep.

Setting foot on the African continent the next day made us feel one big step closer to our destination and many more steps further away from home.

Muted colors of clay buildings, flat roofs and stucco covered walls in burnt yellow, white and dusty orange, cobble stone paved streets, still red with the remainder of dust in the gaps, the sound from mullahs on minarets, calling for prayer, odors of food, cooked in the open, colors and scents from piles of spices and herbs, merchandise rearranged after the storm, the plethora of clay pots, bowls and objects made from copper, brass, tin, jade, precious and-semi precious stones, crafted into beads and jewelry, the amazing variety of woven goods from knotty white Moroccan cotton to intricately woven silks, cotton, and printed yard goods, tanned leather products, the smell of animals, the scent of Turkish coffee being roasted and brewed in open air cafes and the call of the vendors, inviting buyers to touch their wares, stood in stark contrast to our sparsely decorated quarters aboard ship.

Our officer guides were knowledgeable and knew how to fend off unwanted beggars and aggressive vendors.

Maria, Helena, and I bought dark colored, full length, long sleeved

Caftans, like those, we saw local women wearing.

We chose light colored scarves for our heads and faces to make sure, our guides would not lose us in the throng of people, crowding the market. Local females headcovers were black.

The boys did some shopping also:

Wolf chose a gray hooded caftan with white head dress that could cover his face against dusty winds. Walter picked out a tan, hooded caftan with black head dress.

Stefan fancied a blue caftan, with red and white checkered head dress.

We had fun fitting turbans and headscarves on each other, with the help of the merchants.

Our ship's officers stood out in their official, white Stella Maris uniforms.

Red dust began swirling off the flat roofs in little tornados. We walked out of the market, wearing our new garments, trying to get used to our restricted view, but glad to be able to breathe again.

Stefan had found a tennis racket at a leather goods shop. He commented on the excellent craftsmanship and the quality of the webbing.

Highlight of the day was the visit to the spice traders. We were invited to taste spices from black to bright yellow and white in color, like an artist's palette, too numerous to remember names, too spicy on our tongues, to distinguish them in the end.

Excitement came, when a person, who had been following us, decided to pull a knife out and demanded our purses and wallets.

This turned out to be a mistake.

He seemed to focus on me, which was his second mistake.

Like lightning, Stefan used his new tennis racket and hit the robber's hand with an upward forehand, which made the weapon fly high into the air. It landed on top of the roof of a building across the lane. Just as fast, the officers of Stella Maris stepped in and arrested the assailant.

They held him, until they could locate a police officer with the help of the merchant, we had bought our garments from.

The incident took no more than five minutes.

To calm down, we went to a café, where we tasted freshly baked croissants and Turkish coffee and tall glasses of water, while the ship's officers conducted negotiations for a spice shipment, our captain intended to take on board.

What impressed us, was the variety of people from different countries, interacting, trading, talking, and congregating just a few hours after the most vicious storm, we had ever experienced. Everyone acted, as if nothing had ever happened.

We returned to the harbor, where cranes were busy loading and unloading palettes with goods into the hold of Stella Maris. We went to see the purser, who collected our passports and the remainder of our local currency.

Captain Paulus invited us to join him for an evening meal within the hour.

It was time to change back into our own garments.

We shook off the dust from our first visit to Casablanca, Morocco, North west Africa.

After dinner we retreated to our lounge.

Paulus joined us. He had returned to his jolly, friendly self, relieved, to have escaped this unusually dangerous storm.

Paulus was rubbing his hands together, the way people do, when they have finished something important. He began:

"The timing of tides and winds worked to our advantage."

About the attempted robbery he said:

"I told you harbors and markets are not safe. Now you know. You are not in Berlin anymore."

After carefully cutting his cigar with a special tool and making sure, that our boys had done the same, he placed a map on the coffee table and used our tea cups to hold the paper flat.

Then he poured each of us a snifter of cognac from a crystal dispenser with a bulbous bottom and a slender neck. We raised our glasses.

Paulus, with a big smile on his face and with sparkling eyes looking at us, boomed:

"Welcome to Africa. I hope you had a pleasant day and a chance to recover from the excitement of the last twenty-four hours. Cheers, Prosit !!!"

Looking at Stefan, who had by now graduated to be his assistant in all things nautical, he pointed at the map and asked:

" Where did we leave off? Are we done with Europe? What were we talking about last?

Stefan seemed pleased about the next phase of our trip towards the east side of Africa.

Now he was quick to say:

"You pointed out, that Thessaly in Greece, is the gateway between Europe, Asia minor and Africa.

You said, that Thessaloniki is as important a seaport as Constantinople or Venice.

You spoke about embarking from there to the other side of Africa.

We were just leaving Thessaly in Greece and headed towards Alexandria when we saw the two storms approaching, which interrupted you."

Chapter 35

◆

Crossing the Mediterranean

Taking a drag from his cigar, and exhaling with a luxurious puff, Paulus resumed his session. He placed a pointing finger on the map.

"Right. From Thessaloniki, Stella Maris will sail to Alexandria, which became another important trading port, after the Suez Canal was opened, giving us a direct route to India, Asia, the Pacific Ocean. That has shortened travel time, -cost and -distance to ports along the Coast of East Africa, India, and Asia by thousands of miles."

We were very tired. The captain could see, that we were all running out of steam:

"Go to bed and get your quarters in order. Expect a special breakfast tomorrow.

I bid you good night."

The breakfast, the kitchen staff had prepared, was a medley of treats from all over Europe and we fell over them like a hungry pack of wolves. It made us laugh and we began our farewell party in very good spirits and cheer.

After breakfast, Helena and Walter found a gramophone player with a big funnel, that made music good enough for dancing.

Enjoying each other's company and switching partners frequently, we danced into the late morning, while the ship was being loaded and prepared for departure.

We fell into our beau's arms and onto our beds happy and exhausted, ready for a nap.

This evening at dinner, we were very quiet. We knew that now we would learn more about Africa.

Paulus took us to the map room. He had the latest map of Africa spread out before us.

He wiped his mouth with his handkerchief, then used it to clean his glasses. He began:

"Here you can see, how superpowers subdivide the World. Agreements are made with great fanfare, to show the world, who is in charge, who controls assets and who has rights to exploit, extract or trade which part of the African continent.

You will notice, that people still refer to Africa, as though it were a single country.

Check how many times you can fit all of Europe into the African continent and you get a feel of its size and the variety of regions and cultures. You will be introduced to just a few, as we go around the outside. The inside of Africa is filled with surprises, like a Mexican piñata, and the old countries are competing for the biggest stick to crack her open."

He held his belly in a big burst of laughter, at his own joke, then he continued:

Markets in Casablanca are loaded with products coming from skills and traditions going back centuries. Camel trains cross deserts and mountains to bring them out."

Pointing at the map, he remarked:

"You can see, that the German Empire is not a big player. Germany is a young country, created by joining small kingdoms like Bavaria, Wuerttemberg, Hannover and Hessia, under one flag, as a modern nation.

For sailors like us, this is a world in flux. It is still largely unknown to the decision makers representing leading nations. Understanding trade regions, trade routes, trade goods and on what terms they can be traded, is critical knowledge for us.

You are on my ship as guests on a special mission: To study conditions and to make recommendations for better governance of our German colonies and our sphere of influence. This effort is testament to the fact, how new all of this is and how far the department of foreign affairs has yet to go."

This seemed to be a good point to interrupt him and Maria took a deep breath and stepped close to the map table across from the captain. She seemed as determined as she was when she talked to our father back home: She said in a firm voice.

"I have a question regarding the trade with humans across borders and continents.

I understand, that plantations in the New World from South America to North America, Hispaniola, the Caribbean islands, from Barbados to Cuba and the Bahamas, have been a market for the importation of slaves, to work these plantations, for a long time and that Africa was a main source for this involuntary migration. What can you tell us about the significance of slavery in cross ocean trade and the involvement of the city state of Genoa under the Doges? "

Paulus, always surprised about how well informed this young lady was, said:

" Why do you ask?"

Maria looked at me to see if I would agree when she said:

" When we were little girls, Joan and I had permission to share easter eggs with children of mine workers, who lived in company tenements. We brought eggs to them with our housekeeper, helping us carry the large baskets. We had permission to walk into their homes. We were struck by the squalor, some of these families were living in.

The smell of sweat and sour milk would stay with us for weeks. I was compelled to go back, to help these poor people, especially the sick and elderly, with cleaning and nursing tasks. I was curious about health, education, and the languages, they spoke, besides broken German. I was never satisfied with some of the answers I received. I was especially upset about statements like: "They came here, to better their lot."

We were heartbroken about the conditions they were living under, compared to the managers and administrators of the coal mine, our father was the director of.

I tried to imagine, how bad they must have had it, where they lived before, to come into this squalor and call it an improvement. It made me curious about the movement of humans during industrialization. What can you tell us about trade in humans?"

Paulus looked at me then Maria:

"Industry has put new people in power. Labor is defined by them as a natural resource.

In Europe, feudal ownership of land and its people has been inheritable for centuries.

They decide who lives on their land and how they use it. People took it as a God given privilege and accepted it as fate, praying for mercy from God.

In parts of the world, where people are not yet owned, they defend themselves against intruders, who try to annex their land, steal their children, and strip their resources.

Sometimes people, owned by Nobility, migrate peaceably, with the promise of a better life. People are often moved by decree or by force of arms, to satisfy the demands of industry or planters. In Africa, humans became a merchandise, traded at auction like cattle. Relocating labor, is a form of slavery or indentured servitude.

People are not asked for their consent. Industry controls them. That, to me, is slavery.

Slave trade is now on the decline. It began being prohibited in some regions around 1860. In East Africa, the Kalif of Zanzibar banned slave trade during the 1880s."

Wolf now wanted to know more.

"Who was trading in slaves besides Spaniards and Arabs?"

Paulus, looking at Wolf, then at Maria answered bluntly:

"Everyone did. Trade in slaves was conducted by the British (40%), the French (20%) and Spain, Portugal, Italy and Greece making up the remainder."

Helena, coming from a background of local, small-scale manufacturing:

" How did the industrial revolution change the fate of relocated humans?"

Paulus, looking at Helena, then at Herbert:

"In my opinion, relocating people as workforce for industry, is slavery. It is difficult to see, when inexpensive labor is provided by people, who migrate of their own free will to find work, or hope for a better life.

Only rarely were they able to do so without permission by their rulers. Industry will make even more profit, when they can provide them with food, housing, clothing, and consumer goods. Maria has described it well."

Herbert was looking toward Maria:

"Maria is right. Employers often fall short in meeting people's needs, because apparently, industry does not consider labor as humans.

Caring for them, is not part of their business plan.

Labor is an expense. Not an investment.

In my opinion, investment in labor is limited to advertising and recruitment of labor force, unless they need to acquire special skills or specific knowledge for their employers.

Then they will teach them something.

Now I have a question: How did Genoa acquire skills and knowledge in their workforce, to become a world leader in ship building and engineering?

Chapter 36

Wolf was now trying to us get back to the world they were sailing into:

"What is the difference between nations and city-states and how does that affect the population?"

Paulus liked this question. It was touching on his favorite subject: Good governance.

"City-states are flexible. Their leadership does not pass by inheritance. These states are run by elected officials. They must show good results to be reelected. That is how they stay in power.

In Genoa, workers became more educated as their work became more sophisticated: They started building ships. This work has consequences. The workforce must be skilled. Independent thinking is encouraged. Workers demand safe working conditions and earn better wages. Genoa provided all of that. It is an example, how city states can react to change. They operate their community like a business. They are proactive.

Nations are traditionally ruled by people who inherit their power. These rulers depend on information, provided by their advisors. It is a gamble. They do not change course quickly. Nations are surprised by change, and resist it, not causing it as city states do.

Stefan now looked puzzled,

"What do you mean?" He asked.

"I see it as a trader. Look at the crew on this ship. These men may not have a full education. Yet they learn special skills to operate a complicated machine, that must function under extreme conditions. My position as a leader depends on our joint success. Our very survival does. It is a network of collaborators.

Waterways are navigable trade routes, where dams are erected, to raise water levels high enough for ships to travel upstream. Canals are dug to make room for movement of ships, like the Suez Canal. All collaborations. Private initiatives. Some dams are now used to drive turbines, generating electricity. Collaboration is good for progress.

Innovation requires education and skills. Genoa became a world power by making trade easy for all traders. Not just their own. They attracted knowledge, because they used it for everyone's benefit.

Government is slow to respond, as you will see, when you meet the people in our colonial administration. Fast with violence, slow with progress. Short sighted about the benefit of inclusivity, determined protectors of exclusivity and territory. They tend to get stuck on personal gain and influence and thereby miss opportunities for collective gain.

Trade ships are a learning organization. They reach far. Use the same method and your colony will be successful."

Herbert liked this idea. He asked:

"Captain, you travel and have a worldwide perspective as a trader: Do you consider education to be the single most important element, that determines the success of society in a changing world?"

"Yes. Education and health care.

Without these two, no society can thrive.

One more thought, before we go on to our maps:

Growth of industry has changed the international playing field.

Steel processing and ship building are tilting the balance in Germany's favor:

We have the potential of becoming a major naval force, with armored ships and cannon, that are not easily intimidated. This was already recognized by the other players.

Forces are emerging, that old empires cannot control. Mariners on the other hand, trade with people, who have done this for centuries.

We succeed because of well established relationships with our trading partners across empires and across time. To us and to our trading partners, it is incidental, who rules, or which flag is flying over a port. We do not care by which name you call your God. We are the diplomats of the high seas. We avoid conflict, rocks, shallows, narrows, and cannonballs, that can sink ships. Our trading partners help us to navigate this world."

Stefan was eager to get to the next subject. He asked:

"Looking at the map, that was issued during the Berlin Conference in 1884:

What does it tell you?"

Paulus was now getting fired up. He spoke with his booming voice:

"It shows, what participating delegates have decided to do with Africa.

You can see the role, armed naval forces can play, by where names have been posted.

It shows where claims were staked."

He took a deep breath and stepped back as if he was going to jump onto the plan table with both feet to trample this map, then he said:

"It does not indicate, who lives in a region, or by what rules their life is successful.

The conference acted as though Africa was uninhabited.

That was the highest form of ignorance, expressed at the highest level by the most powerful representatives of the most powerful nations on Earth.

To them, the planet it is 'available' 'unexplored' or 'unknown,' unless they have given title and license to some entity.

Until then, the world is theirs for the land grab and the pillaging.

Industry has provided them the means and the mandates, to get us involved in colonizing.

To most politicians, Africa is just one country.

Not over one thousand communities, with languages, customs, and borders, that are defined by features such as oceans, rivers, lakes, mountains, plains, swamps, savannahs, or deserts."

Helena, puzzled by the captain's passionate response:

"Are you suggesting, that the entire population of this huge continent has been ignored?

How can anyone expect a positive outcome, after decisions like this have been made and treaties were signed? Are they not based upon entirely false premises?"

Paulus nodded agreement, almost shaking off his captain's cap: He spoke with anger, his voice, at a low pitch:

"No native Africans were represented at this conference. No signatories had any legal standing on any grounds. There is nothing but potential conflict, not just between indigenous people of Africa, but between the colonizers themselves."

Wolf was incredulous:

"Let me see: Industry needs resources, plants a flag in the ground and makes a claim.

Action is driven by investors, who have financed them and now feel entitled to a return on their investment. How do they not expect their desired outcome?

How do they not want to claim, that it is in the interest of the nation, the economy, and international peace, to force the outcome by use of armed safety personnel and mercenaries in the name of the nation, paid for by the citizenry, that has no stake in this? How is this not the beginning of the end of any nation?"

Paulus seemed to have calmed down, unless it was the calm heart at the center of a cyclone. He said:

"Good question. Three models are used to control a region:

First, annexation after military conquest: A region becomes part of the invading country. A governor is appointed, often with dictatorial power to make rules.

Second, by declaring it a protectorate: Conquerors leave local governance and judiciary in place, while holding a gun to the chest of the existing ruler.

'Protectorate' means military 'protection' in return for trading rights for the 'protector.'

Third, negotiated settlement between superpowers, based on a quid pro quo:

"Build less battleships, and we grant you control over a larger region." This was proposed to our kaiser by the United Kingdom and France. Or: "Give us your mineral rights in Morocco and take control of a major part of the Congo River Basin."

Maria could not believe, what she had just heard:

"How did the negotiators in Berlin arrive at a plan and sign agreements with such limited and clearly false information?"

"Not only did they have insufficient knowledge about the world, but industry and finance were not well understood by them either. The struggle for financial resources and investments, coincided with the struggle to control regions and available resources.

Politics had a role to play. Propaganda was used to influence public opinion.

Together with propaganda, religion was an amazingly popular driving force. Germany sent planters, geologists, botanists, and missionaries to the colony.

They were trying to clone the homeland. Workers are needed for industry at home, plantations are expanding abroad, nation building, to clone the homeland abroad, and markets, that produce resources and consume manufactured goods, to export into the colony, all make for a confusing picture.

Slavery was prohibited. Tribes-people are coerced, to work for planters, to build infrastructure, to dig for minerals. Soldiers of the security force and Askari mercenaries provide protection against upset indigenous natives."

Herbert gave a pained burst of laughter:

"This all sounds like the tried and failed business model of the German East Africa Corporation. Blood was spilled. Lives were lost. Investments failed to show a return. The kaiser steps in. The nation pays the bill. What do you see, captain?"

Paulus related something about himself:

"I was raised by a single parent from a mixed marriage. One parent Greek, one parent German. That made us neither Greek nor German. It made us world citizens. I became a sailor, longing to one day be reunited with my father, who had to return to Greece and took with him my twin brother, to raise him as a citizen of Greece, while I was raised German by my beloved mother. We made up for the loss, by making our world big.

What I see, is a world attempting to become small, concentrated, cloned, and multiplied in sameness. No one knows how to do this, because that is not how it works.

Germany, France, Spain, Portugal, Italy, the British Empire Russia, and others, are all experimenting with different forms of control. Some are using chartered corporations with broad license to arm and control their 'subjects' while pillaging their wealth.

Most use force of arms. Success is defined by the value of the stolen goods, extracted valuables like gold, diamonds and other minerals or by selling humans at auction.

Russia and Germany are late arrivals at the table of colonizers. Gleaning methods of control, others have used and are already seeing the failure.

All follow the same model: Agreements are made at gunpoint and upheld by military force. The Russian empire expanded sideways, east, and north, using annexation. The kaiser is trying to keep his foot in the door in East- and South-West Africa."

Helena interrupted the captain, slapping her hand on the map table:

"Apparently this works well for governors with extensive privileges and power, to distribute opportunity and wealth, backed by military force, rather than by consent, thereby creating a new military nobility, that controls peasants, who provide labor, after being disowned and disenfranchised. To me, these are temporary solutions creating permanent problems."

Maria placed both hands on the table, palms up, forming two bowls:

"Humans, in my mind, are the only force that can create value. Consumption is necessary, to give value to ever-increasing stores of manufactured goods. Now that has become the new challenge, for an investment centered world, that is not reality based. I think we need to rebalance the world and develop a human centered model."

Stefan, looking at Paulus, wanted more of this sailor's knowledge. He said:

"Building bigger ships and larger fleets does not look like an answer for a successful colony. You have shown us how, as a trader, you serve all humans, consumers, producers, and traders. You are telling us, that industry and government will have to bring humans back to the table, or lose control. To me, and I agree with Maria, this is a balancing act, that is best understood, by observing international traders like you. What is your prediction for the future?"

Paulus now looked sad. His shoulders had dropped forward, making him suddenly look ten years older. He spoke softly in almost a resigned voice:

"War is the unfortunate but inevitable outcome, if humans are being ignored.

In Africa, it is a widely accepted practice by the European raiders, to use the population, that does not hold title to their land, as indentured servants.

Until recently, they bought them. They paid for them with weapons, gun powder and bullets as the preferred currency. That was welcomed by people who have no problem with selling their neighbor's children into slavery. Do you sense, how dangerous this makes the African continent of the future?

The British Empire has a "landed aristocrat" class. They live off the land they own and are served by the population that happens to live on it. They are doomed.

Same with "Royalty endowed by God" in mainland Europe. They turned people into chattel and profitable trade objects as slaves to industrialization.

Trading in humans was practiced universally in one form or another. Just the excuses have changed.

Export estimates of slaves sold by European traders have reached as many as 80 000 per year. Revolts have resulted, that have brought empires to their knees.

Rome and the Byzantine Empire have left their mark on the world, but lost power in the end anyway. Presently, the Ottoman Empire is threatened by revolts in the Balkans.

France, the United Kingdom, Russia and lately Germany have begun to move into position to fill the emerging vacuum, left by the crumbling empire. Kaiser Wilhelm has made overtures to enter the fray, offering to support the Kalif of Constantinople. Ceremoniously, he offered help with the construction of railroads, that will open entire regions to development and trade. He promoted construction of railroads, connecting central Europe all the way to Baghdad, thereby reaching newly discovered oil fields in Mesopotamia and the Caucasus mountains, and markets that were before hard to reach.

Kaiser Wilhelm and his administrators favor the collaborative model of protectorates.

You can see, that there is one central part missing in the heart of all these stories:

Humans and Nature are considered merchandise and taking care of them, is considered an unprofitable expense."

Paulus looked at each of us:

"I understand, your mission is, to find a better way, to govern German East Africa. To steer away from a prison colony, with Askari mercenaries, guarding stolen property for planters and forcing natives to work for unsustainable pay. You have work to do."

Chapter 37

World trade

We were beginning to get tired. What moved our imagination the most, was the idea of collaborating with the local population, offering education, health care and infrastructure.

We were surprised by this random subdivision of Africa, made with complete disregard of land and people. We were shocked to learn, how little the deciders knew about Africa or about Africa's interior.

Countries, tribes, independent populations, herders, even hunter- gatherers in different climate zones were ignored. Rivers, mountains, lakes, savannahs, and deserts, were treated as empty space, that came with an available workforce of questionable human status and a doomed biological future, best to be used, while they could be kept alive.

Decisionmakers had no idea how they were impacting millions of people's lives.

After dinner, Paulus spoke about the journey through the Mediterranean.

Like a son of Poseidon, he stood stoically with both hands on his map table, as though he could will the world to stay calm and the weather to hold, until our arrival at Genoa.

He kept on glancing through the window of his command post, then he spoke:

"We are now sailing towards Genoa. We took Timber from Bordeaux to Casablanca and delivered Bordeaux red wine, cognac, and Cuban cigars to officials of government. Now we carry spices, lemons, mandarin oranges, and a load of rock phosphate for agriculture in Italy.

As I told you, Genoa is a city state like Venice and Hamburg.

Genoa made her mark on international trade, by building and deploying ships. Their military is used, to protect their trading posts and fortified warehouses around the world.

They constructed light houses, to guide and protect ships. All the ships.

Genovese scholars have developed the art of map making for navigation and the mapping of river basins and mountains.

Answering the need for more educated workers and scientists, Genoa has developed one of the oldest universities, known as the Atheneum. Genoa is home to two of the oldest banks, to facilitate trade.

They were first to have worker's organizations at their shipyards.

As you know, one of their sons is Christopher Columbus.

Their trade is so profitable, that they could finance extensive expeditions with armed vessels to every corner of the known world.

You get the idea: Humans at the center. Humanitarians at the helm. Everyone benefits."

Wolf wanted more:

"How does Genoa's city-state government influence their economy?"

Paulus was pleased about this conversation. He smiled.

"Very good question, Wolf. As I mentioned, like Venice, Genoa is administered by elected officials, doges, who run their affairs like a business, have built not only a good business climate for other traders, but established far reaching diplomatic relationships.

Genoa has over fifty consulates around the world and forty official agreements of cooperation, with trading partners. Known for its knowledge of finance, Genoa became home of the first banks: The Bank of St George and the Banca Carige founded in 1483, which still exist to this day.

Their traders respond to markets: So does their industry.

Genovese weavers developed the rough cotton cloth, known as blue jean, used for sailor's trousers and protective clothing. Also used as protective cover for goods in port.

We will be taking a load of this cloth to Dar Es Salaam. World-famous and sought after is Genovese lace. This is the influence of people centered, accountable, knowledge-based governance on the economy of the city state of Genoa."

Helena found this hard to believe:

"Did they have a perfect run for hundreds of years?"

"Genoa has suffered setbacks. The plague decimated the population and caused a period of decline under the Doge Andrea Doria in 1528. Genoa then became a satellite to the Spanish crown for a while.

Successful city-states operate outside and independent from inherited kingdoms.

Power, vested under influence of royalty, the Roman Catholic church and even opposing Christian Churches of the

Byzantine Empire, Greek and Russian orthodox communities was limited in time. This top-down form of governance led by a dictator had to be defended by military force, because they did not serve the population, only the leader.

Only for short periods of time, did heads of city-states come from clerical ranks.

Under church governance, massive relocation of unruly tribes and ethnic cleansing took place."

Maria looked around the room, as if to read the other's minds:

"The Genovese fleet practiced slave trade with the new world. Was that not very profitable cargo for ships, before returning with sugar, coffee, cotton and gold?"

"Yes, and yes. For doges of Genoa, the known world was a trading realm, that reached around the globe, across oceans and all established borders. They had profitable trade and the best utilization of their ships in mind. They made no judgement about slavery.

Of course, they also use contract traders, like Stella Maris, to widen their reach.

We will be loading industrial products from Genoa for delivery to Tripoli and Thessaloniki - and blue-jean for East Africa.

Helena found his vast knowledge hard to believe.

"How do you get all this information?"

Paulus was tireless and enthusiastically answering all these smart questions.

"Mariners communicate with flags and morse. And they talk. Each port has traders.

We work with them. They trust us. They share information. Sometimes we carry letters of introduction, if we are new to a harbor or a region. Knowledge flows and fills our mind the way rain water fills a barrel that is placed there, for the gardener to water plants.

There are blind spots. To this day, most of the interior of the African Continent remains undiscovered. We interact with traders at the coast. We know, what people can do at the interior by what they offer to traders. We know what they need, by what they ask for.

As for history, that has been a lifelong passion on mine. I like to have a deep understanding of the world I trade with. I read books."

Wolf was interested in this aspect of his information:

"How do you learn about parts unknown?"

"As I said, what we know about activities of the interior comes from traders, who deliver goods to market at harbors along the coast."

Maria wanted to know about the traders who were able to reach the interior:

"Who are these traders and what religious affiliation do they represent?"

"There are significant Jewish traders. Orthodox Jews maintain their autonomy from secular governments, because they are steeped in faith and have their own laws.

They educate their children, which makes them important communicators and facilitators of trade. There are Muslim traders, who have strong personal connections with indiginous people. They do not try to convert their contacts. They are more like us.

Traders of the seas refrain from involvement with religion or politics.

We are international diplomats, serving everyone. We fulfill orders, placed along our journey. Stella Maris will fly the Flag of Genoa next to the Flag of Italy, beneath the Emblem of the third German Empire and the flag Bremerhaven."

Paulus, pointing at several harbors on the map continued:

"Harbors are windows to our world. They have significance, looking in and looking out. Thessaloniki is a good example. A vibrant community with a strong economy. It attracts ocean traders, because it is protected inside the Thermaikos Bay. Geographically, it is a natural crossing of land and sea routes, going far back to times before recorded history. Socially, it is a melting pot of people from countless places.

That has made this harbor the envy of rulers across the region.

Ownership and control over this harbor have always been contested.

Presently, it is home to a garrison belonging to the Turks.

Greece has never conceded ownership and is valiantly defending her sovereignty there.

Both openly and secretly. We will carry freight for that port.

We will spend several days there, doing maintenance and repairs.

Stella Maris will also replenish her stores of water and food for the journey through the Suez Canal and on to your destination of Dar Es Salaam."

The sea now changed color from the gray green waters of the Atlantic to the deep blue of the Mediterranean, reflecting the green and tan of mountains in the distance on both the European and African shores.

Sailing through the Strait of Gibraltar, we were surprised to see how close Africa and Europe are.

Over land, cumulus clouds were piling up, looking like mountains in the Alps. To the south, the Atlas Mountains of Spanish Morocco topped the landscape, still tinted red from the mistral. Africa, aglow in the same warm colors of the spices, we had seen in the markets of Casablanca, was fading into the distance, as we sailed towards Genoa.

We had a few more hours to study maps and to learn about the path, that would take us to our destination.

Sadly, we were informed, that we would not have permission or time, to explore Genoa.

We were told to stay on board. The freight exchange would take place at night and all our ship's officers would be busy. Time lost at Casablanca had to be made up for, we were informed.

We were not just a little annoyed about the strict supervision, that came with our status as official representatives of the department of colonial affairs.

Captain Paulus explained the dynamics of trade routes, pointing to the flow of rivers defining natural borders, forming safe zones like moats, and making transportation of goods possible and safe.

He pointed out the river Nile, that made Egypt a world empire for thousands of years, by flooding and fertilizing her plains, collecting water from Ethiopia, Uganda, and Sudan.

Paulus clearly enjoyed his knowledge about the world, and so did we, feeling lucky to have a mentor like him.

"The Nile has made Alexandria one of the most important trading ports in the ancient world, serving a vast area of land with a variety of cultures, connecting land routes that reach deep into the heart of this giant continent.

Another important river is the Zambezi in Mozambique, giving name to a region known as Zambia. This river gives access to the East Coast of Africa. Before it does, it fertilizes and waters a vast region. The Zambesi delta is one of the largest river deltas known to man and Portugal was smart, to claim this fertile region.

Opposite, further south and west, you see the origins of the Niger-river that flows from springs in the Sierras of French West Africa, then forms a gigantic loop, touching territories controlled by the French, the British and the Germans, flowing north-east at first and then in a large arc towards the south and finishing its flow into the Atlantic with the Niger Delta, a marvel of fertility and natural beauty, supporting a large population since time immemorial.

A major body of water is the Congo River. The Congo River basin is a tropical forest, reaching into the interior of central Africa near the equator.

It is formed by a vast river basin, second only to the Amazon-river in the Americas. It touches several bordering regions with navigable veins of water, is back-to-back with German East Africa and British Kenya in the east, flowing north at first, then sweeping towards the west and finally draining into the Atlantic.

There are a great number of regions, depending on navigable access through the Congo basin, which makes it a contested region of strategic and economic importance to anyone who controls it.

The map of 1884 looks like a family portrait of Europe's kingdoms.

French and British regions make up the bulk, followed by Portuguese and German neighbors and finally Belgium, who put her name on the Congo Basin, a mostly landlocked area as large as France, Spain, Germany, and Italy combined. Unlimited treasure is expected to be found there.

Plantations are being established to produce sugar, coffee, cotton, spices, tropical fruit and nuts. Precious Metals, minerals timber and slaves are among the goods exported from Africa, together with furs, leather, and artifacts for markets like London, Paris, Madrid Lisbon Brussels Hamburg, and Berlin."

Wolf was spellbound:

"I am curious to understand the difference on how these regions are governed. What influence do the different religions of the colonial powers have and how does their political reality at home influence their trading practices?"

Paulus thought for a moment:

"That is a very good question. At this point, not much is known about the interaction of homeland governments and the colonies. We see how they fortify harbors. We see differences in administrative style. As traders, we limit our engagement to orders received and orders fulfilled. We are of course depending on getting paid."

Paulus glanced over the horizon ahead:

"We see missionaries moving into the interior, also scientists, such as geologists, zoologists, and botanists. Agriculture researchers arrive with sample plants in their luggage, all ordered to find out where treasure, water, arable land, or labor is available."

He had to chuckle about his next thought:

"At home, you have seen exhibits at state fairs and read reports in the financial Times. You might have heard about the debates, between local and colonial administrators and the barons of industry.

Religious groups are very verbal about their mission work. They are used to do fund raising in the name of God, Jesus, mother Mary and all the Saints.

Trade is a mystery to most people, and especially to politicians of all stripes.

The need and use of armed force for protection and expansion of territories is more frequently on people's mind. So are career opportunities abroad.

Then there is the ever-present threat of conflicts between competing governments and industry. This is best publicized, because it has profit potential.

**African Colonies after
the Berlin Conference of 1884**

Chapter 38

◆

Civil war within a national war within a religious war

The captain concluded the tour of maps with a warning: "You must understand, that there is a war going on in the Balkan states, reviving Nationalistic sentiments.

The Ottoman Empire has begun to crumble. We will be getting very close to this war.

Years of expansion by the Ottoman Empire into Europe, annexation, and migration of Muslims into Christian communities, since the end of the thirteenth century, have caused friction. Rulers of this empire have overthrown neighboring governments.

These rulers imposed Muslim religion and religious law. Now this forward motion has been reversed and regions in the Balkans have taken up arms in insurrection against Muslim controlled administrations.

This is far more dangerous than the divide between Catholics and Protestants.

I will have to show you one more map, that shows the migration into areas people hoped were safe havens:

It shows the movement of mostly Muslim families, but also Jews and Christians, fleeing from marauding rogue forces from Bulgaria, Albania, Montenegro, and Serbia.

The vacuum that is created by the crumbling empire has allowed corruption and lawlessness to take hold over civilians, who have lost trust and all hope, but developed hatred, after living in fear for generations.

Everyone is a suspect and it has become easy to hate everyone. Even relatives of different religious faith, are fighting one another. Love does not know religious rules or boundaries. Many are now accused or shunned as traitors, or as partisans in service of someone else's enemy."

Maria's empathy was becoming visible in her eyes:

"What happens to these families? It seems to me, that we have a very naive understanding of the world."

Paulus put down his cap and scratched his forehead. He put his pointing finger on the map:

"A civil war, within a national war, within a religious war are more complex, than the conflict between Catholics and Protestants you spoke of, when we talked about the reason for you being here on Stella Maris.

You were sent to look for better ways not just for a colony, but for the future of mankind.

You have a very big challenge in front of you.

You can see for yourselves how complex this situation has become.

I do not think, that our government officials comprehend the severity of the social and economic tragedy, that is playing out in the Balkans, affecting directly or indirectly many millions of innocent people, and thereby the rest of the world.

I am afraid that the players, who finance this conflict, will wash their hands, when these fires begin to burn out of control and countries, that are standing by idle right now, have no choice but to get drawn in."

Stefan, leaning over the maps, said:

" Tell us about the next stop, after Genoa. You mentioned Libya.

Is that one of the countries standing by? Are they involved? Will Stella Maris be in danger?"

Paulus, developing deep wrinkles on his forehead said, looking at Stefan:

" From Genoa we are sailing to Tripoli, to make a delivery. We have asked for increased security on board. Our pilot knows these waters, the islands, and hazards we might encounter, between Genoa, Tripoli, Thessaloniki, and Alexandria. He will take command of our ship and facilitate landings and freight exchanges all the way to Egypt.

In Thessaloniki, we will stop for a few days to refuel and to make repairs.

The same pilot will guide us to Alexandria, where he will leave us, to guide other vessels back to Genoa."

There was a long silence. Finally, he added in a low voice:

"Libya has been a dependency of Italy since the Berlin treaty of 1884.

Italy did not do much with Libya, until last year, when the Ottoman Empire began showing signs of overexposure and overextension.

Unrest and violence spilled over from Turkey into Egypt and into the interior of Libya. This conflict is intensifying inland.

Italy is engaged in a confrontation at sea with Turkey.

The Italian navy is in control of the Libyan coast now.

These are treacherous times in the coastal waters near the Ottoman empire.

That is, why we use the help of a pilot sailing all the way from Genoa to Tripoli,

to Thessaloniki and back across to Alexandria.

Greece is an independent country, interested in shoring up her northern borders and recapturing Macedonia, which Greece has always considered to be their own.

Bulgaria and Serbia to the North are a new threat to Greece. They want to establish access to world trade, through the Mediterranean Sea, using Greece as a broker, a naval power with her secure ports and centuries of expertise."

This said, Paulus excused himself, to prepare the ship for the arrival at Genoa.

We could hear and feel Stella Maris slow and drop anchors.

A horn sounded, which Stefan knew to be the boat delivering the new pilot.

We were curious, to see how this was to be done. From our quarters, we had a good view on the side of the ship, from which the pilot was approaching.

Stefan stayed behind at the Map room, to be present, when the new Pilot would take over the controls of Stella Maris.

It was beginning to get dark.

We were mystified by the things we had learned since we left Casablanca.

We were trying to visualize the movement of people within the territory controlled by the Ottoman Empire, which was now being challenged from all sides at once.

Sitting on a ship was like being on a remote, floating island.

Reality was humming in our heads, like the engines of Stella Maris in our ears and like the changing colors of the sky above the sea in our eyes, while the pilot boat was making fast to the starboard side of our ship.

We had just learned, that we were traveling straight into a war theater.

This put us on high alert.

We began to pay close attention to every movement on and around Stella Maris.

Stefan remained in the presence of the captain, Helena and Herbert with the purser, Maria and Wolf were with officers in charge of our daily care and I stayed close to chef Jean du Chalet. It was my opinion, that the best-informed person on board was the one in charge of purchasing, preparing, and serving food.

We were disappointed, to not be able to spend time on shore to see Genoa.

We could tell, that things were different now. There was a hush throughout the ship, that told us, that something unusual was going on, but we could not tell, what that was.

It was important enough, to make everyone edgy, reserved, and careful, what they would and would not talk about.

Did this have something to do with the civil unrest in Libya or with cargo we were carrying to Tripoli? We were told, that our new pilot was knowledgeable not only in all the languages that were spoken in this region, but he also knew the rules in every part of these waters.

We had heard, that he was a Greek mariner, who knew of seldom travelled shipping lanes between islands. Somone who could make evasive maneuvers into narrows, to avoid confrontations or collisions with hostile vessels.

He was praised for his personal connections with port officials and light house keepers."

Chapter 39

◈

Twins

Joan paused.

She placed a box of Stefan's papers in her lap and leafed through them.

Then, with an expression of triumph in her face, like a detective, finding the next clue, she pulled out several sheets of hand written notes, holding them up in the air.

"There," she said. "This will give us the story of what happened, when Stefan was by himself, waiting to meet the pilot in the control room of the ship."

She read:

"I stayed behind in the ship's control room with Stan Nord, the first mate.

He was holding the ship anchored, to allow for fastening the tugboat to Stella Maris, that was to tow us into port and the transfer of the new pilot.

My friends had gone to our quarters, from where they had almost as good a view, as I did from the wheel house.

I was still looking at the rigging of the tugboat, when I heard someone enter the control room. Without taking my eyes off the tugboat, I could tell that the person, who had just entered, smelled different from our Captain and even though his voice sounded familiar, he spoke with a foreign accent. At first, I thought Paulus was making a joke.

This person was greeting the first mate Stan, who introduced himself and I heard the pilot give his name as Alexandrou Pavlov.

They immediately began talking about the controls and communications equipment of Stella Maris. I paid no more attention to the hunches I had a moment ago.

The door opened, and Paulus entered, speaking in his usual commanding voice:

"Stan, you have met Captain Pavlov, our pilot to Alexandria?"

To the pilot he said, pointing at me:

"This here is Stefan. Stefan is one of our Guests.

He is watching us run this ship. He is a sailor himself, you can answer his questions, if you like, he may be a captain himself one day."

I was spooked about the two voices I heard, that sounded almost identical, except one was a little softer and had an accent. I turned around and saw the two men from the back, standing at each side of Stan Nord, who handled the ships' controls and did not avert his eyes from the tug boat.

I saw the different uniform jackets, our captain in navy blue and the pilot in a black jacket and a hat with gold cord trim and a short visor, which he wore slightly tilted to the side the same way, our captain wore his. The pilot's uniform had gold stripes on his shoulders. I thought to myself: "In the dark, I would have difficulty telling these two apart."

Now I saw the two men facing each other, as the pilot handed Paulus his papers and I could see the expression on our captain's face change, as he re-read the documents. Under his breath he murmured: "Same date of birth as mine. Born in Bremerhaven, Germany. So was I !"

He reached inside his coat and pulled out of his inside breast pocket a small envelop. He handed it to the pilot. Looking at him as he moved closer to a light to see better.

" Do you recognize this picture?" Paulus asked.

"Where did you get this?" Was the answer.

Paulus again:

" Do you recognize it? This picture was taken, when I was ten years old. It was taken on the day, my father took my brother away to Greece, because my mother was too poor to raise two boys. And here you are. If I am not mistaken, you are Alexander. My twin."

He pointed at the picture. "This is our mother."

Now I saw the pilot reach into his own breast pocket. He pulled out an identical envelop, from which he removed an old photo with the same scalloped edges, just like the one he had been looking at. With a quivering voice he said:

"I have prayed for this moment for forty years." He said softly, wiping a tear off his cheek.

He grabbed Paulus by his shoulders and held him at arm's length.

" Let me look at you. My God, you are my younger brother!"

He threw both arms around our captain and gave him a long bear hug.

"Not that much younger," I heard Paulus say over Pavlov's shoulder, as both broke into uncontrollable, teary-eyed laughter.

There were tears streaming down both of their cheeks.

"How did we stay apart for so long?" beamed Paulus.

"We are old men now. We have missed a lifetime. We must celebrate, when we get to Thessaloniki."

"First, we must survive the journey there." Said the twin with the Greek accent, laughing.

Paulus replied:

"You have a great reputation among merchant mariners. The word is:

"If you are lucky, you have Alexandrou Pavlos guiding you."

Paulus and Pavlov embraced hard once again.

As they spoke, I saw both men holding their photos, touching each other's face and looking at each other again and again as if to make sure, that this was really happening. It was a very touching moment for me to witness. I wanted to let them have their moment. I excused myself to join the others.

Looking back, I see both captains wearing their hat slightly off to the side, making them both look more independent, than the traditional square and centered way, captains wear these hats. Both had the same stance. If it had not been for the different color of their coats, they would have looked identical.

When I arrived at the lounge, the others were observing the lashing on of the tug boat.

The sky had turned crimson to the west, contrasting the deep blue, almost purple of the crystal-clear water and the black of the coast to the north, a spectacular sight, we wished would last forever.

I told my companions about the reunion of Paulus and Pavlov.

I was sure, we would learn more about this German-Greek story, before too long."

"This is what Stefan wrote in his journal," said Joan, caressing the paper, before placing it back into the box.

"Now it was anchors away and Stella Maris was being towed into the harbor of Genoa.

The arrival of Stella Maris at the dock took place in the dark. The gas lights of the city lent a charming touch to the view from our perch, high up on the ship.

We decided to make the best of it, by observing the harbor and the soft city lights. Immediately, the off- loading of cargo from our vessel began and we could hear the noise of cranes lifting heavy palettes out of the cargo hold and immediately lowering new ones into each compartment.

We could tell, that we were taking on extra tonnage by observing the angle of the boarding planks becoming less steep and the kay moving closer to the rim of the ship.

We believed, that some of the cargo, we were loading, besides cotton goods for East Africa, were not just spare parts for machinery, going to Libya and Greece.

Stefan's gut said, and he mentioned this to us, that we were witnessing the engagement of a merchant vessel in business of war.

What supported that feeling, was the sight of armed security personnel, surrounding the dock and several persons in black uniforms, carrying black sea bags, boarding Stella Maris. None of the freight, we had carried up to now, had required this kind of secrecy and security. We could see uniforms and extra personnel at the kay, preventing anyone from getting close to our ship. Stefan and Wolf pointed this out.

We pretended to seem uninterested, by playing our instruments and singing some of our favorite songs, enjoying some wine and refreshments, steward Ed Haller had brought, as consolation for the curfew, the captain had imposed.

Haller did not offer explanations, other than that we were going to leave, as soon as the freight was secured. This he also gave also as the reason, for our having to stay on board here at Genoa. Haller also mentioned, that we should expect the same procedure to be repeated at the port of Tarabulus, the harbor of Tripoli, where we would clear cargo and take on freight at night. Ed Haller ordered chef Jean du Chalet to prepare a special meal, that would make us happy to stay on board, while enjoying another one of his world class offerings.

We could see that unusual freight was being loaded and began to suspect, that this had something to do with conflicts in Libya and beyond.

People are in the habit of talking about wars, as if they were weather events, that break out unexpectedly. We talked about the extensive preparations required, both technically and financially, to send armed forces to war, or to supply them with weapons and ammunition in the field. There had to be a benefit to someone, other than the people who were compelled to take up arms for their leaders.

This was the first time that we felt the reality of war, which Captain Paulus had spoken about. For us the question was: What kind of social order could benefit the people and be sustainable, without the constant threat of war?

Paulus had not mentioned the full extent, to which Italy was engaged in a war with Turkey, over control of the province of Libya, known as Tripolitania, which Italy considered one of her provinces, dating back to the Roman Empire.

We knew that Italy's claim on Libya was confirmed by the Berlin conference in 1884.

We were told, that in 1902, Italy and France had signed a freedom from intervention act. This was done in private, concerning their respective interests in Tripolitania and Morocco.

Now, from rumors spread by the food chandlers in the ship's kitchen we learned, that Italy's sovereign rights had been challenged in 1911 by forces loyal to the Ottoman empire and from inland by insurrectionists, supported by Egypt.

From what we were able to observe, we concluded that we might have just become involved in this war.

Stefan, Wolf and Walter were sniffing the air like blood hounds and Helena and Maria were adding observations of their own, which confirmed, what I had divined from small talk in the kitchen, from remarks by our chef Jean du Chalet and remarks by the chandlers, who delivered provisions. The chandlers were the only outsiders with access to Stella Maris at this port. I kept a keen ear for information, coming from these vendors.

I saw it as my duty to inform my friends. Together, we sought to confirm this information.

Would the new pilot be a source of information? Even though we did not think so, we listened carefully, the next time we were invited to the captain's table.

With both Paulus twins present, Stefan might be able to ask questions the right way.

He knew to ask a question in such a way, that the answer "no" meant "yes."

At the port of Genoa, unloading and loading freight happened under tight security.

We observed from our quarters the loading of boxed shipments, that arrived at the dock with a military escort. The placement of these containers in the center hold showed, that the crane operators were handling these items with extreme caution.

Soon, we heard the horn of the tug boat signaling the departure of Stella Maris.

Once the tug boat was detached, Captain Pavlov steered Stella Maris south into the Ligurian sea. We could see the Apennines mountains to the north and traveled close enough to the islands of Corsica and Sardinia to reward us with a memorable sunrise and a view of mountainous islands, bathed in the brilliant light and the glowing reflection of the rising sun in the clear waters of the mediterranean.

Unforgettable nature in an increasingly troubled world.

We were now very tired, having feasted late into the night before. We retired into our sleeping quarters, knowing, that we were going to be crossing seas for five hundred nautical miles, which, according to Stefan, would take a little more than three days at an average speed of ten knots.

Plenty of time to sleep before sighting Mt. Etna in Sicily on the south side of the ship, after crossing the Tyrrhenian Sea. Pavlov told us, that Mount Etna had just seen a major eruption on its north east flank and that it was still active, visible while we sail by it, at the end of the following day.

Events like volcanic eruptions, according to Pavlov, are seen by the local population as the wrath of a deity, in response to human disobedience and the commitment of sins.

That is why despite the shock, rebuilding usually begins immediately after things cool off. What we saw from a distance, out at sea, was eerily beautiful.

We arrived at Tripoli at night. A tugboat came to tow us into port.

This time, dinner was served at our quarters.

We played music and went to sleep again, trying to calm ourselves in the knowledge, that we were in the care of two of the most experienced captains alive, with a loyal crew running Stella Maris.

Unloading under cover of darkness looked like a ballet and was, according to Haller, accomplished in record time.

The horn of the tug boat did not sound, until after we were back in open waters, moving across the Mediterranean Sea at the fastest speed, the hull of this vessel could maintain.

Except for a couple of evasive maneuvers, around some small islands, the crossings were uneventful.

We anchored in the lee of a small island at the mouth of the Aegean Sea, when an impenetrable fog had moved in leaving us zero visibility.

We had to wait, until mid-morning, to let the sun burn off enough fog, to let Stella Maris sail safely into Thermaikos Bay, where the harbor of Thessaloniki is located.

Stella Maris dropped anchor in the middle of the bay.

We spent a night without engine noise or vibrations. A well-deserved respite from the fast crossing at top speed that had rattled us to our bones.

Our spiked emotions and the need for shelter, comfort, and closeness, in the safety of our love's arms were intensified by the sudden calm, that made our ears ring and our hearts pound.

The sense of danger during the last few days, intensified our passion and left us spent, as though we had experienced the eruption of Mt, Vesuvius inside of our bodies. At breakfast, hungry like a pack of wolves, we were still flushed.

I was amused, how the Paulus brothers were exchanging knowing glances and smiles, which made us blush once more.

On board ship, there are no secrets, but also no judgements.

What happens on board, stays on board. That is the law of Captain Paulus.

We now learned, that we were going to spend eleven days in this beautiful town of Thessaloniki with a view of Mount Olympus across the bay.

Chapter 40

Thessaloniki

Thessaloniki is protected by a walled citadel, overlooking the bay and a fortified tower next to the docks, armed with cannon, capable of sinking any hostile vessel, before it could even move into position to fire a shot.

The following day dawned with a fog, once again disguising the land and its hills from view.

We could hear the chatter of captains, officers, and crew. From their voices and the way everyone moved around the decks in a more relaxed fashion, than we had seen since leaving Genoa, we felt a sense of relief, that felt good, especially in the arms of our partners, and companions in the safety of our salon.

We enjoyed a rather lavish breakfast at the captain's table, witnessing the celebration of the reunion of the twin brothers, that would last the entire time we were present at this port.

By mid-morning, the fog began to thin and mid-afternoon it had burnt off.

A grand view on this beautiful city was emerging one building, one feature and one tree at a time, followed by views of the hill with its citadel, churches and mosques, dominating in size most residences, office buildings and warehouses next to this bustling harbor.

We were hoping to be offered escorted tours with opportunity to follow our interests and curiosity in the culture and life of this beautiful city. We were sure, there were going to be boats to return us to the ship every night.

Instead, during the first breakfast, our captain and his brother reminded us, that the region was at war:

"Thessaloniki is presently occupied by a Turkish garrison of the Ottoman Empire." Paulus reminded us:

"This port is so important, that the partners of the Balkan League, presently at war with Turkey, cannot be trusted, to free Thessaloniki and to return it to Greece.

Even France attempted to take this port by force, a few years back.

Greece was able to fend them off. But the fires, that were set during the fight, cost countless lives, and destroyed too many houses."

We learned, that an attack by the Greek army on this Turkish garrison was imminent.

Most of the population was Greek, a wide variety of people from all faiths and regions around the Mediterranean and the Adriatic, made up a smaller part.

The church was in support of a peaceful settlement, so that history would not have to repeat itself.

The allegiance between the Balkan League and Greece was fragile.

On the surface, there was no resistance to the Turkish authorities. Resistance had gone underground.

"My brother has informed me, that the underground resistance is growing, supported by the Greek Orthodox church. The high priest is hoping to achieve a negotiated liberation of his town, with minimal bloodshed and no destruction of buildings by fire this time.

The clerics are preparing to help in the final stages of this liberation.

Whatever role Stella Maris is playing in this effort, remains under strictest secrecy.

Do not pry. The less you know, the safer you are.

Your presence and your status on this ship, must be kept secret. You must be invisible to port authorities or the gendarmerie on land. By suggestion of Captain Pavlov, we will dress you the same as all the other sailors on this ship. You will appear to be running errands, in preparation for the next leg of her journey.

This means, that whatever we do in this town, cannot raise eyebrows, or be in any way unusual. You will be issued the same papers as the crew of this ship and your quarters will be prepared for the possibility of an inspection.

Your personal belongings will disappear. They will reappear, once we reach Alexandria.

The less you know, the better, in case you get picked up for interrogation.

This is not out of the question, as the situation has become very tense over the past six months. If it happens, cooperate, and show no signs of resistance.

In the extreme, they will contact me to come, to vouch for you and to pick you up," said Pavlov, adding:

"As you know, in my position as your pilot, I am the harbor authority, presently assigned to Stella Maris. You are working under my command, just like the other sailors of this ship. I would not be in this position, if I did not have excellent relationships and friendships with key individuals of authority in Thessaloniki.

I grew up here and our father was laid to rest here a few years back. He was given a sea burial, as was his last wish, giving him the feeling, the ocean would connect him to the love of his life, our mother."

Pavlov crossed himself three times and kissed the tips of his fingers.

"While we are doing maintenance on the ship and taking on freight and supplies, we will have errands to run all over this town. You will be assigned either to myself or to my brother as an escort. We will mix it up, so you can see as much of this town as possible, visit churches and attend services as you desire.

To the authorities of Thessaloniki, you will be invisible, blending in with the crew of Stella Maris. We will come together in different groupings for meals at eateries in the food markets. Trust me, you will like the food. That is all you need to know. Welcome to my home."

We felt privileged to be invited to several very festive and elaborate dinners, in which the brothers were celebrating their reunion. This took place at crowded restaurants near the markets. Alexandrou was tempted to introduce his twin to his friends. Long separations are part of seafaring culture and celebrating the safe return of a loved family member is not just a tradition but a way of life. We were witness to a heartfelt reunion, that lasted throughout our lay-over in Thessaloniki. Privately, everyone was guarded. We enjoyed meals with many courses and delicious specialties from sea, hills, and gardens, served with wines and liquors made from grapes and fruits of the land. These beverages gave these meals a softness and emotional richness, that evoked the desire to dance in both men and women. Musicians were always at hand to play string instruments and drums and to sing melancholy love songs and joyous dancing tunes late into the night. This seemed to be the general mood in the market halls. We did not stand out but blended in with the flavor of the moment.

The sound of bells, calling for prayer, was mixed with the sound of mullahs, calling the faithful to prayer. They streamed through the town, dressed in traditional costumes of their confession or their region of origin.

Next to the bustling port, the harbor was laid out with a promenade along the shore and a single railroad track, a road with four lanes parallel to the seawall and avenues reaching up towards the hill with the castle, lined with houses tightly tucked in behind walls, from which the eye can roam over the generously laid out town and the very expansive bay view to the west. Parallel to the seawall, wide avenues with electric street cars and a colorful mix of motor vehicles and horse drawn carriages, giving delivery service to a variety of stores, offering wares of the region and from around the world. Buildings varied in height from three to five stories, with flat roofs on the lower structures and dormered mansard roofs on taller, more stately buildings.

Yellow, white, tan, and dusty rose facades were adorned with balconies, supported by ornate stone braces or intricate cast- or wrought iron braces and hand rails.

Both Captains gave these instructions to us and to their officers:

"Our guests must blend in with all the activities of Stella Maris' crew during the next ten days. We want them trailing our sailors. We want them carrying things.

Maria and Joan, I assign you to join the chef and his kitchen crew. You will accompany them on their visits to food vendors, markets, and warehouses. In your hand, you will hold lists of provisions, required for the ship. Wolf and Stefan, you will be with the ships mechanics, doing maintenance on engines, tackle, gear and drinking water. You will accompany the engineers wherever they go. Helena and Herbert, you will be assisting the purser with financial transactions and paperwork for import and export. If a translator is needed, ask our pilot, captain Pavlov. To keep the ship safe, I ask you to defer to your assigned crew members in any interaction with vendors and local authorities. If you are asked questions you cannot answer, say nothing. Insist on contacting Captain Pavlov and wait for him. He is Thessalonian, knows the customs, the authorities, and speaks the language.

Enjoy your visit. We will let you know, where and when you will be served meals during the day and where we will meet for dinner. You will be assigned transportation back to the vessel each night. Never leave the side of your assigned crew member."

This understood, we filed into the purser's office to pick up our papers. Then we collected our sailor's uniforms. That night, we sat together in our lounge and spoke about our expectations, and about the role play we were ordered to perform.

Chapter 41

Melting Time

Helena was confident that this was a good plan: "I think we are in the best hands at this moment."

She looked at each of us to be sure we were listening.

"This is a dangerous time for this region, for Thessaloniki and for Greece.

It is also dangerous for us. We owe it to each other, our mission, our captain and to his brother to be invisible, by merging with the crew as requested.

Paulus is more than a captain to us. He is our mentor. We owe him gratitude and loyalty. I see this as an opportunity to show gratitude and to learn from the masters."

Trying on the clothes the captain provided for us, was a riot. We shed tears laughing, as we modeled for each other. It was badly needed comic relief, until finally, we looked like the ship's crew. Long skirts for the women with dark blue scarves and capes for rain.

Straight cut trousers and vests for the men, with hats, rain slickers and work jackets.

We were soon tired out from travelling back and forth, from late nights at the tavernas, where activities never began until after dark and did not end until the wee hours.

God help us to stay serious. We danced in our new fashions and made adjustments for fit and comfort. The look on our faces made us break out in bursts of laughter.

The following ten days were busy for us, doing our assignments. Once on board, we sat together, sharing our stories and observations about places we had seen and people we met.

We were keenly aware of the pressure, that was building from all sides on the population of Thessaloniki. We could feel it in our bones. Something was about to happen.

No one dared to say openly what they thought this something would be.

Everyone was guarded.

Memories from previous assaults on the city were still haunting people.

The population was not only a melting pot, we observed the vast disparity of class and wealth from merchants, clergy and business owners to laborers, peasants and hungry children, begging for coins and food.

People were friendly in their interaction with the sailors from Stella Maris.

At the end of each day, we were led to different eateries located in market halls and in passages between blocks of buildings, sometimes in houses of friends of Alexandrou Pavlov, where elaborate dinners were served. There we were able to be ourselves. We enjoyed these private feasts behind closed doors.

This is how the reunion of the brothers was celebrated.

Emotional toasts were exchanged, large quantities of ouzo were consumed.

Stories were told about years of separation and the heartbreak of the parents.

We noticed that the twins were referring to both parents in the past tense.

At one point there was talk about the sea burial of the father's body in the center of the Thermaic Gulf, the bay in which Stella Maris was anchored.

We heard Paulus speak about the great fortune of finding his twin.

He was carrying on his ship a coffin containing the body of their mother, who had asked for a sea burial. It was her last wish to be reunited with the love of her life, her children's father. She had asked for a Greek Orthodox service to be performed to unite their soul. She was hoping to have the same priest perform the rites.

This would conclude a forty-year story end a thirty-year painful separation, finally putting two souls to rest.

Our time in Thessaloniki melted away like butter in the sun.

An elaborate transfer of the sarcophagus to the basilica of Hagia Sophia was performed by most of the ship's crew, serving as poll bearers and forming a large honor guard in long black robes and black caps two days before the ship was to sail for Alexandria.

The ceremonies were stunningly beautiful, the voices of the quire angelic.

We could feel that the spirit of both parents was present and reunited in their soul.

The plan of Captain Paulus to hide us in plain sight amongst his crew and to make us invisible succeeded. During the last night, we quietly slipped into our bunks awaiting the hum and vibration of the engines and the slapping of waves on the bow of the ship.

But first we sat together in our salon exchanging thoughts and ideas, playing music, and letting our minds daydream. This night, the ship was going to move out. Chef du Chalet outdid himself, preparing a feast with all the best food Thessaloniki had to offer. Before baclava and coffee, captain Paulus thanked his brother for this important visit to his town and to his country. He finally left to go to the wheel house to order anchors away. We could see the lights of the city fade away as the sip began picking up speed.

Soon the bay slipped from view behind a headland. Stella Maris left the port of Thessaloniki under cover of darkness, guided by Pilot Alexandrou Pavlov.

The mountains of Greece disappeared behind the horizon as the ship steamed under full power towards Alexandria's port of El Dekheila, aiming to make this run in four days.

Stefan noted that we were flying a German flag with Egypt's and Britain's flags above Greek's pennant.

At dinner, Paulus thanked us for our cooperation at Thessaloniki. He said:

"You have noticed the safety precautions we have maintained since Genoa.

We were carrying freight to support the liberation of Libya and the defense of Thessaloniki. Discovery of this cargo would have meant certain imprisonment for all of us and the confiscation or destruction of Stella Maris.

Your cooperation has made these important deliveries possible."

At Thessaloniki, Paulus had finally leaked a rumor, that some persons on board were on a mission from a foreign power, but that we were not at liberty to disclose who they were and what their mission was.

Eyes of the harbor authorities were focused on our crew, trying to detect, who these persons were. Meanwhile, no one noticed the undeclared cargo, we smuggled into port right under their eyes, while reprovisioning the ship."

Wolf seemed irritated, he felt used; now he wanted at least the truth.

"How did you transport the contraband into port undetected?"

Paulus smiled at him:

"We had on board goods to support the resistance against the Turkish garrison and potential invaders. We have no idea, who the recipients were.

That was part of our protection. We communicated with the priest of Hagia Sophia through Alexandrou Pavlov about the funeral and the memorial for our mother.

He also had ideas about how to move these goods from ship to shore and how to make them disappear, once they were on land."

Stefan was incredulous. He did not think anyone could have done this, without his noticing something:

"How?" He asked in a commanding tone, that meant, he wanted an answer.

"We did not notice any delivery of goods. We were everywhere, all the time."

Paulus was very pleased with himself: He was glad to answer:

"We had a sarcophagus with the remains of our mother, to perform the sea burial, she had asked for in her last wish.

The priest reassured us, that the rites, he was preparing for her, did not require for her remains to be physically present at the church. He insisted, that it was possible, to make a spiritual connection through his ceremony, candles, and prayers, offered at Hagia Sophia.

He disclosed, that a secret underground tunnel exists, through which persons can reach Agios Dimitrios and Hagia Sophia."

We were given the honor of attending the mother's funeral services. We were given long black robes; the kind choirs use for singing at church.

"The entire procession will wear these,'" we were told. Heads covered with hoods, monk style. We were led to the tender, that takes everyone to shore. Near the kay, we followed the procession in single file down a narrow stairwell, leading to a souterrain room, which was lit by many candles. It looked like a sacristy, or a room for baptisms in a private setting. As we stepped inside, we saw the end of a movement of a wooden wall altar, that now exposed a door, that lead into a subterranean tunnel.

Priests in white robes, holding golden crosses, stepped two by two into this tunnel, which was also brightly lit by candles, singing a hymn, as they walked step by step, setting the slow pace for the procession.

They were followed by eight people, carrying the coffin. Slowly, the remaining congregation filed into this tunnel. Behind the last mourner, the altar moved back into its original place and the tunnel entrance was once again hidden by the altar.

The tunnel made the voices of the choir sound louder and more beautiful, than in the room, where they first started singing. Finally, we arrived in a wide underground chamber, that had several doors. We followed the other mourners into a sacristy, two at a time, where we were handed lit candles, with a grip, that has a circular top to prevent hot wax from burning the bearer's hands.

Holding our candles, we followed the procession up a wide stairwell into the large sanctuary of the church.

There were columns supporting the very high ceiling, covering the length of the room. Outside of these columns was a wide corridor, surrounding the entire space of the church.

We walked one entire circumference, before the procession turned down the middle, to end up at the table, upon which the coffin was to be placed.

Now we noticed something unusual: We saw the bearers of the coffin pick it up and shoulder the load. It seemed less heavy than an ordinary coffin with a body inside.

Now this coffin was placed on the viewing table. It appeared to be only a fraction of the weight from before. It made us think. Now we had to ask the captain. Stefan spoke:

"You used your mother's empty coffin as a decoy to hide and transport freight to shore through these ancient catacombs?"

"Not only the coffin," the captain beamed, the pallbearers and the entire procession of the crew as honor guard, wore black robes, as did you. Each was loaded with bags, strapped to their bodies, ready to drop them, as they filed one by one through the backroom, behind the sacristy of the church. Each was met by a receiver, also in black robes, who took the bags away. The entire honor guard reappeared, carrying lit candles, as did you. Our shipment made it safely to its recipients.

The orthodox church was protecting her freedom, to carry her religion into the future and increased the negotiating position of the liberators," Paulus concluded.

Then he added: "May it provide reassurance to the resistance, to negotiate a transfer of power back to Greece, without having port and city burned to the ground once again."

All of us said in unison: "Amen."

Stefan could not let it go:

"You will not discuss what was delivered?"

Paulus, with a defiant smirk on his face: "No! "

A long silence. This subject was now closed. We turned our eyes towards the future.

For the six of us, experiences and discoveries continued in the privacy of our bunks, under blankets, that had been returned to us, together with our belongings and our musical instruments.

"I missed you" were words, whispered over and over in the bliss of three young couples celebrating the joy of being finally free again to express the passion for each other, to have the privacy, caused by the humming of the ship's engines and the vibration of the twin screws, moving the vessel southeast towards Alexandria.

Chapter 42

Leaving Europe

At the captain's table, it was now time to prepare for the end of Alexandrou Pavlov's control over our vessel. We became witness to a new separation of the twins.

In Greek fashion, this was done with wonderful food, cheers with Ouzo, followed by servings of baklava and strong Turkish coffee. Paulus, trying to make light of things, told us:

"There is an Arabic saying about how to recognize good coffee:

"It must be as hot as the kisses on the first night, as sweet as the embraces during the second night and as black as the curses of the mother, when she finds out about it."

He laughed hard about his joke but the laughter soon turned teary eyed, when he looked at his brother and saw the heartbreak in his eyes.

We thanked captain Pavlov profusely for everything, he had done and said our good byes before taking leave and returning to our own lounge, for a long evening of music and quiet conversation.

Wolf offered this observation:

"Two cities, two harbors with very similar populations and activities, that take advantage of the strategic location for international trade, being watched and fought over by the powers controlling the world, because they are trade hotspots, critical for a world of emerging industrialization.

Thessaloniki is open to the Balkans and central Europe via the Silk Route; Alexandria is serving the Middle and Far East and East Africa through the Suez Canal.

Railroads and ships are the companions of an ever-expanding and ever shrinking world.

Both cities are now a powder keg, ready to explode, as soon as someone lights a match.

New forces, new possibilities, new needs, and no recipes in the old play book.

I am glad, we have as our guide a captain who sees the world as a dynamic phenomenon rather than a static one.

All I see is confusion. Academically, philosophically, politically, economically, and socially.

The world is torn between those, who want to have regulations, but cannot see the target, because it is moving- and those, who take advantage of the confusion, who thrive on chaos and movement, by immersing themselves in it, rather than fighting it."

Stefan, always looking for a more practical approach:

"Big pictures drawn with a broad brush. That is the way of politics.

I think we must focus on details, get close enough, to see everything with our own eyes and follow the tiniest movements, in real time.

We must invent a new canvas, upon which a new world order will be drawn.

I may not have academic, philosophical, or legal skills, but I think I am a good student of reality, who pays attention to detail.

From tennis, I have learned to focus and hit a target, even when it is moving faster than most others can see.

We are leaving Europe now and nothing we will find, will have any resemblance with what we were told by those, who make life changing decisions, even as we speak."

Stefan stretched his limbs, until they made a cracking sound. Then he put his hand on Helena's arm. "What do you think?"

Helena looked at her fingernails as though she was counting them.

"I think you both have a point. To me, it feels like I am riding on a fast-moving train. I can look straight out of the window and the world is rushing by, creating a blurred image. I look far, to slow down the image and ignore the rush in front. I look forward, to see the world approaching, even though I do not know, what to expect. I look back, to see the world disappearing, even though I had no time to understand it. I look inside my compartment and notice my travel companions. I must look inside myself, to see if I am still here. I think I will start there."

"Tea anyone?" I asked.

Herbert nodding yes to tea:

"Let me bring music for mezzo soprano and piano. I want to hear Joan play and Maria sing. You can break our hearts with your delivery of your tragic ballades. "

Maria began to hum her favorite tune of the day. She remembered, hearing it sung by a child at the curb in the vegetable market of Thessaloniki. She did not understand the Greek lyrics but she remembered the song. Maria turned towards our companions:

"I am having trouble understanding the fate of children. We see them with their mothers. The world seems to be in order. Then something happens and they reemerge in a state of abject poverty. Begging for crumbs.

How is it not our first order of priority to provide for children and for each other? I see magnificent churches, basilicas, mosques, and temples.

Houses of worship to a merciful God and his countless saints. Are we waiting for God to step down to us, to restore order and to set things right?

Is our sense of purpose and justice already so distorted, that we begin arguing, the minute we step out of the house of worship and into our own field of influence?

Are we spending our thinking time, justifying the double standards by which we treat people of different faiths, ethnicity, skin pigmentation and social class?

When did we decide to drop the children? When did we agree to slice up the world? How can there ever be peace? When will the heartbreak end?

When will our prayers begin to ask for wisdom, patience, and strength, to do the right thing instead of asking God for the favor of doing the heavy lifting for us?

Oh, and yes, I would like some tea also. Do we have Moroccan mint left?"

The tea distracted us and lightened our mood, as we began to sing and play music.

From where Stella Maris was now anchored, we could see a launch approaching, that would drop off two new pilots from the Port Said Canal Authority and to take our pilot Alexandrou Pavlov to shore.

The harbor launch driver handed our purser a stack of newspapers. Each one of us took a paper to our quarters to read. At breakfast, we would compare notes of what was in the news, before giving the papers to our captain.

Before we said good night, Stefan informed us:

"Sailing through the Suez Canal north to south, will take at least forty-eight hours.

The canal goes from Port Said to Port Taufiq, south of Suez at the Gulf of Suez, where our pilots will leave us once we have reached the Red Sea.

Our next port of call will be Djibouti, in Ethiopia. Then on to Mombasa, Kenia, and finally the island of Zanzibar.

We will exchange freight at Zanzibar, a kalifate under the protection of the kaiser. The Kalif of Zanzibar was given extensive powers to govern almost independently. He has abolished slave trade in his region during the late eighteen-eighties. We should find out more about him. First, we must travel the 200-kilometer length of the Suez Canal."

We were relieved, that the journey from Genoa to Alexandria is finally over. We were not comfortable with all the secrecy and the constant threat of possible entanglements with war ships from countries that were either engaged in the Balkan war or in the conflict between Italy and Egypt over Tripoli.

This was our first carefree night. We were ready to celebrate.

We had read the newspapers.

The new day brought us to the captain's table for breakfast. We wanted to discuss the news with him.

Especially the sinking of the Titanic, the unsinkable ocean liner, on April 15, 1912, when almost 1600 souls were lost and only 745 could be rescued, mostly women and children. We had many questions about what mariners would have to say.

The captain's face looked ashen. He was sunk deep into his own thoughts.

This separation from his twin must have been as hard for him this time, as it was the first time.

We remained quiet, until he was ready to look up from his plate, to look at the newspapers laid out before him and to face the world again.

This happened sooner than we expected.

He raised his eyes and looked at each of us in turn. He began:

"I am glad to have you on board of Stella Maris. I know, I am showing you a world that is confusing. It can overwhelm the smartest minds. Change is happening at increasing speed in every aspect of life.

Someone was smart enough to send you people into the field, to make observations and to find answers to questions that have not even been formulated yet.

This is your opportunity. There is a big gap between what people are being told and what happened. Both about the past and about the future but especially about the present. Image and reputation are becoming more important than facts.

Take the tragedy of the Titanic:

Mariners are claiming privately, that there was a fire inside one of the coal bunkers, that started before the ship departed on its maiden voyage to New York.

This fire made the Titanic sinkable."

He looked again at the old picture of his brother. The image raised his emotions:

"To find my brother, after a thirty-year separation, made me remember the total collapse of my world, when he was taken from me at the age of ten. I now find out, that it was like that for him also. At least now I know where he is. That makes me even more concerned."

Paulus paused and looked around at us again with piercing eyes.

"There are two possibilities at moments like these: Lay down, get depressed and die, or rise and face the world, using everything in your reach, to pull yourself up, stand tall, find new ways to act. We are talking about the survival of the smartest, not the fittest. Choose a mentor. To me, my brother is such a mentor. We had the good fortune, to be raised by parents, who never got in the way of our curiosity.

No preset ideas, no local customs, no traditions, or behavior to guide or to intimidate us.

Our parents were outsiders and keen observers.

That is their legacy." He thought for a moment.

"They never assumed, that what was presented to them, was the truth, not even if it was printed in black and white and no matter how loud it was shouted from a pulpit.

They told us, to go out and find our own truth and to avoid people with opinions.

"Go seek those, who have gained knowledge from experience," they would say.

That is how we both ended up in positions, where we do not have to take sides, but can help those we meet, to succeed with what they aim to accomplish.

We do not argue about national origin, customs, race, or religious affiliation. We observe what works, then make our best decision. We both became deciders." He now took a long glance forward at the canal.

"We will travel through the Suez Canal for forty-eight hours. Lots of time to talk. I will have two canal pilots in charge of Stella Maris."

He fell silent, returning to his own thoughts.

We saw Alexandria in passing from the decks of Stella Maris. We learned, that France, Britain, Egypt as well as many other countries were interested in Alexandria, just like Thessaloniki.

We observed, that multicultural, religiously tolerant communities were wealthier and economically more successful, than dictatorships, run by fanatics of all stripes. These communities have in common that they support institutions of learning and Science, with libraries and universities, attracting visionaries." Wolf put his hand on the stack of newspapers. "I think the industrial revolution has power to change the world, yet it is more Dangerous than anything we have seen so far."

Herbert stepped between the captain and Wolf:

"Another element, which our captain has pointed out to us, is the fact, that a Project, like the construction of the Suez Canal, is larger, and more costly than any country could design, construct or finance by themselves."

Helena picked up on this train of thought. She took it further:

"Egypt had to give up some of her control over this important asset: This canal saves every ship thousands of miles and weeks in time on their way to the far East and India."

Stefan agreed:

"This canal is of critical economic impact and importance to the entire world. It is changing politics, influences economic defense strategies and raises military objectives beyond territorial conquests and national defenses. " Wolf enjoyed this kind of conversation.

"Economic interests have become an objective for all military forces. The world has given weight to international thinking. Maybe there is hope in that?"

We saw a mosque with five cupulas and two minarets, we saw the buildings that house the Suez Canal Authority, complete with warehouses, tug boats, canal maintenance gear and residences, that speak of the history and importance of this central part of the Silk route, shared distinguishing elements of port cities like Istanbul, Alexandria, and Thessaloniki.

We were now moving through one of the busiest harbors, we had seen so far. We could see the wisdom of having two pilots guide us through this aquatic bee's nest.

Once we cleared the port area, we entered the canal itself.

Dredging gear and excavation dunes lined both sides of the canal. Houses here looked improvised compared to the stately buildings of Port Said. We were amazed by a remarkable bridge, that was designed to pivot on both sides, to allow traffic to cross the canal, without holding up the shipping lane for too long. We saw irrigation canals and structures that would lead small boat- and barge traffic into bodies of water connecting to the river Nile. Paulus pointed this out on the map:

"The Nile is one of the longest rivers in the world, still used for transport of goods and

for irrigating and fertilizing its flood plains for extensive plantations of cotton, coconut palms and other crops," he explained. "The rest of the landscape looks like a desert. Green is limited to irrigated farmland." We met the captain in the map room, where we hoped to discuss forms of colonization, used by Europe's empires and kingdoms.

Paulus wanted to discuss the news first, even though they were already weeks old. " You must have read the press." Pointing to the stack of papers. "Tell me what you found in these papers."

Wolf put his hand on the item that had caught his attention. "The Reichstag has increased defense forces by 515 000 troops. Great Britain has ordered five new battleships.

The German navy has ordered two new biplanes from America. I think, the whole world is preparing for an armed confrontation."

Maria had noticed something else, she found note-worthy:

"Portugal has voted to separate church and state. They have granted voting rights to women for the first time. I think that secularization of government and giving women a voice, is a victory for the people and a defeat for the Catholic church in Rome."

Helena recalled an item that was of great concern to her:

"Owners of a garment factory in New York were charged with negligent homicide for locking workers into their workspace and blocking the exit during a fire, in violation of building codes and labor laws.I think that corporations are suffering from the confusion, that has turned humans into a natural resource, corporations into legal persons and money into a form of speech."

Herbert focused on events in the region we had just passed through: "Italy is asserting ownership over Tripoli and is at war against Turkey over control of the Mediterranean Sea, while Egypt is supporting forces in a land assault against Turkey in the region between Egypt and Libya. Italy has raised her flag over Tripoli. Germany has dispatched a war ship to Agadir in Morocco, to protect her interest in copper ore and other minerals in that area. Germany and France are presently negotiating a swap of influence, by granting France the right to make Morocco a French protectorate in return for Germany's control over almost 100 000 square miles of land in the Congo region of central Africa. I think this it is an example of Empire building far away from these countries.

Politicians who gathered around the table in Berlin during the 1870s, had little or no knowledge of the countries and regions they were dividing among themselves. They were responding to mandates from industry and relied on information that came

back from Christian missionaries, both catholic and protestant, who were hoping to have their extensive mission properties defended by armed government forces. Scientists provided evidence, that it would be of national interest, to secure resources for manufacturing.

The companion part of this information is the claim, that there live only homeless savages, humans- that can be recruited, after being tamed for plantation work, the land for which was taken from them, after being declared as "available" and "free," because there were no holders of legal title to these lands. Colonizers have been illegally claiming for themselves grants and title to areas suitable for planting coffee, cocoa, oil palms, rubber and cotton and raising cattle for hides."

Helena spread her arms wide:

"We have not even entered the continent of Africa and we can already see, that the Coast we have visited, is not one country but a variety of regions with different climates, topography, customs, religious traditions, and sovereign governments. How can this world possibly be developed and exploited by foreigners, who are not native to a region? How can one establish sustainable communities, without knowing anything about them?"

Herbert put his hands on Stefan and my shoulders. He said: "That is why we are being sent. I think conflicts have erupted in German East Africa, right from the beginning. Practices of our representatives and of our commercial planters have met resistance from the native population right from the beginning.

These are the same planters, who are now leaning on our government, to send more troops to control people, who feel that their identity, their culture, their language, their land and their lives have been stolen by invaders, who treat them as primitive sub- humans, unfit to govern themselves and incapable to manage their own affairs. Now they want to turn them into proper Germans, as productive, tax paying members of an orderly community. They have announced:"These savages need to be civilized first." That is a powerful group we will have to avoid, while we do our investigation. Otherwise, these racists will sabotage our mission.

Maria remembered the conditions that had shocked her at home. She said: "This is not so different from the plight of industry workers at home, who were moved to where they are needed and must now live in squalor and unacceptable living conditions in housing provided by the owners of the factories that employ them. I need to see conditions in German East Afrika with my own eyes and speak with People personally, instead of going by impressions people get at trade shows and from entertainment acts, displaying people like circus animals, to make us believe their lies. Circus Hagenbeck, at their zoological gardens, put "primitive" people on display, together with exotic animals. That is what people at home remember. I think our foreign policy is informed by the misinformation such displays have created. Promoters of industrial interests use them for propaganda."

Wolf answered with a frown on his face:

"I am concerned about Christian missions, both protestant and catholic. They have acquired thousands of hectares of land and are constantly raising funds to help peddle influence with policy makers at home. They ask for military protection. God is nowhere to be found. I hope to God I am wrong about this. Stefan, you are awfully quiet this morning. What do you think?"

Stefan moved off his perch, from where he could observe the landscape next to the canal, as it seemed to move past at a steady pace. He had not taken his eyes off the sand dunes and features that contain clues of human activity. Returning from afar in his own thoughts, he said: "Did you know, that the French were thinking of building the Suez Canal during the reign of Napoleon, who visited the area in person, to see for himself, how this would give him access to the rest of the world? Did you know, that the reason, they did not do it then, was that the surveyors had made an error in calculating elevations, and believed that the difference in sea level between the Mediterranean and the Arabian Sea was ten meters?"

Herbert, always curious about history, had this to say:

"The purser told me, that someone in France did not believe in the accuracy of the first Survey. In 1854, the French obtained license to construct this canal.

Ten years later it opened to commercial traffic with the United Kingdom becoming a shareholder of 44% and French syndicates controlling the remainder."

Wolf was still in a serious mood:

"This will be a hotspot for the rest of time. Economic control is important to all industrial nations. Whoever has the biggest guns, will be in control here."

Chapter 43

Land of Empires

The captain looked out of a forward window: He said:"You may want to see this. Dolphins are riding our bow wave." We went to the bow to watch the movement of several dolphins. These intelligent ocean dwellers were enjoying life. We were mesmerized. When this day came to an end, the light drew a line near the horizon.

Colors transitioned from almost black to night-blue to dark purple, to red, orange and finally a bright yellow, before merging to deep blue, without getting blue and yellow mixed up. The intensity and beauty of nature took our breath away. No one spoke. The ships engines hummed at low frequencies.

The dinner bell rang. We took our places at the captain's table, still concerned and curious, how Paulus was doing after the second separation from his brother. Now a grown man, after a lifelong career as a mariner, he seemed to snap back into his element, now that he knew where his brother was living and what he was doing, another survivor from the same cast as his. He was ready to share more of what he knew.

He began speaking to no one in particular: "Relationships between my crew and you have changed in Thessaloniki. We merged you into our crew, to avoid detection. You did very well. Thessaloniki is still controlled by a Turkish garrison. But not for long.

The fact that I found my long-lost brother, was not planned. It came as a happy and shocking surprise to both of us." He pulled the faded photograph of his ten-year-old twin out of his breast pocket and placed it in front of his plate. He smoothed it caressingly. It had accompanied him all these years. It was his good luck charm. "Stella Maris agreed to carry freight, the nature of which cannot be disclosed. It had to be handled with the secrecy of war time operations. The idea was, to help liberators and to avoid suffering and to save civilian lives." He thought for a while, his eyes scanning the horizon.

"Presently, involuntary migration of people is going on in the entire region of the Ottoman Empire. People live in fear for their lives from religious, political or economic persecution, while nationalistic sentiments are rising, without restraint by any humanitarian principles.

Hatred is an offspring of suppression. We see it everywhere. Fanatics are dangerous. So are believers and fundamentalists. They delegate responsibility to others or to a higher authority.

We can see the benefit of collaboration in cities like Thessaloniki and Alexandria, being connected to a greater world and therefore less narrow minded in the acceptance of people of different faith, race, or origin."

Wolf put his knife and fork down and wiped his mouth with his napkin. "I am wondering about the life-span of empires. From what we have learned in school, recorded history is very brief. We tend to slip from history into philosophy, then into theology. We are led from someone's personal take on what they believe is known, to oral history, that would later be recorded as fact."

His eyes glanced over a stretch of desert and sand dunes. "We are looking into the distance. We see colossal monuments, built by someone before recorded time, with means and methods unknown to us. Despite all this knowledge, some of these empires have not been able to survive."

Stefan:

"I think, that maps are a good place to start. We measure topography and natural features like oceans, rivers, and mountains. We have come a long way, since the time, when people believed the Earth is flat. I believe, that this came from the presentation of early maps on flat papyrus. There was always an end to the known world, where the viewer reached the edge of the map. I suggest that now is a good time to look at maps, to see what they can tell us."

Looking at his friends and the captain, he continued:

"Captain Paulus will agree with me when I say, that we owe most of our maps to Mariners, who have recorded their observations. This is how mariners made sure, to find their way home, after venturing into previously unknown parts of the world. Inland, in Africa, surveys are being conducted right now and maps are being made by geological societies, interested in locating natural resources for industry and the establishment of zones of interest, influence, and protection and expansion of territories for settlers."

Pointing to a green, irrigated stretch of land in the desert, Paulus said: "We know, the Romans are gone. They have left behind Roman Law, which contains the idea, that land, that is not owned by someone with a legal title, is available to anyone who can write and record a deed. Now the owner of "record" is entitled to defend this claim by force of arms. The romans used for this event the word PRIVARE, which means to rob or to steal from someone.

Privatization is a universal problem, because it violates the commons and takes assets, owned and paid for by the public and moves ownership into the hands of individuals orlegal persons, corporations, thereby making it private property."

Our two canal pilots were steering the ship south through the Suez Canal. Our captain was free to spend time with us. Outside, there was not much to observe.

Seeing that everyone had finished eating, Paulus moved our meeting into the map room. He picked up on the subject of privatizing: "The concept of private ownership of land was basically unknown in most parts of the world. Conquest was practiced everywhere, yet ownership of land remained communal."

We could see natural sand dunes for hours on end, also mounds of excavated material from digging the canal and creating the occasional trenches for water, used to irrigate croplands. Paulus pointed them out to us. "These are plantations were made on arid soil, that was no longer usable, until Irrigation was installed. You will find land inside of Africa, that was turned into plantations, on fertile soil, where the indigenous population had to be removed, to make room for industrial agriculture. That was privatization Roman style."

Herbert was stumped.

"Last I checked, we were raised by a nation of laws, with a strong moral code. How are we to make sense of this?"

Paulus looked at Herbert, then he said patiently:

"The six of you were sent to study changes in land ownership and its consequences on the profitability and stability of colonies. Colonies, used for agriculture, have been underperforming for investors, mostly because of revolting native populations and a resulting labor shortage.

The concept of land grants- and title, given to someone else in the name of God and emperor, is having failure written all over it. A plan, that was supposed to save savages from going to hell is not a plan. It ignores the ingenuity of all humans, other than us Europeans."

Herbert was visibly upset:

" Government has invested a lot of money in infrastructure. We were led to believe, that we were going to create a second industrial revolution there. Railroads and infrastructure worked at home. It made sense to our leaders, to do the same in Africa. To have it paid for by the state, and built with labor, recruited from the local population, giving them employment, instead of selling them into slavery in foreign lands.

They saw this as a win, win proposition. I have doubts, that we can have it both ways: Call Africans a sub human, genetically flawed species and cloning our fatherland on land that needs to be privatized, while these sub humans provide the labor, to build another German province."

Wolf agreed and added:

" All this at starvation wages, that do not add markets for export- goods from our homeland into the colony, as the claims were made so loudly. All we know, is that even the meager profits were taken by private enterprise and that tax payers at home were asked to pay for both infrastructure and protection.

Someone said that we are privatizing profits and socializing losses of our colony." Maria, after looking straight into the eyes of our captain: " You have said earlier, that indigenous populations were removed from their land, to make room for plantations and that they were moved onto marginal land. How are they maintaining health and nutrition, if their traditional lifestyle is no longer possible?"

Paulus thought for a moment, then he replied, with as bitter burst of laughter: " Missionaries claim to have done a lot to supplement the native's food and nutrition and in the process, making them aware of God and teaching them proper work ethics and industrious behavior, elevating them from lazy savagery to mission-owned plantation workers."

Wolf, blowing out air:

"Missions competing with planters and industrial farmers for labor? How did this come about?" No one knew whether to laugh or to cry.

Paulus moved a hand across his maps to smooth out the creases. He looked at each one of us and said: " See the lines of borders, outlining territories and delineating countries? These are not actual borders of actual countries or communities. These are fake lines, drawn with a ruler on a piece of paper in Berlin, London, Paris or Brussels."

Stefan, who had studied surveying and cartography, seemed offended by this statement.

Seeing this, the captain changed his approach. He said:

"Now let us look at the picture from the point of view of a trader. For arguments sake, follow goods from the port, where they are loaded onto ships like Stella Maris back to the place where they were collected, made, caught, harvested or grown:

To get the idea of what I am about to say, look at this map of the African Continent. It was created by participants of the Berlin conference in 1874, during which ownership and control of Africa was assigned among conference participants."

Chapter 44

Chopping the world order

Stefan made himself even taller by rising onto his toes. Interrupting Paulus, he said: "Without a single inhabitant of any country from Africa present, no less. This map was still 50% blank at the beginning of the conference. The word used for remaining unmapped territory, which together was larger than all the participant's countries combined, was 'available'."

Paulus nodded in agreement. He liked how engaged Stefan was. He said: " None of the participants in Berlin considered, that goods from African kingdoms, tribes, families and nations have reached markets around the world for millennia. Goods traded in Africa were picked up by ships from trading nations and delivered to ports around Europe and Asia. What made it even harder for the participant's imagination to grasp, was the confusion about the origin of goods. Traders, who bought and transported goods, knew basically nothing about trade routes and support systems from the beginning of their journey to the market, from the far East, from Africa or from elsewhere on this planet."

With a long look at Stefan and Wolf, Paulus added:

"Consider how many people still think the earth is flat. Now add the fact, that people from different parts of the planet have different hair color, skin pigmentation and complexion, speak different languages and embrace different cultures and traditions."

Looking directly at Wolf and Maria, he added:

"To make the confusion complete, consider that humans around the globe worship dozens of different deities and that many have no written language or documented history. Scientists have collected as many skeletons and body-parts, as they could legally obtain, to find explanations for the laws of evolution, just to prove our supremacy that gives us the right to be the masters of this world."

Helena took a deep breath and said, after looking at each of us: "I remember, that our quest was born from the growing divide between people of two different faiths: Protestants and Catholics.

Now we are beginning to see what the truth is. From what we have seen on our journey so far, is the fact that the assumption of a world divided in just two faiths, is false.

More than half of the known part of Africa is governed and inhabited by Muslims.

France has turned regions governed by Muslims into protectorates rather than

annexing them to their Homeland. These communities have culture and tradition, that predate most other European countries. Earlier science, older libraries and more intriguing architecture and refined art and crafts.

France found it unnecessary to replace their government or judiciary and saw it possible to benefit from knowledge, that was stored in their temples, universities, and ancient libraries. This is what I have taken away from this journey.

Wolf agreed and, taking a deep breath, he added, scanning the sandy desert horizon:

"Christianity was used by the Roman Empire as a weapon to cs around Europe and parts of Africa, giving people they had defeated in battle the choice to get baptized or to die. We have learned well and now we are doing them proud.

This was the early version of what now is 'gunpoint diplomacy' we are using today.

You know more about this than I do," he said to Paulus.

"Slavery was a way to distinguish not between races, but between Heathens and

Christians. Land owning classes and vagrants.

If I am not mistaken, the word Slave originated from dislocated Slavic people, forced to become chattel, privately owned and from indentured servants, after their countries were defeated in battle and persons were carried off by the victors.

Today's slaves are humans, captured and sold to traders, who supply workforce requirements on plantations and industrial operations, designed to make a profit for investors.

I understand, that the British East India Corporation serves as the

model used by other nations, who are undertaking expansion of their empires into areas like Africa and Asia. Some colonies are run like military reservations, using natives, traid against their own people.

Helena picked up Wolfs train of thought:

"You remember the slogan:" A Place in the Sun?"

It was used to find German investors for the German East Africa Corporation, which has failed investor's expectations and had to be taken under the protection of the second Reich by the kaiser.

The German East Africa Corporation failed, because Africa was not as wealthy or as rich in treasure as India. It was not possible, to simply raid the wealth of this annexed territory and bring the treasure home, the way the British East India Corporation was able to do in India, pillaging the continent under license and protection, to the benefit of their investors, including the crown.Paulus nodded agreement and returned to his original thought:

"Look at of how Afrika functions:

Start with Africa's shape; it looks like a leaf. Her rivers are veins and arteries. They provide life. They challenge life.

Mountains, valleys, forests, swamp lands and deserts are features that determine thelife humans live who inhabit each region. These features give them opportunity and force them to enable the development of specific skills. Features of this leaf made inhabitants live far enough apart from each other, so that land ownership or shortage of space, have rarely been an issue.

Territorial expansion was seldom a necessity.

Some are herders. They move with the seasons. Some live on land that gets flooded annually. Rivers leave behind silt and fertilize their soil. Then they plant.

Some live in forests and forage in the shelter of trees. Some live on rocky terrain, findgem stones, dig up silver, gold, and diamonds for trade. Water is a treasure, recognizedby indigenous people and colonizers alike. And yet, there are desert regions where people have learned to live with barely a drop of water."

Stefan, pointing at regions on the map, showing mountains, both in the northwest and the East, he said:

"I have a vague idea, how high some of these mountains in Africa are. Especially in the East African region, we are about to visit. The German surveying team tried to reach the top of what we believe to be the highest mountain on this continent, sent to map its topography, they found, thatno indigenous people ever ventured, into the cloud covered region, because theybelieve, that the mountain is the home of Gods, who protected her from human intruders.

The people say that those, who go up into the mist, never come back. A new attempt is planned and I will be part of that team."

Paulus retrieved the thread of his thought:

"It is a matter of skills, required for life in each region, that determines the size and nature of nations, kingdoms, fiefdoms, tribal lands, and spheres of influence. There are hundreds of these, independent from each other, except for trade.Islamic states have succeeded in establishing larger Empires, because they support their communities, encourage trade, build schools, hospitalsand universities. They have their own military protection, enforcement of laws and edicts. Some of these Kalifates are centuries old and have wisely created free trade zones like Venice, Genoa, Bremen, or Hamburg.

Complex modes of transportation are used to bring trade goods to trading centers and to market.

These goods are surplus, things people make or harvest beyond of what they need. Since there are only a few regions controlled by a formal state, taxes are still widely unknown. Labor for wages is not known in most parts of Africa.

People trade, what they have plenty of and return with things they need.

Moving goods by river, requires different systems and skills than moving goods by camel donkey or in bundles, carried on people's heads.

Modes of transportation are supported by personal connections, relationships and established trust. These are the nerve system of our leaf. You have seen the offering in markets we have visited. You can appreciate the promise of wealth, someone visiting these markets can expect, especially those, who do not understand what it takes, to keep camels and their keepers alive while crossing deserts like the Sahara or the Namib or what it takes to navigate the Congo River, the River Nile- or their tributaries.

Most of this was widely unknown during the Berlin Conference." Stefan pointed again at the Map. He seemed furious. He raised his voice and stabbed the map several times with his pointing finger. He almost shouted, eyes blazing: "All this ignorance is visible on this map."

Wolf liked Stefan's passion:

"The idea, that there is only one true religion, adds insult to injury, it has caused all these false assumptions. I think, that all of us understand, that from assumed superiority can only come violation of human rights. Violation of social traditions and of personal relationships.

Integration, needed by people to thrive in their different climate zones, together with their adoration of the creator in different religions, is a more reasonable expectation.

Money-making plantations, investment driven factory-farms colonizers are attempting to create, using cheap labor, recruited at gun point, are bound to fail.

Slavery was prohibited by Islamic states and is condemned in our homeland. It is my opinion, that rights assumed over people, who are considered a human labor resource as part of a business model, is not economy. It is a crime. Just as is pilferage of natural resources, found in the colonies, wrestled from people, whose inherited livelihood has been destroyed by force of arms."

Maria responded to Wolf. His way of seeing things made her feel close to him:

"Violence and imprisonment are no incentives for collaboration, after the best soils have been taken and villagers were relocated onto marginal land, that makes it impossible for them to stay nourished, as they were before colonizers arrived with their outrageous claims."

Helena replied with her focus on missionaries:

"Missions are no help either, because they want to teach wild savages the fear of God in the name of Jesus Christ, and work ethics suitable for working their plantations, while forcing them to give up part of their meager compensation in taxes, to finance security forces needed to keep these savages from revolting or from running away.

Herbert was in line with her on that thought:

"Raising lower humans to the level of Europeans is an argument, that has not kept colonial governors from enforcing two sets of justice:

One for colonizers and one for the colonized. None for the offspring of mixed "Races" There is no oversight from home, since all communication takes at least ninety days, causing scandals to reach the attention of the public at home far too late to do anything about them."

Chapter 45

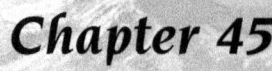

Into the red sea

Paulus put his hand on Stefan's shoulder, a sign of affection, sounding apologetic:

"Look at this map of Africa. What administrators do understand by now is the fact, that there are multiple climate zones, river basins, mountain ranges and deserts and that there are sites, where ships can land on all sides of this Continent at the mouth of most rivers, where traders can dock, where nations can send battleships with cannon to open or shut trade, to negotiate favorable terms with coastal kings and chiefs, offering them protection, in return for the illusion of sovereignty. I sense, that corruption will be a heritage, we are now creating.

That is the outside view of a trader. The inside view is still largely unknown. You, my friends, may be able to shed more light on the real Africa, after you finish your investigation. You will enter the continent from the east side, where Kaiser Wilhelm II has supported building more infrastructure: Railroads, harbor facilities, town halls, hospitals and schools."

He added calmly:

"At home, people are impressed. They have only Europe to compare. They have witnessed the fact, that laying a million kilometers of rail all over Europe has accelerated the industrial revolution and in doing so, has improved everyone's life.

In Africa, such improvements are not really serving the indigenous population, but the planters, while destroying traditional trade routes and many of the skills and relationships that came with them. That is a great loss to Africa and the world.

You will find it difficult to explain this to the public at home, more willing to believe than interested to know. I know this, because I am part of the system, designed to export and deliver the overproduction of fabricated goods from Europe to the world and to return the riches, created by planters, together with the results of the collective ingenuity of indigenous populations. In Africa, investments have had good returns only from regions, where precious metals and minerals were discovered and mined, but not from agricultural production, with a labor force that must be whipped like oxen, to stay upright and to keep working for the master race."

We were by now so deep in our own thoughts, that no one had any more comments or questions. The passage through the Suez Canal was almost complete. We had cabin fever. We saw the Canal pilot tender approach Stella Maris to pick up the two pilots.

Stefan explained:

"We will now sail the length of the Red Sea, until we reach Djibouti, an ancient Port, that serves traders from Somaliland, Ethiopia, and Eritrea and across the golf of

Aden, -from Yemen.

One more dinner, one more evening in our quarters and one more good night's sleep and we will finally be able, to set foot onto solid ground, while Stella Maris is taking on freight, after unloading cargo from Germany, Genoa, and France." At dinner, Wolf asked the captain:

"From what I have seen on the map you showed us, Djibouti must to be another key port for trade. I am curious how it is governed. What do you know about that? Is this another case of a territory protected by France, but left to be more or less self-governed in their own traditional ways? You mentioned that it is a free port?"

Paulus pushed away his plate, took a long drink from his goblet of red wine and sat back in his chair to think for a moment. The pilots had left. The ship had once again picked up full speed. Land was beginning to disappear on the distant western horizon, showing us the glorious colors of the setting sun over arid land. He said:

"This is a very good question.

Djibouti is an ancient market place.

Consider where it is located. This market has a network of trails leading to it, by water-, ocean from the east, rivers from the west. For traders, this is ideal, because of the vast area this port is serving. Djibouti is a nerve center, where we find raw materials, artifacts, and woven goods from the other half of the world. Traders know the law of supply and demand.

As you have seen, we are not connected or bound by the laws of just one land. We feel our way through space and time. For us, this market is a treasure trove. Here you can see, how the world works, when it can function without special interests or hidden agendas interfering or obstructing. You can see in the offering of this marketplace, what works and what does not.

This is where you see what really matters: People.

Take people away from the table and you have no place to put them but in prison." After we had tasted another fabulous dessert, the chef had prepared,it was time for us to return to our salon and do what we do best:Make music, tell stories, and recite poetry, until it is time to go to sleep.

For a long time, we stood by the starboard railing to observe the stunning afterglow to the west. My work in the ship's kitchen was an intense course in French cuisine.The benefit to all of us, were the endless variety of special desserts Chef Jean du

Chalet had perfected:

Crème Brule, doused with hot chocolate sauce in a footbath of honey, to be flamed withaged cognac. This was the grand finale of the celebration of another Suez Canal passage.

Champagne flutes and a few bottles of the finest chilled champagne had appeared. Our captain never missed an occasion to turn his- and our life into a special celebration.

Chapter 46

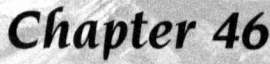

Djibouti

We were amazed We were amazed What followed would linger in our memory as the night, when eros shot his arrows

without ever missing his target. My feelings for Stefan had bloomed into deeply rooted trust, wrapped in a blanket of hot passion with a bouquet of breathless joy, that defies description in mere words.

Such poetry has yet to be written. All of us must have gone to that land of bliss this night. We exchanged no words in the morning, when we finally emerged to return to face the intense light over the immense ocean, that surrounded our ship. Our faces were still flushed and even the captain could not suppress a knowing smile.

We all had overslept breakfast.

Knowingly, my friends in the galley had anticipated this and set aside trays with a scrumptious European breakfast for us, including freshly brewed café au lait.

If sunrise could have an after-glow, this would have been a good time to show it.

We were still drowned deeply in feelings and thoughts and exchanged timid smiles and blushes, while devouring this treat with ravenous gusto.

Was the world still there?

Before we knew it, the ship's horn sounded and Stella Maris slowed down to take on a Pilot to guide her into the harbor of Djibouti Stan Nord announced a six-hour port stay and assigned officers to escort us on a tour of harbor and markets. He cautioned us: "Stay on guard for pickpockets. Crafty merchants will accept any currency, but have tricky ways to calculate exchange rates. Best to make purchases on your way back."

Stella Maris was securely tied to the dock. Unloading began immediately.

We felt excited to visit the first true African trading post. We noticed smaller vessels in the harbor, busy unloading freight from Yemen, loading goods arriving on camel trains and offload barges, tied to the docks, from canals linked to rivers from the interior.

The mood at this port seemed buoyant.

The hustle and bustle of the market was dizzying.

Paulus was right: Muslim governance favored free trade.

As he had put it, this gave nourishment to the leaf of the African Continent.

 dazzling display of artifacts, crafts, cut stone, fine metal work, fabrics, garments, leather goods, spices and agricultural products was offered to countless traders.

People were wearing a wide variety of traditional garments, men sitting on low chairs, sharing cool smoke from mysterious contraptions with central smoldering chambers and gurgling water traps, sipping black Turkish coffee from tiny ceramic cups with gold rims and -handles, held delicately with thumb and pointing finger, pinky pointing off to one side, deep in conversation, enjoying the moment.

We saw manufacturing shops inside market stalls.

Amazing skill was on display from metal work to jewelry making, fiber art as spinning, knitting, and weaving to preparing spices for mixing, storing, and transporting.

Mouth-watering scents flooded our senses, calling for a taste of freshly roasted Turkish coffee or cups of tea offered everywhere. Sweet treats shaped like large marbles made from dark chocolate, honey and spice were among the irresistible temptations.

Rich colors of merchandize were enhanced by wafting scents of meat, roasting on vertical mechanisms in front of hot charcoal fires and the scented steam from large pots, offering food for every taste or diet.

Trading was accompanied by social rituals that made an impression as though everyone was glad to be in the company of someone.

Our shore leave flew by like a flock of pigeons, and before we could catch our breath, we were back on board of Stella Maris. The horn sounded to announce our departure.

We were famished, thirsty, and exhausted all at the same time.

A very elaborate meal was our reward for waiting, until the pilot had left the vessel and we could see the wake, made by the departing tender.

Chapter 47

A new threat at sea

Paulus seemed to be in a somber mood.

The folds on his forehead and above his nose had deepened.

He took a deep breath, which prompted everyone to look at him and to pay close attention:

"I have news, concerning sailing in the Gulf of Aden and along the coast of Somaliland. There have been reports of pirates active in this region. They are not just prying on fishing vessels to steal their catch any more, but have expanded to hijacking entire vessels and their cargo."

He looked at each of us to be sure we were listening.

"Times have changed. We are facing a new threat: Commercial vessels have come under attack. Piracy has increased. They are also better armed.

Boarding parties have taken hostages, holding them for ransom."

He paused to let this sink in.

"Your safety and the safety of our crew and officers are important to me.

He looked at each of us again.

Then he motioned Ed Haller and Stan Nord to listen to what he had to say:

"Our vessel was built with a new, state of the art steel hull.

We are equipped to defend ourselves, with modern, powerful weapons, part of a program, we worked out with our insurance company Lloyd of London.

I am sure you have been wondering, what the tracks on our deck are for and what is underneath the blue tarps at the end of these tracks."

He rose from his chair. Pointing toward the stern of the ship he said:

"Stella Maris has enough engine power to outrun most ships in these waters.

However, we might have to defend ourselves. These pirates are very clever.

Port side, we have a rapid-fire cannon, that can shoot fifteen 30 mm rounds per minute.

It can sink most ships within fifteen hundred meters.

On the starboard side you see two separate tracks. These are for 20 mm weapons capable of discharging hundreds of rounds per minute to fend off small craft, attempting to deliver boarding parties from their mother ship.

They try to quietly climb aboard a ship, after creating a diversion, like a flair or a rocket shot to another part of a vessel. We will have to prevent that."

He sat down and took a long drink of water.

Herbert rose, pointing at Stefan and Wolf:

"You know, captain, all three of us had some military training:

All to do with BTS: Ballistics, technical and strategical.

We are familiar with, and trained on modern state of the art weapons.

We know, that these types of weapons are not yet widely accepted by standard armies, because they represent a type of warfare, unknown to most traditional war manuals.

We were trained in the use of machine guns: We have been trained on Maxims, Vickers, and Bushmasters.

Tell us, which of these guns you have on board. We can help you to set them up.

Give us a few minutes. and we will be able to make these weapons do, what they are designed to do.

From what we think you have, we will need one person to feed cooling water from one side and a second person on the other side, to feed ammunition and to keep the belts from buckling. Then two more each, to deal with surprises and as backup.

We will hit any target you ask us to hit, once they are in range.

They will not have a chance to survive an assault on Stella Maris."

He was a little breathless, then he said in a low voice:

"We want to help. I suggest we place the ladies in observation posts, to blow the whistle, when they see pirates approaching.

Show us what kinds of boats these pirates are known to be using and how they go about attacking ships."

Maria got up and stepped forward to face the captain:

"We will need low light binoculars, if you have them. Show us the influence of wind speed and direction and ways these boats might approach Stella Maris.

We will let you know when we find them, and how close they have come."

She thought for a moment. "We have all sailed around marks during regattas. We are familiar with guessing distance over water. Direction we call by the time on our wrist watches. We call the Bow twelve o'clock and the Stern six o'clock. Starboard three o'clock and Port nine o'clock.

Distance, we can call pretty accurate up to two miles.

Do you have pictures of the shapes of boats we are looking for?"

Maria sat down and exhaled. Her concern was visible between her eyebrows and her eyes had turned even darker. She seemed calm. She looked first at Wolf, then at Stefan and finally at Herbert. She grasped my hand under the table and I could feel that she was hiding her state of excitement and fear. She nearly squeezed the blood out of my hand. I had to pull my hand away. Shaking my hand and facing the captain, I said:

"We understand strategy on the water. We know Stella Maris is the mark. We know the mothership is hostile. Describe for us, what these pirate ships look like and how they find us in the dark. Tell us how they board a vessel. The more we know what to expect, the better we can help. How do they get enough light to see what they are doing?"

I sat down and took Maria's hand again. She had calmed down.

Helena rose from her chair. Addressing all present in the room:

"We are all sailors. We are here, because we are a team. We know, we represent the Country, which makes us targets for hostage takers.

So far, you have protected us, during every shore leave, even though sometimes we would have preferred to roam freely and without supervision. We understood.

Maria and I have nursing training. We know, how to dress wounds and to apply splints. We trust each other and we trust our captain and the ship's crew.

Now is the time for us, to pay you back: I suggest you put Wolf in charge of the port side cannon. He is a ballistics genius. Let him use the 30 mm weapon.

Put Stefan and Herbert on the 20 mm guns, they can work together, to protect our flank. I have seen them stand at the end of the two tracks by the railing, inspecting the possible purpose they might serve. You might consider letting Stefan be the commander of this detail, leaving you and your crew to deal with whatever the pirates will bring to this fight." With emphasis she continued, pointing at Stefan:

"Stefan has nerves of steel; we all have seen him in action. He and Herbert will keep our flank covered."

Helena sat down and looked into Herbert's eyes for approval. He nodded consent.

The captain took a deep breath:

"It seems to me, that you have thought about this already. Let us go to the map room and I will show you photographs of various Dhows, used by pirates in this area."

Twenty minutes later, as the sun was preparing to set in the west, the blue of the sky turned to a magnificent dark red near the horizon, setting the sea ablaze.

We began to scan the horizon. The captain had to draw us in to the map table, to look at the images:

"This is a Dhow. It comes with variations in size and height of build ups at the stern. Some smaller ones are one masted. Two masts are typical son larger ones.

The rigging is called lateen rigging, it maximizes the sail area of a single main sail per mast, that can be hoisted all the way to the top of the mast. It is a slanting triangular sail. The color of the sail can vary from white to a reddish brown. You recognize them by their slanted triangle shape.

The mother ships of Somali pirates usually deploy small vessels, like whaling boats, used for a stealth approach, to get close to their target.

To board the target, they use lines with enter hooks, to fasten their boat to the vessel they want to board. They climb up often undetected, surprise the sleeping crew and overpower the watch.

Lately, they have begun to shoot hot flairs, to cause fires on decks to create a diversion from the boarding-party."

He displayed several images of dhows in port and at sea under sail.

"We have powerful flares of our own. We can light up the sky and the sea around our ship, to expose even the smallest skiff.

To be harder to locate, we will be sailing without running lights."

"How do they find us in this vast ocean?" Helena asked.

Paulus pointed towards the stern of the ship:

"They travel with a low search light and steer an intersecting course, until they see our wake. Then they follow us, with an observer in their bow, who signals to the driver, if there are course changes. Many unsuspecting ships have been captured this way. Lately, they have taken hostages and kept them prisoner for ransom.

We will sink and disable the boarding parties. Then we sink their mother ship."

Stefan took over the conversation, and the captain agreed to have him be in charge of gunners and observers.

While there was still daylight, and Stella Maris gained distance from the coast of Djibouti, we inspected the stations and were given gear and instructions, including life vests, partners assigned, for relief in each station and signals we were to use in various events.

Now came, what felt like the longest night of this entire journey. It was difficult to keep our eyes open. We were positioned, to have eyes on four sides of the ship, until we were far enough from land, to expect no pirates to approach us from the east.

Stefan consulted with the captain, to get permission to have two lookouts at a time until activity was detected in our wake. He set up shifts of two hours on and two hours off.

The gunners set up reclining deck chairs, so they were able to be at their position in just a second from an alert.

Just the hum of the engines and the bow wave. Flat black water. Only the forward motion of the ship, seemed to move air. The night was completely quiet. We were on the second rotation. I lost track of who was where. I had to keep reminding myself where we were and what we were doing. I was in love with Stefan. We had gotten so close during these past weeks, that there was no question about our relationship being committed. Two souls merged for life.

I felt lucky and warm in my heart.

The whistle blew.

Maria went up to the wheelhouse.

Paulus:

"How close? What position?"

Maria:

"Six o'clock. One thousand meters. Following in our wake.

Paulus sent word to the gunners:

"Prepare to engage. Stefan, stand by with both weapons. We will turn hard to starboard, when they are getting into range. They are running under power as well as sail.

Wind speed now 4 knots from the north-east. We will let them come closer.

Make them think, we did not see them. Are we ready?"

"Ready."

At this moment the area between the ships lit up with flares coming from the pirate's mother ship. It made several small boats visible.

Helena:

"Two small craft 2:00 O'clock, 250meters."

Stefan:

"Ready to engage," then

"Fire!"

I see a flair landing on our deck. It came from the boat Helena had spotted. I said:

"Small craft, 1:30 150 meters flair landed on our foredeck.

The ship did a hard turn to port,

I could see the crew douse the flare on the foredeck. The light died down.

Now I could hear the papapapapapap of our weapons.

Our own flares went up.

The boats, Helena had spotted, were sinking.

Stella Maris turned hard to point Wolfs cannon on the pirate's mother ship.

It was taking a series of hits on the mast. The sail collapsed.

The slow tock, tock, tock continued, until I could see a gaping hole open at the waterline near the pirate's bow.

The mother ship began leaning forward.

I could feel the ship turning hard. I could hear the captain shout over the roar of the engines. He began to push us into a course, that would put us broadside with the pirate. Both 20 mm guns were now close enough to inflict severe damage on the pirate; with our flares, we could see all the boats she had deployed.

One after the other the small boats followed the first one to the bottom of the sea.

There was no one left on the pirate's tilting deck.

Again, the ship turned hard and Wolf sounded his tock tock tock tock.

He was facing the pirate broadside. His gun fired at a steady rate.

The engines of Stella Maris slowed, giving Wolf time to cut a series of perforations just below the waterline, after disabling the steering mechanism of the pirate's mother ship.

Paulus ordered more flares, to be sure, that no more pirate boats were left afloat. We had now disabled the pirate's mother ship and it was beginning to sink

Wolf set his gun to single shot mode. As the pirate's ship sank, the last thing visible was the flag, he was flying on a short mast, mounted on top of his wheelhouse.

Wo

It hit the center of the flag and made it explode.

The dhow and its boarding party had disappeared in the sea. Paulus turned Stella Maris back on her course towards Mogadishu.

Wolf took aim and fired one last shot.

Chapter 49

After the attack

According to Stefan, it would take just over two days to round the horn and three more to reach the port of Mogadishu, given a travel speed of 10 knots.

To him, the world was composed of movement, distance, and time.

We needed sleep after the guns were cleaned, ammunition and equipment were returned to the captain and we were relieved of our duty.

Paulus was pleased with the outcome of this night's event.

He ordered breakfast in ten hours, time to let the adrenaline bleed off and for our nerves to settle down. His crew took over the watch.

"Have some tea" he suggested "Your throats will need to be moistened. You can sleep well, knowing that you have kept us safe. You should be very proud of yourselves. In the name of the owners of Stella Maris, I will instruct Emil Holt, to waive all your personal expenses since Bremerhaven- until we reach your destination. You have earned it. Good night."

Once we were back in our quarters, Stefan spoke:

"Excellent job, everybody. Now I will go back to the captain and suggest a series of watches, beginning after breakfast tomorrow. I suggest 6 hours on, six hours off, if you all agree.

We have no reason to believe, that this was the only pirate and we have six more days to reach Mogadishu in Somaliland, then two more days to Mombasa, Kenia and one more day to Dar es Salaam in Tanganyika. Once we reach the waters of Kenia, we can turn the watch back to the ship's crew.

If everyone agrees, I will offer the captain extra watches for the next eight days, starting tomorrow."

We all nodded yes in agreement and waved him to go ahead to see the captain. We sat, holding our tea mugs, and waited for Stefan's return. We sat in silence, trying to keep our knees from knocking from adrenaline.

I was watching Herbert, who was white as a sheet and Helena who did not let go of his hand. I took them aside and asked:

"What is the matter? "

Helena, instead of answering, reached into Herbert's jacket and opened a few buttons. There was a hidden vest underneath, that looked like a series of wooden handles set in a series of pockets magazine style at a diagonal with the top of the handles to the left. The top pocket was empty. She took the second handle and pulled it out. It revealed a sort of knife with a sharp point and razor-sharp cutting edges on both sides.

"Wat is this?" I asked. "Why is there one missing?" Herbert responded with a faint grin:

"That one is inside the pirate who was trying to tie up Helena and throw her overboard to his partner in a small boat. It was connected to our railing with a line and hook, opposite of where Helena was stationed."

"How did you know?" He put his finger to his lips, then explained in a whisper: "I saw him. I am a knife thrower. That was my sport, since I was twelve years old." He took a deep breath, then buttoned his shirt.

"I saw this figure climbing up on a rope near the bow at the very moment when their flare hit the front deck. I left my position at the gun and ran to confront the intruder. He was already placing a muzzle over Helena's mouth, when I reached them.

His back was turned towards me. He heard the door slam shut, after I stepped out.

He turned around. I threw my knife into his chest, hitting his heart.""What did you do with him?"

"We threw him overboard and we think that he fell right into the skiff, he had come from. Stefan and I later sank that boat with our Maxims.

We have not mentioned this to anyone.

It is over.

We need time to recover from this.

Look. You can see the welts on the corners of her mouth.

Let us not talk about this to anyone.

We had enough trauma.

It is over."

We joined the others.

We sipped tea until Stefan returned. He gave the thumbs up sign.

Now we got up to find our beds, to try to get some rest.

I could not sleep. I needed to be held.

I needed to be consoled over the loss of life that could not be prevented.

I needed to calm down. The world had shown me a face that I was not prepared to see.

Stefan was as sweet as I knew, only he could be.

I did not need to explain. I slipped under his cover and tears began streaming.

He did not say anything but held me for a long time. We listened to each other's breathing. Love was present. It was met by gratitude. Our intimacy rose to a new level.

We found the balance between self-love and love for each other.

I could tell, Stefan was processing tonight's events in his own way. He was our captain.

It was not possible for him to see himself separate from us.

As long as there was potential for this type of danger, his mind was holding him to his obligation as our captain, to stay alert and to feel responsible for the outcome.

For me, it was a slow and disturbing process.

I lay awake for a long time.

I was aware of my heartbeat and my breathing.

I could feel strength coming from Stefan as he finally fell asleep.

His breathing was deep and regular.

I tried to breathe with him.

It calmed me.

Deep down, my mind was too far from calm and my heart was in deep distress.

I had found myself in the middle of a deadly fight, brought on by attackers, who are known to take hostages for ransom, burn ships, steel cargo, and use deadly force.

No, they do not ask. They take. By force. Our preparedness surprised them.

They had no ship to return to, even if they did survive our response.

I knew Stefan, Herbert and Wolf acted in self-defense and in protection of Maria, Helena, myself and of course our captain, his ship, and his crew.

I now needed Maria, her wisdom and insight.

I finally sank into a restless sleep and woke up to the bell that called for breakfast.

I looked at the other's faces, as they appeared at the breakfast table.

Ashen faces, deep-set eyes, signs of restless sleep all around.

No one was able to speak. This will take time. I looked at Maria.

Her eyes were almost black today. Her hand was resting on Wolf's hand.

She looked at me and I could see, she was fighting back tears.

I have not seen her like this, since the day she decided, she could no longer go to confession, when she left the church.

I could tell, she was as wounded by this experience as we all were. I looked for the door to open and for the captain to come in and show us how to return to life. He did not. We were on our own.

We were beginning to see another side of Africa. We knew now, how Africans must feel when foreigners come and take their land. This was not the Africa, we were told about by promoters and officials, who claim possession of parts of the world, as if they had inherited it directly from a higher authority.

We now had a taste, of what a taking might feel like and what a response might be.

Reflecting on our days aboard Stella Maris, we could see the reality of the different facets of the vast and magic land and its inhabitants, called Africa.

We had seen many things, that were brought to market for sale.

We saw the influence, different religions, nationalities, and tribes have on trade and the skills required, to make articles both manufactured and grown.

We could see how different regulations enable or hinder the creativity and ingenuity of Africa's people, who have inhabited this huge continent, since the dawn of time.

We saw places with institutions of learning, research, and science, that have shaped Europe.

Now we have encountered the exact opposite:

Armed predators. Existing without collaboration or fair exchange, soaked in violence.

Is that what we have come to expect to be the new norm?

Is this the reason for our failure to create colonies that function?

Are we the perpetrators, committing the same type of violence?

Maria took me into her confidence, when we ran into each other in our night gowns before dawn. She whispered:

"Wolf is extremely upset. He told me about his feelings, after sinking the pirate. He was shocked about the excitement and joy he felt, and the satisfaction when he sank our attackers, especially the moment after he had fired the last single shot to take down their flag, before the waves sucked down the splinters and shreds of a symbol of terror.

He was acting the trained ballistics expert, doing battle. It had changed for him, when he became aware of the attack on Helena over the speaker. He said:

"It became personal at that moment and I felt rage well up inside myself.

That was new to me.

I had no other response but to kill. These terrorists had pushed me over a line that I could not retract from."

He finally fell asleep and now I am wide awake.

The two of us held each other in a very long embrace, until we both stopped vibrating violently.

Later at breakfast, Maria mused:

"Are we the terrorists that have introduced asymmetric warfare and robbery with the angelic smile of the innocent and the entitled?

Have we just seen the mirror image of what we are doing here?

I am deeply disquieted. These thoughts will be our companions on our watch for the next eight days, until we reach Kenia. We are either going to sleep or hold watch in our assigned stations. No. I am afraid, that these thoughts will be with us for the rest of our mission here in Africa."

Stefan tried to be all business as usual:

"The captain has announced, that we will not leave the ship in Mogadishu.

This is the third time since we left Bremerhaven, that we were forced to react to warfare, that is coming to us from outside our ship, from a world in upheaval."

We had short conversations, mostly concerning our well-being. Too exhausted to spend time together. Six hours on. Six hours off. Watch around the clock. Distorted sense of time. Time to think.

More than ever, I now needed my big sister Maria, who can shed light where all I can see is pitch black darkness. I felt lucky to have her by my side.

With red eyes and deep dark rings under our eyes, we stumbled into a world that was different than the world we thought we knew the day before.

Yes, we thought we knew about all the hazards of our time, the myriad of uncertainties, the conflicts of interest, territorial claims, lies, propaganda, economic and scientific justifications, and the questionable legal foundation, that was being guarded by force of arms, and yes, we were also witnessing magnificent achievements of mankind.

Not just architecture and philosophy, medicine, and science, but the little things that make life easier, more delicious, more beautiful, and more meaningful.

We were able to see light and shadow and we felt, that it was our destiny to try and turn these two forces into color and texture, as long, as we find a way to not violate life itself.

This act of terror changed all of that for us. It felt, like a curtain had dropped and all light had disappeared. Nothing but a black void was left and we had no power to counteract it. It raised the question in all of us: How can anyone live, after taking the life of another human being? What do we have to do, to reconcile what we have learned in Sunday school with what we have experienced?

Where was God last night?

Where was God, when some countries claimed ownership over land and resources, that was already inhabited by indigenous people since the beginning of time?

Where was God, when they made these decisions thousands of miles away, without representation of the people at the table, whose life is being changed from old traditions to new forms of slavery?

Where was God, when it was decided to take humans away in chains on ships, to work on plantations on different continents?

Where was God, when we began to bring plantations to their homeland?

Where was God, when we took possession of arable land and moved colonized victims onto marginal land?

Where was God, when we began using Christian missions to educate and instill Christian work ethics and discipline in the name of Jesus Christ?

Where was God, when we saw different justice applied to non-whites?

Is God only merciful, provided you are white, free and hold in your hand a modern machine gun? What if in the future industrial production mandates, that such weapons are sold to anyone and everyone? Where will God be then?

I was not the only one harboring such dark thoughts. We moved about our days and nights, guarding the ship six hours on, six hours off, until we reached the port of Mogadishu.

Here, we were not given leave to see the harbor. We were being kept safe by our captain, his crew, and the port authorities, who could not afford to have embarrassing incidents at their harbor. For us, it was a chance to sleep and to let the events of the last days rest and our minds try to calm down and come to peace.

Maria suggested:

"Words will not help in this situation. Music will re-harmonize us."

She took out her guitar, Wolf brought his violin, I played the piano, Herbert and Helena brought their guitars, flutes, and song books. We played, sang, ate, and slept, creating distance from the past, trying to recompose ourselves for the last phase of our journey.

Maria finally said:

"Look for potential, not for failure. Look at what we saw in Djibouti.

Arabic influence in dress, especially from arid regions. European and African costumes in present and past styles.

Mesmerizing music with pentatonic sequencing. Instruments, made with rich decorations to reflect the beauty and happiness they were designed to emit.

Poetry like the Garbay, an epic, with over a hundred lines.

Libraries, older than any on our continent, containing treasures of ancient wisdom, protected under Islam.

Rich cuisine, reflecting the full palate of an international trading post, where people were catering to individual tastes and traditions.

We learned, that on this side of Africa, Arabic is an official language, supported with Swahili. Of course, Sudanese, Somali, and Ethiopian are spoken.

There were interpreters, capable of speaking six to ten languages fluently including dialects from India, English, French, German, and Italian.

Look for potential.

We all understand music. That is the international language, that connects us on every emotional level. Then comes dance. Then come painting, sculpture, and architecture.

All potential."

Wolf agreed:

"That is where God resides."

Wolf continued his musings out loud, he sounded depressed:

"God does not reside in colonial prisons. Not in the halls of European governments and not in the Vatican in Rome and not in protestant missions around the world and not in board rooms of international corporations."

Herbert added:

"Control over natural resources is not for the benefit of people here or at home. Pretending it is pursued in the name of the God adds insult to injury."

Chapter 50

Cyclone

I was worried about Maria. She looked tired. She was spent. I knew it was Maria, who would find ways to show us the light. I also knew, that Wolf was seeing it her way.

We went on making music together until we were tired, relaxed, and able to find sleep once again.

We knew, we had to stay vigilant about pirates, until our arrival at Mombasa, Kenia. To make our journey there uneventful, Paulus chose a course further to the East, to stay out of range of coastal raiders. For us, this was a great relief.

We had calmed down a little, during the short stay at Mogadishu.

Finally, we heard the long sound of the ship's horn, announcing our departure.

Another outstanding breakfast.

We resolved, to treat the pirate episode as part of why we were here:

To observe, experience, see the world from six pairs of eyes and to find meaning in all that we experience, without being judgmental.

Survival just became part of life for Maria and Wolf and personal for Helena and Herbert.

I could see Helena's hand pressing Herbert's hand so hard, he had to shake it, to get his feeling and circulation back, survival is also essential also for Stefan and me.

Stan Nord entered the room. He made this announcement:

"You have noticed, how calm the ocean is this morning.

Do not be deceived. It is the calm before a storm. Look to the east. There is a black line on the horizon just below the sun.

See the intense orange of the sunlight. This is the outside cloud formation of a cyclone headed our way. The pilot says, this cyclone is moving west towards land over Somaliland at about seven knots, with wind speeds exceeding eighty nautical miles.

The rotation is counter clockwise. We are at the southern side of this rotation around the moving heart of this cyclone.

This will be to our advantage in two ways: There will be no pirates and we will have the wind from our back. We will run with wind driven spray and waves and head straight into large, rolling ocean waves at a slight angle to the south-east. There will be heavy seas and captain Paulus orders are for you to prepare your quarters and close your battle stations, tie up all loose items and return the weapons to their storage places under the tarps. The crew has orders to help you.

This storm will pick up sand and dust off the Somali desert and off the mountain plateau and send them into the sea, making streaks of golden silt.

Seal all windows and keep the hatches locked. This cyclone is more powerful than what you have seen in the north Atlantic or in Morocco. You will need to wear breathing protection from the air born dust, even inside."

With this, he left the room.

The heat had begun to become oppressive, ever since we left the Suez Canal.

Now, Stefan reminded us of the energy, emanating from warm ocean currents:

"What we have seen in Morocco is child's play, compared to what the warm waters of the Pacific will do to energize a storm. There will be wind gusts, exceeding a hundred and twenty miles per hour.

Waves will build to epic proportions. We must secure everything that can move.

Moving objects become as dangerous, as strong winds and waves.

Let us eat breakfast after we have prepared for the storm."

Almost imperceptivity, the light changed, as the outer rings of the circular clouds moved over the ship and towards the coast. We were steaming towards the open sea in a south-easterly heading.

Once the pilot had left our ship, Paulus sat down at the breakfast table with us.

We felt that he had adopted us as his family and now he was facing another separation, once he had delivered us at our destination.

Meals he ordered, were increasingly festive and this breakfast was no exception. Stake, eggs, roasted potatoes, and garnishes with many side dishes made from local fish, meats, sauces and produce of the region, spiced, and made into edible works of art.

We were absorbed in this delectable feast, when the bow of the sip suddenly rose and fell into a deep valley with a thunderous clap, followed by a wave of heavy spray washing over the entire ship.

The food and our plates became airborne. Breakfast was over.

Winds had begun blowing from the west off the Somali plateau, loaded with fine sand, tinting large rolling ocean waves with streaks of gold color from white foam on top to black, almost metallic looking water of the deep.

Countless breaking waves were chasing one another into the wind, giving the impression, that the next seventh wave could surely swallow Stella Maris.

The deafening noise that wind, water, and the rigging of the ship were generating, ranged from a high-pitched shriek to that of rolling thunder. It was a terrifying sensation to even the most sea hardened, salt crusted mariner.

Our sense of time, being distorted by the six-hour on and six-hour off shifts the days before, together with the turbulence and cross currents, grinding and gyrating the ship, confused our sense of up and down.

Torrents of water and dust made a staccato, that made us feel like we were inside a drum doing a big drum solo.

Thanks to the great skill of our skippers, we reached the back side of the storm safely.

We had to adjust to the motion, that seemed to continue inside our bodies, as a drunken person would feel, even after the seas had finally calmed down.

Stella Maris was headed south once again. We had lost track of time.

Finally, we arrived safely at the port of Mombasa, Kenia.

Once again, we were treated to another special feast, our chef had prepared.

Ed Haller paid special attention to every detail in selection and presentation, to please his captain and his guests.

We were given a full day of shore leave with escort in Mombasa.

Paulus himself had some special visits planned, to personally deliver some of his most prized possessions from his Bordeaux wine store and from the humidor, with priceless Cuban cigars. As he explained, this attention to detail was his secret for maintaining his trade relationships. He returned to the ship with boxes of carefully packed glass bottles, containing exquisite essential oils, treasured by perfumers in London, Paris, and Berlin.

We became once again aware of the trading mission Paulus was passionate about:

To know and to find the rarest and most treasured goods along his circumnavigation of planet Earth.

No one ever mentioned the events in Somaliland, or the cyclone again.

We were now looking forward to our final approach towards our destination:

Dar Es Salaam, provisional government seat and port of German East Africa.

At the captain's table, Paulus introduced the port of Mombasa:

"Mombasa is a port inside of a deep and very secure bay.

It was established as a trading port hundreds of years ago.

In 1570 a mosque was built here.

The British East Africa company has received license to operate trading business from here, reaching across the waters to India and beyond, expanding existing trade connections.

They established plantations with slave labor.

During the eighteen nineties, the British Government took over Kenya as a protectorate. They have since built towns, railroads, and government office buildings, expanded the harbor, and added steam cranes for loading and unloading ships.

Trade from here includes Ivory, Millet, Sesame seeds, Coconuts and Coffee as well as goods brought in from India such as Silk, Cotton, Brass and Bronze objects, Terracotta.

From India came merchants, building market stalls, restaurants, and banks.

You will find Indian traders everywhere in East and South Africa."

We were happy to finally step onto solid ground, to feel the constant inner motion slowly subside, while we visited the markets. We were fascinated by the rich offering of goods, produced on plantations, hunted on safaris, and delivered by camel train and railroad from the interior of Africa to this vast market.

We had time to enjoy coffee, tea, and pastries, offered everywhere. India trade was visible and we could not resist purchasing silk saris and learning how to wear them, while the boys enjoyed Turkish coffee and Greek baklava.

We wore our saris, to see, if the boys liked the colors of these delicately woven and embroidered silks, we had chosen.

Europeans, Asians, and African tribes-people, wearing their traditional dress, streamed by the café we had chosen as a meeting place. Some of the Europeans stood out in their pristine white safari helmets.

People from a plethora of countries, Jews, Muslims and Arabs, traders from as far away as Zaire, Southern Sudan, Uganda, Rwanda, Ethiopia, Egypt, the Sahara, and the Savannas of Africa, as well as traders and merchants from Asia and India crowded the narrow lanes between market stalls.

Wolf was pointing at the crowd. Excitedly, he exclaimed:

"Look at this! I think that proponents of segregation and nationalism are already on the losing side of history."

Helena picked up her own view:

"I cannot see inspiration or peace in arrogance or ignorance. We have yet to see signs of advantage or success in forms of governance that restrict or tax trade and movement of people and goods in and out of the areas of their origin."

Herbert, looking at armed security personnel, parading through the crowd, observed:

"I cannot see a trace of justice coming from the muzzle of a gun."

Our day came to an end much too soon. We had to return to our quarters on the ship to await the horn that announced our departure.

We enjoyed our visit to yet another trading port very much, with its ancient roots and traditions, reaching from centuries back into our present time.

Maria was happy about this day's events:

"For me, harbors are classrooms, where humankind is demonstrating its potential."

We were getting ready to make landfall in German East Africa.

The setting sun presented with a spectacular display of colors, the like we had never seen before:

First stars appeared to the east in a sky clear and black, merging to dark cobalt blue, that changed seamlessly in the west to crimson red.

It looked, as though the water had caught on fire. The sky line of Mount Kenya drew a sharp black silhouette into this stunning sunset.

This explained the love, people feel for this part of the world.

Everyone breathed a deep sigh of relief. We agreed, that we were lucky, to have been in the care and under the watchful eye of a captain, who saw the world with curiosity, practical knowledge, experience, and empathy, rather than with judgement or greed.

Captain Paulus had demonstrated to us, that his ship could be run without suppressing part of the crew. He maintained a sense of purposeful order, that assured him of the attention and loyalty from his team. A complex operation, looking simple and safe in an environment that was neither.

Paulus does not just navigate oceans. He navigates human life, talent, desire, ambition and folly in a way, a conductor leads an opera production with orchestra, singers, tech support and an adoring audience.

He believes in the magic of cooperation, anticipating and meeting needs, before they are expressed. He approaches life with infectious enthusiasm.

We felt privileged and lucky, to have made our journey with a man like Captain Paulus.

Testament to the success of Captain Paulus and his command of Stella Maris, was the way he was greeted and supported, wherever she made fast or dropped anchor on his navigation around a very confused world, that was amid both the most dangerous and promising phase of evolution, the world has seen since the invention of the wheel and the discovery of time.

We were exhausted.

We went to bed on a gently rocking ship, that could have lulled a baby to sleep, after each of us had said grace in our own language, to our own God.

Chapter 51

German East Africa

After a long blissful sleep, Stefan came to wake us up to share with us his enthusiasm about this morning's sunrise. He made us get out of bed to see it.

The air over the Pacific Ocean was like hot salty soup. Almost completely saturated with moisture.

The water was flat, a soft tremolo of slow vibration seemed to come from underneath the surface, like ripples, created with a repoussé hammer on pure, thin gold.

All of nature was in harmony at this moment, as we stood by the railing, holding each other in gratitude, soaking in the sparkle of diamonds on top of each of millions of tiny wavelets.

We had arrived in the waters of the Indian Ocean near Tanganyika.

To the west, we saw the end of the blue hour; hills delineated delicately in shades of blue before a massive mountain, seemingly detached, towering over the horizon with a pure white elongated cap, contrasting a dark blue, cloudless sky.

Stefan pulled me close and whispered:

"This is the highest mountain in Africa. Mount Kilimanjaro.

We will appease its spirits and clime to the summit this time.

The geographical society is once again sponsoring an expedition and my climbing partners are already on their way, to meet us in a about three weeks."

I pulled him over to the side, away from the others. Then I whispered, looking straight into his steel blue eyes:

"This time? Are you telling me you have been here before? No need to mention it?"

Stefan whispered back:

"Have I not mentioned it? I thought I had. I did not make a big deal of it. It was unsuccessful. I also did not want to lord it over you and our friends, but rather tried to take a fresh approach, with all of us together, seeing things for the first time, with our quest and our investigation."

He paused to think.

"I was just a student then. Through my family, I was offered the opportunity to tag along with an expedition, sponsored by the German Geographical Society.

We were sent to fill in some blanks on the map. It was my father's opinion, that I could make myself useful with my mountaineering skills and my enthusiasm for adventure and for being first at things, turning my competitiveness towards something useful."

He pulled me close, with the floating mountain above the clouds reflected in his eyes, he whispered:

"Will you forgive me?"

"Of course, I forgive you. I love you. You are my life."

I kissed his eyes.

We knew from the hospitality, the captain had shown us, that his feelings for us were more, than what he had contracted for.

He had grown to care for us. We had become his other family.

Now Paulus looked at us, the way he had looked at his twin brother, before it was time to say good bye to him.

He could not hide his upset over being separated soon from his new adopted family. Our final breakfast on board was testimony to this.

For the first time, our captain could not find words. His gaze into the distance, his fork and knife poking around on his plate, finding nothing of interest.

His coffee was getting cold. He reached for water, like a person, whose mouth is getting dry. Without a word, we watched him leave the table to go to the wheelhouse, motioning Stefan to follow him. We did not see either of them for a long time. Soon a pilot came on board.

Paulus ordered us to the map room and asked us to make statements, regarding the pirate incident. He gave us the option to sign his very complete account, or to add details from our point of view and to fill in what might have been omitted.

Seeing, how shaken we were about this experience, Paulus assured us, that the captain's log was confidential and that this report would stay on board, for the life of his ship.

Paulus looked to Maria and Wolf for leadership in finding the spiritual side of armed conflict and death, the way he had noticed their ability, to help with the ceremonial part of the sea burial of his mother.

Maria suggested, we gather in our quarters and play a few hymns plus Tchaikovsky's Greek orthodox chorus to the Virgin Mary, which, together with soothing candlelight, helped us to find closure to this event.

Now we began preparations for our arrival in German East Afrika.

A boat arrived, to take us into Dar Es Salaam.

We were no longer under the watchful eye of Captain Paulus and his officers.

Instead, we were met by delegates of the German East Afrika administration.

They had come to welcome us and to offer their support.

We requested a few days' time to get our land legs back.

Accommodations at the Grand Hotel were as European as any first-class Hotel in Berlin could be.

We enjoyed space - and time for ourselves, after the long confinement on board of

Sella Maris. We were assigned the luxury suite on the top floor of the Grand Hotel, with views over port and city, which, from up here, looked like a typical port in Germany, with long piers, street cars, railroad tracks and cranes by the kay. On the inland side, we could see a new market hall, outside of which were the traditional sprawling market stalls spreading like fingers into the distance.

Chapter 52

Dar Es Salaam

Paulus had taught us to read markets, as an expression of need meeting talent, to answer the demands of traders and to connect humans to one another.

Captain Paulus could not have been prouder of his students.

He did not linger on good byes.

He left without another word, after giving each of us a long, hard bear hug.

The purser said his good byes and, as ordered, handed Helena an envelope filled with bills in Reichsmark, redeemable in gold.

During the following days, we went out to explore town and harbor in various groupings.

We made sure, to be accompanied by government agents for protection, while we navigated the mayhem of the markets and the bustling intersections of this fast-growing, almost German looking metropolis.

It was damp and blisteringly hot.

Mornings played out differently for each of us, depending how "sleepless" or "dreamless" previous nights had been with Eros once again shooting arrows wildly and accurately at all of us.

During the day, we tasted all kinds of food, offered by vendors, who were always cooking something interesting, using exotic ingredients and spices.

For supper, we met at the hotel dining room, where we were seated around a table in a space, defined by a large bay window. It was made to look festive with a variety of exotic potted plants.

Lighting was provided by a large chandelier above the center of the table.

Individual candles were lit in front of each place setting. We were made to feel at home.

No chef, of course was able to match the culinary art of Jean du Chalet on Stella Maris.

The food served here was good, solid German fare, the kind you would expect at the October Fest in Munich.

After dinner, we retired to a small, comfortable living room at our suite on the top floor.

Our investigation into German East Africa had officially begun.

Helena began her report, after settling into a large, overstuffed chair, with matching footrest:

"Maria and I visited a local hospital today. We saw a state-of-the-art healthcare facility and maternity ward. Very impressive."

Herbert was curious:

"Did you see any African patients? How is modern medicine received by the natives?"

Helena looked at him and without smiling said:

"Doctors and nurses mentioned the high infant mortality rate in the region. They said:

"We have yet to find acceptance and a way to build trust in our way of doing things."

They explained. "We are planning to train native nurses and midwifes. We are thinking that missions can help us recruit apprentices from their flock of Christianized Africans."

Maria, pacing the room.

" For tomorrow, we made an appointment to see the new elementary- and the middle schools. The headmaster will personally open doors for us and show us around.

We decided, to also visit mission schools and educational facilities of Jewish-, Hindu- and Muslim communities."

Helena stopped Maria's pacing, holding her by the hand.

"We noticed, that there are stories, that need to be told. To do that, we must establish relationships. I am afraid, we do not have enough time here, before we start our journey inland.

Maria finally sat down and glanced into space.

" We were told, that the mission, to improve and raise natives and non-whites out of savagery and squalor, is motivating Protestant and Catholic nurses, doctors, and administrators. We could not see much evidence in that respect.

"It goes along with the need to gain trust and acceptance with the native population.

It is easier for Asians and Indians to accept European Medicine than for Africans.

We are up against voodoo and evil spirits, who need to be appeased through dances, drums, burning incents and potions, administered by voodoo doctors," they said.

Helena was glad that Maria had settled down.

"I think that the foot in the door will be more success in saving babies and decreasing infant mortality, through pre- and post-natal care, feminine hygiene and infant nutrition."

Wolf wiped the sweat off his face with a handkerchief.

" This is the status here at the coast. Inland, malaria and sleeping sickness are still raging. I say we suggest, to widen reach and impact of medical services in GEA."

Stefan was as usual thinking about practical steps:

" Railroads will have an impact on the health of the population, by accelerating accessibility and supply of medicine and access to healthcare facilities for an increasing number of patients.

Research in epidemiology is still in its infant stages here. Improving healthcare will be more helpful, than recruiting and arming Askaris, for security purposes.

Herbert agreed.

" I understand from conversations, I had with veterans of the security forces, that Askaris, as they call African mercenaries from various regions, as well as native porters, who transport weapons, ammunition and supplies during troop movements, who are not as smart, or as educated as combat forces, are ordered to infirmary-duty, and are experiencing firsthand the benefits of European medicine. This will help to spread the word to their supporting followers, during troop movements, when wives and children of Askaris and porters are accompanying them by consent of the military command.

Wolf, fanning himself with a folded newspaper.

"I heard that security forces are still using scorched earth, torture, cat tail punishment and public hangings, to spread fear in the native population and to assure obedience and collaboration. I disagree with those who tell me:

"Fear weakens the resistance to our taking of land and designating it for plantations. Fear helps with "voluntary" employment of villagers, who have never paid taxes and are now being compelled by decree to work for wages, to pay taxes, to avoid punishment and eviction," as one of the officers of the security forces told me, under his breath and in private.

I understand that natives are encouraged to use small lots, worthless to our planters, to have their wives and children grow subsistence food. Apparently, planters cannot afford to pay living wages, if they want to make a profit. Security is a costly burden to our planters, who would like security to be shouldered by our homeland tax payers."

Maria looked puzzled.

"What is cat tail punishment?"

Wolf made a movement mimicking the snapping of a whip.

"Cat tails are a form of whip, originally used on slave ships, to punish, or suppress disobedience or revolt. Cats are made from five strips of cowhide, attached to a short handle, with knots or even metal beads at the end of each strand. A strike with this whip causes deep cuts on the skin of a victim. Fifty strikes will make a body bleed out.

It is a spectacle so horrible, that just the mention of "letting the cat out of the bag" will cause most victims to comply with almost any demand or rule.

Herbert turned pale at this thought.

"I heard stories about such practices, which are not published in newspapers at home: Planters are paying slave wages, while administrators are writing and enforcing policies that would never be condoned or permitted by the public at home.

They are acting with impunity, feeling protected by distance and isolation.

Lack of accountability results. I have this to say about what I have learned:

We may have succeeded in banning slavery. Trafficking in humans has slowed down considerably, answering demands made by the public at home.

Instead, we have brought plantations to Africa, thinking that "homeless" natives would flock to the recruitment offices of planters. Surprisingly, labor has become difficult to find, after removing people from their ancestral land by force, to make room for these plantations on arable land and pushing the former inhabitants to the margins, onto untillable land.

Our mission cannot possibly be that of suppressing traditional ways of life in the name of lifting savages out of misery, squalor and godlessness, a condition, we have caused ourselves, the minute we have arrived here. We have in effect turned natives into slaves on their own land."

Stefan thought about this for a moment.

"This explains, why conflicts have been constantly erupting across this region.

Sentiments of the public back home, are influenced by the reports issued by administrators and missionaries.

Praxis and policies of the Schutztruppe and their Askari mercenaries, are diametrically opposed to what the nation has been told about this colony.

Military objectives are supported by the armaments industry at home, by planters, and by investors, but not necessarily by the emperor, who has sent us to study GEA.

This confusion, we have already found, is irreconcilable with the mission, to build a new commonwealth and to expand the wealth and space of our nation.

What our colonizers are doing right now, cannot be condoned and cannot justify the public investment, our nation is asked to make.

We are far from working for the common good of this community or for our fatherland.

Maria tapped Stefan with her pointing finger on his forehead.

"That is the reason why we were sent here. I think that merely writing a report of our findings is not going to effect the change we are assigned to propose. We have much to learn.

As a nation, we are acting just like the pirates in the waters off Somaliland.

And people here are responding exactly the way we responded, when we were being attacked.

I dread the day, when the type of weapons we used to defend ourselves, are in everyone's hands.

To accomplish our mission, we will have to acquire land and set up an experiment to demonstrate that a new approach can be found and is possible:

To build an integrated community based on acceptance of racial and religious differences and on granting everyone the right for religious expression.

Here, we must replace dominance with participation and embrace the vast variety of talent this population can offer, to contribute to a common culture and to share the benefit of that, which has begun to take root: Health care facilities, hospitals, schools, and vocational training. Improving infrastructure, such as roads, railways, steamship services and port facilities may ultimately be a bridge builder, especially, if it is done without murdering countless conscripts, losing them to fatal accidents, starvation, epidemics or torture and murder. In a study, done by a small-scale, integrated community, we might be able to build an example, of what is truly possible:

A federation of independent people, who enhance each other through collaboration, rather than suffering from murderous conflict and mutual oppression."

Helena did not seem convinced.

"Creating security for enterprises, such as planting on a large scale, mining gold, extracting diamonds or minerals by pointing guns in the face of Africa is not promising an enthusiastic response. We can expect the same response, we gave the pirates. Time will not be on our side. Christianization, that begins with robbery and dislocation, has a poor chance of leading people to accept our concept of God.

I believe, that protecting all groups of this diverse population with their traditions intact and simultaneously encouraging progress, building an economy, that enhances what has existed for millennia, seems to bear more promise to me. Opening new markets, sponsoring production of trade goods for export, growing traditional foods, and importing goods for consumption in GEA could be affecting such growth. Promoting arts, crafts, and trade, by offering education, literacy, and health care and most importantly, protecting human dignity and religious freedom, as well as protecting women, children, and elders, seem to be the key ingredients towards such an end.

Our presence here is changing everyone's life. It could be for the better, or it will be a disaster. The mood we felt, coming around the Mediterranean, was not encouraging.

I believe, we must find ways, to do this without further murder and robbery.

An educational community would be helpful in an expanded version of a facility like the estate, where we met and where this conversation began.

The question is, who will grant us permission to do so, when local customs do not provide the right to sell land to any individual? Will we have to step in as mediators?

Or do we continue to commit theft or bribery, justified by our good intentions?"

Maria, more hopeful now, said a resounding

" These are the questions we must ask.

Yes! Government by consensus, rather than by poorly informed decree, issued by persons, unfamiliar with local customs and blinded by the idea of copying German ways and forcing them on people, who are native only to Africa. Enforcing such decrees violently, using Askaris, armed with modern weaponry to suppress dissent, is a recipe for disaster.

Is Europe ready to mend its ways, are we not still desperately justifying the old ways?

Giving a place at the table to all members of this multifaceted community, making agreements enforceable by consent and providing a currency, capable of accommodating local and international trade and most importantly, guaranteeing freedom of religion, are elements we should develop and propose, as an alternative to the genocidal ways, everyone is copying from the playbook and business model of empire builders."

Stefan, practical as usual:

"First, I see us splitting up, to save time, to go on separate expeditions, to study different regions and activities we find, from here all the way to the lake region and up to the summit of Kilimanjaro, at the foot of which I suggest, we look for land, to establish our experimental community. We must do this by making agreements with the local population."

At the end of this day, I asked Stefan to remind the others again about his previous visit to East Africa during his surveying expedition and about his failed attempt to summit Mount Kilimanjaro.

Also, that he had already planned another summit bid on Mount Kilimanjaro and that his partners from Bavaria were already on their way.

We finished the night by bringing out our instruments to play music, sing, recite poetry and enjoy each other's company.

Stefan promised, that this time he was going to summit and ski on the snows of Kilimanjaro. Now we felt, that we had arrived and that our adventure could begin.

My desire to see Africa from the highest mountain on this Continent had grown, ever since it first appeared to us on the western horizon, standing on board of Stella Maris.

I announced, that I was joining the expedition to the summit. Stefan was thrilled.

He was disappointed that not all of us could join him.

Only he knew, how hard this trek would be, through uncharted terrain all the way up into thin air. It was settled, that I would go up with him. And that we all would help with preparation of food and medical supplies, which would give us extra time for planning our excursions, starting with a visit to the foothills of Kilimanjaro.

Here, everyone would fan out to see different parts of this enormously large area.

Stefan had arranged meetings with the representative of Chancellor Bernhard von Bulow, Bernhard Demburg, who had been sent to GEA, to work on reforms to the colonial administration, together with Governor Albrecht von Rechenberg.

A lot of information had begun streaming in on us. Stefan kept reminding us, that the area of GEA is three times the size of the existing German Empire.

It was hard to imagine.

Stefan reported:

"According to newspaper archives we saw, the population of this region is estimated at seventy-five million inhabitants, of whom one third are Muslims and the rest are Jews, Christians and Tribal groups practicing various rituals, customs, traditions based on their inherited beliefs.

There are eight hundred planters from Germany here in GEA, who employ seventy thousand African workers on their plantations, guarded by German Security officers, who command Askaris, African battle-hardened mercenaries, with no local ties.

Under cultivation are one hundred thousand acres in sisal, two hundred thousand acres in rubber plantations and two million coffee trees. There are Sisal processing plants and recently geologists opened gold mines in the western lake region.

Dar Es Salaam has one thousand German residents.

The Colony counts ten thousand Europeans, of which thirty-five hundred are German immigrants.

Helena gave her impressions from her day's discoveries:

"Work on schools offering primary and secondary education, as well as trade schools, hospitals and agricultural research facilities is considered exceptional, according to press-reports we read at the German Language newspaper. What we saw was truly impressive and confirmed these reports."

Chapter 53

The dark side

Wolf spoke in a low tone, almost whispering:

"There is a dark side, that is not on display. Only, when you talk to people privately and off the record, do you learn, that in the effort to build infrastructure, like the rail road from Dar Es Salaam to Morogoro, Tabora and Kigoma, employed draconian methods of recruitment, including forced labor.

I think this is cause for concern, if the colony were to become successful."

Both Stefan and Herbert reported, that railroads and towns were still being built with forced labor, at the cost of countless lives, caused by bad sanitation, food supply shortages, lack of potable water, topped by severe punishment for disobedience, all designed to frighten laborers into submission to brutal and arbitrary rule making.

Herbert was noticeably irritated and upset.

"It is a reign of terror. Lack of food supply was improved, by having wives and children of workers follow their mates, foraging for food, planting crops to feed their men. This was encouraged. Workers were less likely to run away, with wives and children nearby. Lack of rest for workers is responsible for illness and exhaustion. Some missions are said to have stepped in, providing comfort, shelter, and medical care for the sick and injured.

Stefan waved with his hand to calm him down:

"None of this can be verified at this moment. It is not our mission to look backwards, but to find a good starting point going forward. As the wisdom goes:

"There is no future in the past."

Herbert had to agree:

"People we have talked to so far, are living away from the hinterland. Little of what happens there, is officially known to the public at the coast. And nothing in Germany.

Helena, ignoring what Stefan had said:

"More openly discussed are revolts, that broke out under Gustav Adolf von Goetzen. His administration experienced resistance against expansion of plantations and land grab of the best arable land in the region. Von Goetzen and his Schutztruppe, together with their mercenaries, have practiced scorched earth warfare, starving people by destroying their crops and burning their villages.

The death of over three hundred thousand Africans could not be kept secret.

It had to be presented as a victory. News of revolts reached Europe, since neighboring Kenia, the British Crown Colony, and southern Africa had seen similar methods, used to achieve the same kind of "victory."

We cannot just brush this away. There is no way to white wash these events. I was told that the landscape was "littered with skulls and bones. "

Maria said with a sad and serious face:

"There are libraries full of books, I found even in Berlin, books that justify the treatment of colored and indiginous people on this planet.

Many explain genocide with biological or philosophical justifications.

Missionaries have used slave labor in their stations.

Neither Protestants nor Catholics approve of murder.

That was left to the security forces to do and to defend, as having been necessary to avoid bloodshed on settlers and missionaries.

Soldiers could always be blamed for brutality and overreach.

Missions raise money at home, for Christianizing and Elevating Savages, to be Saved and Civilized in the name of Jesus Christ and the holy mother Mary."

Stefan once again explained his prior visit to East Africa, as a member of a survey team. He now added to our task list his plan, to complete mapping of Mount Kilimanjaro. He had been given orders to climb Mount Kilimanjaro with help of surveyors, who had been part of the previous attempt. He was promised the support of a couple of dozen porters and cooks, who had agreed to go up as far as the cloud zone.

Now we prepared our meeting with representative Bernhard Demburg Stefan, in his capacity of captain, organized his team:

"I suggest we base our research excursions in Dodoma, establish headquarters there and work out our excursions with Demburg from there.

Remember, we decided, to direct our guides on how we will plan our expeditions. We must take charge of what we wish to look at and what questions we will ask.

Only then can we draw good conclusions.

Let no administrators direct a single one of our steps.

Bernhard Demburg has agreed that Dodoma is a good base for our explorations."

Stefan laid out maps he had obtained at the newspaper office.

Pointing to Dodoma, he began:

"Here are the areas that can be reached from Dodoma:

The Serengeti, a region still untouched, to the North, teaming with wildlife.

Mount Kilimanjaro to the North East, now ready to be surveyed.

Roads ray out from there, leading to Dar Es Salaam via Mnguni, Mbundu. Pandambili, Ukwamani, Mtumbatu, Magubike, Maguha, Magole, Morongoro, Chalinze, Mlandizi and Kibaha.

Old Ivory and slave trade routes from the Congo and from the lake region and the rift valley to harbors on the east coast run right through Dodoma."

He pulled up a detailed map and said:

"Here is the road to Arusha and Moshi and south east to Tanga.

At Tanga begins an old coastal trade route, that took caravans north to Mombasa in Kenya.

Herbert and I suggest we travel by train to Dodoma."

We were careful, to treat our meal time as personal time.

Evenings were kept free to be together to make music, sing, share ballads, read aloud, and recite poetry.

Wolf and Maria went to the library, to see, what was offered to the public.

Wolf was curious about the difference between what the public was told and what we were able to glean from our own observations and from conversations with people from different walks of life, people who live here, or near Dar Es Salaam.

We were able to gather information from traders in the old market alleys.

We had been taught well by Captain Paulus, to understand the world by observing its markets.

Paulus would say:

"The market place is where the truth is difficult to hide.

You learn, what talent and opportunity justify the risk of trading.

You notice, how personal relationships make it possible, to succeed against a myriad of obstacles."

We conducted work sessions to share our discoveries:

Stefan started:

"I was interested in harbor facilities and ports. There are about 3500 German nationals residing near the coast. Harbor facilities were improved with steam powered- and electric cranes, to load and offload ships, serving 350 freighters and over a thousand coastal trading vessels each year. Rails are laid to most warehouses and rail service is almost complete all the way up to the lake-region, where armed steamships have been assembled, expanding transport of troops and goods further into the interior. The new market hall is being completed for this year's State Fair of Dar Es Salaam, the temporary capital and seat of the GEA administration."

Helena added:

"Still existing, and spreading far into the distance, are the narrow alleys of the old market, with the inherent mayhem of vendors, byers, craft shops, tea rooms, small and large animals and goods from all over Africa, India, Asia and Arabia."

Wolf was happy to report on time spent with Maria.

"Maria and I had tea in a spice shop. The vendor, a descendant of Indian traders, introduced us to a gentleman, who was having Turkish coffee and a smoke from a very ornate waterpipe.

He is an attorney and money lender. He explained to us, that only a small number of contracts on business, credit and loans for building shops and houses, are done in writing. He said that letters of credit are based on personal referrals, rather than official documents.

"The economy here," he said, "is based on trust and traditional relationships, passed from generation to generation. Defaults are punished, by financial retaliation or by the taking of property." He explained.

We overheard a loud and excited conversation in a mixture of French, English and German next to us, about the revolt of the HeHe people under Chief Makawana, who fought against the expansion and expropriation of land by German planters with the help of African mercenaries, followed by the Maji Maji revolt of 1905.

"This has interrupted trade in the entire region and our caravans had to go underground, travel at night, or make very long detours, to avoid getting raided by either side of the conflict. War is bad."

One said, who wore a turban and a wide, sand colored caftan, with a fringed, red and white checkered shawl over his shoulders.

"There are no winners," said an old gentleman, whose face was wrinkled with the traces of a long, hard life. He did not say much, but when he spoke, everyone listened. To us, he seemed to be a sage. We wished, we could speak to him in private, but without personal introduction, that was not possible."

Stefan reported on his exploits:

"The region from the foot of Mount Kilimanjaro to Lake Victoria and the boundary between Tanganyika and Kenia have been surveyed in 1910.

Information about revolts was whispered to Herbert, Wolf, and me by Askaris during our visit to the German Garrison. These were older soldiers, who spoke some German. They only spoke, when they were sure, not to be overheard or seen, speaking to us, by members of the Schutztruppe.

Officers of the Schutztruppe proudly showed off their new automatic rapid-fire weapons like the Gatlin Gun, once they learned, that we had received training on this modern weaponry back home."

Wolf added, making himself sit up straight and tall:

"I was shown their arsenal of horse drawn cannon, once I mentioned, that I was a ballistics specialist with cavalry training."

Herbert added proudly:

"I was impressed with the Variety of ammunition for the cannons, that included a variety of explosive charges, that could cover terrain with deadly shrapnel, or take down a small house in one strike. We were showing interest, but gave no indication of what we thought about the use of this type of weaponry on the native population."

Wolf was more critical about his discoveries:

"Proudly, officers pointed out, that the use of modern rapid-fire weapons such as the Gatlin Gun, had made it possible to win battles, by causing countless casualties, decimating enemy forces and completing the clearing of land, still using scorched Earth against civilians, as had been ordered under the previous governor."

Stefan cautioned:

"We must be extremely careful, when we speak with military personnel.

They are jumpy. They have strewn a region twice the size of Germany with skeletons. They do not want to be found guilty of genocide."

Helena, Maria, and I visited health- and educational facilities. Schools are teaching German and Swahili as a common language, useful in a region, that has a population speaking dozens of different languages. Muslims, speaking Arabic, are better educated than Hindus. Jews are educating their children in their own schools in Hebrew.

Ethnic groups consider language classes essential for success in commerce and trade, that reaches around the world from here.

Helena was ready to bring the conversation to a positive place.

"The success of German Hospitals and medical services was made possible through collaboration of educators and religious missions. Leaders of different faiths are benefactors to those, who are lucky enough, or who have the courage to use European medical services, rather than relying on local customs or ritual healers.

Especially successful is the introduction of pre-natal care and -hygiene after assisting with the delivery of babies. For many mothers, it is ending the problem of multiple early infant deaths. Indian women are most open to using modern German medical services.

Herbert was looking for middle ground:

"Wolf and I wanted to find out about government practices. Very visible of course is the garrison of Dar Es Salaam. We learned that there are also garrisons at Moshi, Iringa and Mahenge.

German officers are outnumbered one to twenty by non-whites in the schutz truppe. The native soldiers are strictly organized by rank, from porters, to cooks, to the different stripes of military authority.

The garrisons have in their ranks almost twenty-five hundred Askari.

Askari are mercenaries with prior battle experience, for different masters, in different campaigns.

They are known for being brutal and merciless, sparing no civilians.

They are not tied to any social or tribal group.

With their help, land has been cleared of indiginous inhabitants to establish and expand plantations for cash crops:

One hundred thousand hectares of sisal with processing plants. Land for two hundred thousand rubber trees and countless coffee trees.

As we had already suspected, activities of the Schutz Truppe have disrupted traditional trade routes, like the street of caravans.

As far as Germany is informed, purpose of the colonizers' efforts, is to end and suppress slave trade."

Chapter 54

◆

The search for social justice

Wolf provided more details:

"In 1887 a revolt was put down in collaboration of British and German forces, called the Abushiri revolt. The mission to end slavery is popular in Germany.

When Germany finally learned about the scorched earth policy, governor von Goetzen was recalled and replaced in 1906 and governor von Rechenberg was appointed.

Von Rechenberg is jurist, diplomat, and politician, not a warrior.

I have heard rumors from sources at the newspaper, that von Rechenberg is being recalled and replaced by another hawkish governor, who is a soldier."

Stefan was as always focused on immediate action:

"I am preparing myself for the expedition to summit and survey Mt. Kilimanjaro. I am very happy that Joan has agreed to join us."

Maria and I share an interest in sustainable food production. At the library, we made the acquaintance of a biologist and botanist, who is concerned about the introduction of monoculture- farming. We came away with information about a possible location for a research station in the foothills of Mount Kilimanjaro 10 000 acres of hilly land, suitable for small scale experimentation.

Maria is trying to find any possible way this might be possible. She said:

"Wolf and I are adamant about using local knowledge and careful observation of people, plants, and animals to develop methods of agriculture and horticulture in harmony with society and nature."

Wolf expanded on this idea:

"People who have lived here since time immemorial are an important source of information and knowledge, that we can tap into, rather than forcing European ideas and methods of agricultural production on an area, in a climate, we know nothing about.

Bringing industrial methods of agriculture to Africa is enslaving the indiginous population right at their home at a time, when the world has begun to prohibit slavery."

During one session on farm- and general labor, we agreed that involuntary relocation of people as a 'resource for labor' is as old as there were empires, but has always devastated communities. It must therefore be seen as a crime against humanity.

Herbert expanded:

"Empires, even before Rome, have done the same thing. Progress was built on the backs of subordinated people, causing them to search for a savior from a lot, that was a consequence of eating from the apple of truth. They were told, that it was this sinful behavior, that had Adam and Eve expelled from paradise." He laughed.

Wolf agreed, bringing his point one more time:

"Supply of labor, wherever labor was needed to cultivate land or to build empire, was provided with the speed of shipping merchandise around the world, even by fleets of sailing vessels. It was for many decades the most profitable enterprise for owners of large sailing vessels, to buy, transport and sell slaves at auction for plantation labor.

Humans have become a commodity, that could be traded, permissible under Roman Law and adopted by all of Europe. The legality of this practice has not been challenged to this day. People are not ready to look this situation straight into the eye."

Herbert agreed and picked up on this thought:

"Chartered Corporations, with authority given to them by governments, kings and emperors maintain human resource departments, treating labor like other natural resources, required for production. They are authorized to hire, arm and train mercenaries for resource security and to smother dissent, calling those who object terrorists. Conquistadores did it in the Andes, in India it was done by the East India Corporation and the Hudson Bay Company did it in North America. All to protect the interests of their investors.

Helena summed it up:

"While we march under the banner of social justice, we have granted Corporations the right to call dissenters anarchists and to use lethal force to suppress them.

Africa is no exception. Anywhere you have plantations or large factories, you find this to be true. Alternatives are difficult to construct in theory.

We must find ways to build a commonwealth, rather than another slave colony."

Stefan, trying to bring the conversation to the present:

"The industrial revolution has almost failed, because factories can turn out goods faster than society can consume them. Industry, unable to match consumption to production, is running up surplus of manufactured goods, paying workers so little, that they have no money to buy the goods, they make.

Factories flood markets with goods, causing prices to plummet, threatening profits, and alienating investors. This is the vicious cycle of our new industrial age."

Herbert widened the view:

"This did not become visible right away in Europe, because a million miles of railroads have opened vast markets all over the known world. Saturation was reached, while industry was producing goods at a speed exceeding consumption, something, that never had been thought possible."

Helena, trying to reign in the discussion:

"Let us remember our mission: We are here, to observe German East Africa.

We are asked, to suggest policy changes, to make GEA successful. The need for military protection is making the colony unprofitable and unsustainable.

We must try not to upset government officials, who will be hosting us. They are hoping to convince us, not to look beyond the New Market Hall.

They would like us to say this: What they are doing, is as good as it gets, and that they deserve financial support and military protection, while replicating our old world in a new location, promising something, that only they can deliver."

Wolf cautioned us again:

"Remember, that according to our sources, governor von Rechenberg is being recalled and that his replacement is aligned with military security and the weapons industry, which in Germany, is gaining political influence right now."

Herbert shared this observation:

"Military and Navy are friends of Industry. They are the only part of modern society, that can consume everything and more, than what industry can put out.

It is the only sector of society, where oversupply is not an issue.

It is a form of welfare economy, not for profit, but for the benefit of investors, who are privatizing profits while socializing cost.

Winning or losing in their world view, depends on how fast they can push weapons into war theaters.

I remember Paulus saying, that the world is headed for a conflagration of unprecedented magnitude and that no one will be able to escape from the resulting tragedy."

Maria, showing how painful this prospect was to her, answered:

"I heard Paulus say, that he expects violent conflict to begin with fights over the remains of the Ottoman empire. He said:" Nationalist sentiments in the region are growing. Land grab will be next. Bulgaria will want to annex Macedonia. States will rise to regain their independence and Greece is afraid, that the first land grab their neighbors will attempt, is the region around Thessaloniki, a prize, that would be a feather in the cap of any new nation. Greece is still celebrating her recently found independence. There is no room for diplomacy, where dictators or nationalists rise to power."

Wolf recalled these conversations:

"Paulus insisted that colonialism has strapped a heavy yoke on the backs of the subjects of conquest. He said that this will be no different here in Africa. The future, he said, lies in finding a balance between old traditions and new possibilities."

Maria nodded:

"I think Paulus is right. The kettle has been boiling for at least a generation already, even though here, along the African coast, there is little visual evidence of uprisings. Battles take place further inland or are fought elsewhere in the world. Here we see polished boots and clean uniforms on parade grounds. We see non-white police, uniformed, and trained to keep order around markets, harbors, railroad stations and government buildings. All slick and clean."

This is how we wrestled with the world we were trying to observe and to understand.

After ten days at the coast, we were getting ready to depart by a train from Dar Es Salaam to Dodoma.

We enjoyed one last elaborate buffet meal with all the best German food, presented and served to impress us and to make us feel at home. They succeeded. We were impressed,

Chapter 55

Dar Es Salaam to Dodoma

Stefan, now again in his role as our captain, summarized our visit:

"We now have seen Dar Es Salaam, a city, that has been made into a show peace of GEA, since Germany took over from the German East Africa corporation.

They delivered masses of all things German:

Order, power, progress, infrastructure, railroads, steam cranes harbors, market places, and delicious food, just like this German breakfast.

We have heard rumors, that in the hinterland things are quite different, perhaps with the exception of some mission stations, where, just like here, crews consist of a mixture of volunteers and displaced, coerced natives, making armed protection unavoidable.

We found Askaris to be friendly and open, as soon as we were out of sight and earshot of officers, who are stone faced and appear stone hearted in their white, German style two story officers' quarters, next to the parade grounds. Housing for recruits resemble a prison camp with gates, guards, and barbed wire, where terror and fear is used to achieve and maintain order and obedience."

Herbert added:

"We learned in the market place, that the interference from the schutz-truppe and German immigrants, with the help from the authorities, has become a thorn in the thigh of established caravan traders.

In the opinion of several merchants, we talked to at the old market, this is neither good for Germany, nor for Africa. Also, not helpful, are pillaging, taxation, forced labor and scorched earth methods of expanding plantations. We must find ways to bring all these different people and their concerns to one table."

Helena looked worried.

"The sponsor of our assignment, Baron von Rechenberg, who was sent to make administrative reforms, is being recalled. I wonder what that will do to our project.

In Germany, his reports, as they appeared in the press, were labeled "propaganda" and missionaries here were silent about his findings, since existing security forces are also protecting their "acquired" holdings."

Wolf added in his stern voice:

"We better ignore all precedents, rumors, experience, and established policies.

We must open our minds and hearts to potential that exists here.

What we need, in my opinion, is a safe zone, that can be kept free from contamination by traditions, both at home and in the colony.

A Utopia, for long term study and experimentation. I do not see quick answers.

We are as unqualified as other observers were before us.

This colony requires time, integration, and assimilation in the Spirit of Africa.

Joan and Stefan can look at the Kilimanjaro foothills, to see if there is available land.

Land that is not being fought over by planters or claimed by corporate interests, who proclaim, that the mission for Germany is to raise native savages to the civilization of our of gun toting, cat wielding, earth scorching brutes, and investors looking for profit."

Helena, following wolfs train of thought:

"This Utopia would be demonstrating ways to halt the continuation of violent conflict and to prevent further loss of truth and humanity at the hands of persons holding modern weapons, rather than informed ideas."

Herbert agreed, looking at Stefan.

"We will talk more about this, when you return from Kilimanjaro and after we had a chance to look around some more ourselves."

Maria, now speaking to everyone;

"I Like to see the world move away from the misguided theory about the supremacy of races. What we have seen in the markets is the result of ingenuity, wisdom, and talent."

Wolf, having calmed down some, put the challenge into perspective:

"Scientists have been trying to sort out the logic of the superiority of the white Anglo- Saxon race, compared to other races. There are societies, who study these issues: The Ethnographical Society, the Anthropological Society, and the Sociological Society; most of them funded by people and entities some of whom believe, that the destiny of mankind is to end up, in the fate of species, with only two surviving races: The Aryan and the Semitic race. The rest of humanity, under this theory, is destined to disappear like snow in the sun. This is how imperialism is being justified as a Law of Nature."

Stefan, glancing into the distance:

"The sheer size of the African Continent, and we know it only from circumnavigating half of it, puts this attempt, to create a 'civilized' world, at a loss.

We have created a legacy of fear, mistrust, and violence. We pretended to be civilizers, who are motivated by a mission idea that is impossible to realize, because of the mental and physical distance to the known world.

The civilized have suffered trauma and disease at the civilizers' hands.

Wars waged, and loss of life inflicted, is being considered a legitimate means to an inescapable outcome. I think, that to go forward, we must create such a safe zone somewhere, as Maria and Wolf have suggested.

This amazing world deserves quiet, thoughtful, integrated study over some years, to include nature and the people of this great continent in all its manifestations.

This is not a short-term project but will take a lifetime commitment."

Helena, spreading her arms enthusiastically:

"I agree. The hope of a colony, organized by military and corporate principles, with ranks, that can never permit equality for ninety eight percent of the population, with ranks, that cannot change, and require the dehumanization of individuals, to become obedient extensions of modern weapons or corporate security and industrial production, is far from what I imagine possible or desirable.

I am afraid, that we are right now creating a systemic human rights violation, and Africa deserves better."

Helena looked at her watch.

"It is time for us to go to the train station. The porters have left a while ago to deliver our luggage. It will be a long journey on a train, that runs through the coastal mountains until we can see the plains and the expanse of the river basins of the hinterland."

We filed out into the blistering heat and humidity under a glaring midday sun.

Missing the sea breeze, familiar to us from our long ocean journey, caused us to turn around one last time, to take a longing look back over the Pacific.

We now turned towards an uncertain future, with more surprises and discoveries ahead than any of us could imagine.

Wolf had suggested, that we must open our minds and hearts to this magnificent world.

At the station, we checked our luggage, presented our papers, and boarded a special railroad car, reserved for government officials. It included a galley with a Stuart, who introduced himself as Johann. He explained, that he was here for our comfort, food and drink. We settled into a compartment for six, with overstuffed seats and windows on both sides.

Our railcar featured a lounge, a formal dining room, a kitchen, and an open-air platform. High gloss varnished Mahogany paneling was used throughout, lending a feeling of established European class and substance.

The car's bedrooms were equipped with queen size beds, large closets with overhead suitcase storage. Two large windows for enjoying the scenery made it tempting, to stay in bed and cuddle dreamily, while the world was rolling by.

Each bedroom had an attached toilet and shower room, that drained onto the tracks.

We met the porters and after deciding, who was to be in which room, Stefan showed them where to place our steamer trunks.

Johann and his team were attentive and prepared delicious, traditional German food.

The impression was, that we were enclosed in a German time capsule, rolling through a new and magical world.

Chapter 56

$\diamond$

Johann

The whistle blew and the train began moving steadily inland, towards Morogoro. It stopped at every station. We could see how railway access had encouraged the development of little trading posts.

Johann was helpful and knowledgeable, talking about the emergence of these settlements.

He explained:

"The country is very much in flux, with memories of recent uprisings still fresh.

The arrival of European and Indian traders, competing for market share and for property to build warehouses and shops for wholesale and retail trade is favoring Indian traders, even though the German administration treats them with the same contempt, as native Africans. The administration is favoring whites over colored people and endeavors to set aside land, to segregate markets. The difference is, that German merchants have no relationships with inland traders. That has stalled their efforts. Promoters back home do not know this. Using force of arms is problematic, the economy is doomed because it is disrupting trade routes, that have taken centuries to develop."

Wolf was surprised at such frank language. He said:

"I have noticed that racism is still very much a fact of life here. We have learned, that Indian nationals and their descendants have built their own schools and hospitals. They call themselves Khoja traders.

A merchant I spoke with at the Indian market at Dar Es Salaam, told me that despite German hostility, the Khoja population is continuing to grow.

Their resiliency is due to well established trade- and business networks and personal relationships."

Johann, nodding agreement:

"Germans have a lot to learn and must overcome arrogance and their sense of superiority. Indian merchants have established their position here a long time ago.

They grow their community over time: A new worker will be brought in by a sponsor.

He works for his benefactor for several years as an apprentice, establishing his credentials.

Eventually, he will have a reputation and earn trust in the business community.

Soon he can receive goods on credit and receive loans to establish his own store in the hinterland of Dar es Salaam, near a new railroad station. That is what I see."

Wolf, pleased and surprised with this account:

"Once established, he will probably return to the village in India, where he has family.

His elders will secure him a bride. These merchants have family, in-laws and religious communities, to fall back on. They are keen to educate their children."

Johann was glad to have someone who would listen to him. He remarked:

"They are being ignored by our administration. The German administrators are too fixated on the ways things are done in Germany.

Here, with traders from India, this will be repeated with friends and relatives. New apprentices arrive. Living quarters are built above stores, making housing and work efficient and affordable. They need no administrators from India to help them."

Helena, who was listening to this conversation showed agreement:

"Few people from other countries can compete with this tradition, because it is personal, not institutional. These merchants do not use the German commercial development bank. Everything is based on time-tested relationships.

Their credit is based upon trust, experience, and it is interest free. Everyone benefits from their trade. There are no hidden expenses."

Maria was glued to the landscape. Pointing outside she exclaimed:

"While we are enjoying this journey through this incredibly beautiful country, I would suggest, we spend time in the evenings preparing for our meetings with the administrators. This is not a fast train and we will have plenty of time to decide what we want them to show us. Look at this amazing world!"

Stefan, also interested in the landscape at this moment agreed, together with the rest of us and we began to take in the unforgettably beautiful landscape during daylight hours.

Once it was dark outside, Stefan assembled his team around the table.

He summarized his understanding, of what our team would do:

"Maria, you are interested in plant production, plant propagation, seed and food preservation. Also, you have been trained in, and understand prenatal healthcare and the education of children.

Joan, you are interested in food production, cooking, baking, vocational training and in the culinary arts.

Helena, you are interested in health administration and school development.

Wolf, you are interested in labor relations and social justice issues, science, religion, anthropology, and education.

Herbert, you are a weapons expert and -scientist, you relate to- and understand the schutz-truppe. They tell you things, once they see, that you are interested and understand the work they do, that they would not share with outsiders.

I am interested in all of it, once my survey expedition on the mountain is complete.

I am interested in possibilities for the acquisition of land, where we can develop experiments in agriculture, with a community, that embraces all parts of the population.

I visualize a large village, to realize the true potential of this colony, without murder or genocide, scorched earth, or land grab. I see a long enough table for all the stake holders present, to work on consensus-based decision making."

Looking at Helena, he continued:

"I suggest that you will continue to be our facilitator and that we ask Herbert to be our spokes-person with administrators."

Chapter 57

Dodoma

We explored more of our ideas about the next phase of our adventure.

Before we knew it, the gong sounded and dinner was served.

Herbert pointed out, what an engineering feat it was, to build a railroad through this hilly, rocky, swampy terrain, gaining altitude as we moved away from the coast.

Each of us found a quiet place, after the evening meal, to formulate ideas.

We knew that Governor von Rechenberg had received assessments about us from the department of colonial affairs in Berlin. Now we wanted to be sure to direct the steps of our expedition, by having a program ready to present to our contacts at Dodoma. We had a hunch, that it would not be as easy as people in Berlin had suggested.

The train journey had been long, but very pleasant. We began to realize, how vast this country is. We did our work in the evening, when we were not gazing at the breath-taking landscape. Stops at stations along the way made us compare the impact, railways had here, versus back home on development and commerce.

Johann was very knowledgeable and helpful.

We retreated to our sleeping quarters for little naps, the clackety clack of the rail carriages put us to sleep. Gentle curves along the way made the train rock back and forth. Walking inside the moving train reminded us of walking on the decks of Stella Maris.

The air inland was not as damp or as hot as near the coast. Dark blue skies displayed occasional thunderheads, sometimes backlit by the afternoon sun like giant lamps with silver linings. We saw every shade of green of vegetation, contrasted by gray and orange rock outcroppings and blue bodies of water, silver flowing rivers, azure lakes, and swamps, often flat like mirrors, indicating to us that there was not a breeze, other than the air moving along the train. We enjoyed standing on the open platform at the end of the last car.

Looking back along the rails, we had an unobstructed view of the world we were about to explore. The scale of space was enormous, making German landscapes seem like a toy display in comparison. Or as Wolf said: "Mama, someone shrank my friends."

We were too excited to sleep, when it got dark at the end of the day. Johann kept us supplied with tea, cookies, and little snacks; luxuries unknown on our trains back home.

We were arriving in Africa and could not help but to compare everything we heard, saw, smelled, and touched with the world we had left behind only a few months ago.

The train whistle sounded, followed by the conductor's announcement: "Dodoma! Dodoma."

Grinding brakes on steel wheels, echoed by the walls of the railroad station roused us from sleep, that had finally found us.

The fragrance of tropical plants and wafting steam from the locomotive reached our senses, as we were escorted off the train by our hosts, who had arranged transport for our luggage to a hotel near the station.

So far, we had been enveloped in a German time capsule, everything displayed here was meant to remind the traveler, that Germany was being recreated by the colonizers of German East Africa.

Police officers, dressed in immaculate white uniforms, donning white helmets, shouldering muskets and sabers, made us feel safe, but surprised us by the fact, that they were dark colored Askaris from Dodoma's Garrison, reminding us:

"You have arrived at the home of law and order."

After checking into our quarters, we washed up, selected light clothing for the tropical heat, that met our faces and were led to the dining room, where a buffet style breakfast was laid out. Servers were eager to hear what we had selected to eat or drink.

The manager of the hotel announced, that the kaiser's delegation would be arriving at noon, when a banquet style meal was to be presented as an opener for our mission to German East Afrika.

We noticed, that our colonizers knew how to live a good life.

We were impressed. We looked forward to having representative Bernhard Demburg introduce himself in his function as the assistant to governor von Rechenberg.

After breakfast, we had a couple of hours' time to put our paperwork in order and to

check out the vehicles we had been promised for our excursions. A large Daimler for road travel. For off road, safari style travel in the back country, there was an all-terrain capable tractor vehicle. These items had been shipped ahead of our departure from Germany. We found them parked outside our hotel.

We reminded Helena, that she was our facilitator and Herbert our spokesperson and administrator.

Stefan, myself, and his team were preparing to leave shortly towards the foothills of

Mount Kilimanjaro.

Men were going to inspect the garrison and Women were planning to visit missions, both Lutheran and Catholic.

We were ready to go to work.

Chapter 58

Was this Africa?

German punctuality. Set your watch. At Noon sharp, the governor's delegation arrived. A separate dining room was reserved for this festive occasion.

Tables were set in a circle, with traditional German place settings, white porcelain plates stacked in the order that food was being served, with polished silverware in the order that they were to be used from the outside in, spoons at the head of plates from soup to dessert, everything according to official protocol with silver rings holding white napkins. Candles in festive looking silver candle holders, being ceremoniously lit, once we had taken our seats behind two-sided name cards, held in little sterling silver stands. Curtains were drawn to dim the glare of the noon day sun. We were impressed.

Was this Africa?

Small bouquets of mixed wild flowers in front of each setting, added a festive flair.

We were met by the delegation with introductions and handshakes followed by the invitation to take our seats. Formal but friendly, maybe a little stiff for our taste, but a good starting point in traditional German etiquette, leading to a soft transition to wild Africa, as it was still being discovered and colonized by people, whose vision was clearly to replicate Germany.

We took our seats.

Helena began by thanking our hosts for this wonderful reception and for the arrangements, that had been made for us ever since we landed at Dar Es Salaam.

"We were pleased with the ten days you gave us, to acclimate and to explore the many impressive achievements this administration has accomplished at our port of entry."

She suggested, that we go around the table, to make our introductions, handing each delegate a folder that contained our curricula vitae together with our preliminary schedule of inspections and investigations.

Bernhard Demburg spoke for his team:

"I am pleased to welcome you to German East Africa.

I trust you had a pleasant journey and found our arrangements at Dar Es Salaam to your liking. I am here, to offer you my personal support for a successful visit.

Let us remember the order, given by Governor Von Rechenberg and Chancellor von Buelow. To do everything in our power to make your mission successful and to be helpful to you, so that you can report your findings and make suggestions to our administration for the development of policies, that can meet the expectations of our emperor and our nation.

Out meeting was cordial and the introductions were made in the spirit we intended.

Together with Maria, Helena, Stefan, Herbert, and Wolf, we began to lay the foundation for creating Utopia in German East Africa.

We worked on developing action plans, designed to become a model for the future of this region. The more we learned about German East Africa, the more we discovered, that we had a principal conflict with the idea of purchasing land in a region where land was not used by the population as a commodity, that can be purchased or sold.

So far, land had simply been assigned and license for use granted to planters, municipal planners, railroad engineers and port facility officials at rivers, lakes, and at the seashore. To purchase land would have meant, to disown the population, give title to their property to a licensee and to make a buyer believe, that they had legally obtained the full bundle of rights to go with this land, just like in Germany, and to use its inhabitants, as they see fit, like German counties of the nineteenth century.

Soon we were informed, that Governor Baron von Rechenberg was being recalled and that a new, more hawkish Governor was sent to replace him and his entire team.

We decided to begin executing our mission as ordered.

While Stefan and I, together with his survey team and our expedition crew of porters moved up into the clouds of Mount Kilimanjaro, the inspections in the region took place as planned. I told you about the Kilimanjaro experience earlier. Now, the expedition to the Summit of Mount Kilimanjaro was successful.

Stefan's glacier accident caused him to have an extended stay at the hospital of Dodoma, where necessary operations on his toes were performed. I never left this side. We held meetings by Stefan's bedside and later in our quarters, to keep him in our conversation and to lift his spirits.

It turned out, not to our surprise, that the new governor was not interested in having our report and findings published, but he did not interfere with our orders, since they had come from the emperor himself. Stefan was not ready to give up, he told us his thoughts:

"The industrial revolution has almost failed, because factories can turn out goods faster than people can consume them. The inability to match consumption to production, has run up a surplus of goods into the marketplace. The pay workers receive for their services is so low, that there is not enough money in their hands to buy the goods they produce. The market is flooded with manufactured items, causing prices to plummet.

Over-supply is threatening the existence of this new economy. A successful colony might add millions of new consumers to the table, if we find a way to give them buying power."

Herbert widened the view:

"This did not become visible right away in Europe, because a million miles of railroads opened vast new markets. The saturation point was reached later. Industry can produce goods at a speed never thought possible. Now the hope is, that the colony is not just a resource for raw materials, but will become a market for export."

Helena, always the moderator, said:

"Remember our mission. We were asked to suggest policy changes to make GEA successful. The need for military protection has made the colony unprofitable to investors. Our government officials appear to be hostile to changing their thinking.

I think, that instead of as an investment, we must think of this region as an opportunity to add a new district to the German Reich, that has unique features, that do not require to be suppressed, but can be integrated together with her population, with all their talents and unique abilities. Key is, to use the innate ability to learn and to reach them by respecting them, not by arming them and making them defenders of their own old ways. We must educate their youth, not radicalize them. The present administrators are hoping to convince us, not to look beyond the new market hall or the many improvements they have made during the past twenty years. What they believe in, is their ability to create another Germany in a region four times the size of our home land.

They would like us to say, that our colony has become as good as colonies can get.

They want us to testify, that the colony deserves full financial support, to replicate the old world in a new setting.

We say: You would have to replace populations to achieve that. That is what we cannot recommend, because the country was already populated by millions of souls, when our colonizers have first arrived here."

Herbert, as meticulous as always in his background investigation:

"Military and Navy are sent to serve the colony, while by design, they are friends of Industry. They can consume everything our industry can put out. It is the only sector of the economy, where oversupply is not an issue. Winning or losing battles, depends on how fast one can push weapons into war theaters. I remember Captain Paulus saying, that the world is headed for a conflagration of unprecedented magnitude and that no one will be exempt from the tragedy of such a disaster."

Maria, always concerned about the fate of families:

"I heard Paulus say, that he expects a violent conflict to begin with a fight over the remains of the Ottoman empire.

He said:" Nationalist sentiments in the region bordering the Adriatic are growing. Bulgaria will want to grab Macedonia. Small states rise to independence and Greece is afraid, that the first land grab, someone will attempt, is the region around Thessaloniki, a prize that would be a feather in the cap of any newly restored nation. All of this is being acted out, as though there were no families with children or elders. When the love of power is greater than the love of people, the future is lost. Greece is finally celebrating her independence as a kingdom.

There is no room for diplomacy, where dictators or nationalists get a hold on power."

Wolf, passionate and compassionate about the way workers are treated, added:

"Paulus insists, that colonialism has strapped a heavy yoke on the backs of the subjects of their conquests. People were owners, before they were discovered and conquered. They did not make claims of ownership, but worked together as a community.

He said, that this is no different here in Africa. The future, he insisted, lies in finding a balance between old traditions and new possibilities."

Maria, Wolf's companion as well as his soulmate, said:

"I think Paulus is right. The kettle has been boiling for several generations, even though here, along the African coast, there is little evidence of uprisings and battles.

Here, at first glance, we see nothing but polished boots and clean uniforms on parade grounds. We even see non-white police, uniformed, armed, and trained, to keep order. Looks very integrated to every newcomer."

Herbert, always looking for what works and what does not, had this to say:

"We learned, that interference with trade by the schutz-truppe and German immigrants, with the help of colonial authorities, has become a thorn in the thigh of caravan-traders. In my opinion, this is neither good for Germany nor for Africa. It is our task, to find ways to make things better for both."

Wolf, always embracing the concerns of the most vulnerable and the need for their protection, said:

"It is imperative for us to ignore all precedent, claims of experience and established policies. We must open our minds and hearts to the potential that exists here.

The human capital that is fragile, but resilient in its integration with nature. That is not something we can transplant from Germany to Africa. It is already here.

What we should consider in my opinion, is the creation of the safe zone, we talked about, but making the entire region a zone that must be kept free from contamination by traditions and regulations, both from home in Europe and from colonial Africa.

A commonwealth, capable of sustaining justice and peace for all humans, with biological diversity and economic resiliency. That is my vision.

Helena was now all fire and flames:

"Being able to prevent violent conflict and loss of life, using truth and humanity, committed, and perpetuated by persons holding no weapons, but informed ideas and open hearts. That would be my vision."

Herbert, the keeper of order:

"Let's talk more about this, when Joan and Stefan return from Kilimanjaro and after we had a chance to take a good look around down here."Maria, our human rights protector:

"I Like to see the world move away from the theory about the supremacy of races.

What we have seen in the markets is the result of human relationships, ingenuity, wisdom, and talent."

Wolf, visibly aggravated by ideas coming from the scientific community, needed to get this out of his system:

"Scientists have been trying to explain the logic of the supremacy of white skinned races

over races with darker skin pigmentation. There are societies who study these issues:

The Ethnographical society, the Anthropological society and the Sociological society; funded by people, who believe, that the destiny of mankind is to end up, like the fate they claim to be inevitable for all species in nature, with two surviving races: The Aryan and the Semitic race. Consequently, along this line of thinking, we will use this excuse to dominate nature and humans and destroy our planet in the process they have designed as a self-fulfilling prophesy. Theirs is a new, materialistic religion, that does not create, but ends the existence of our planet. The rest of humanity, under this theory, is destined to disappear, like snow under the sun. This is how imperialists are justifying their actions: They keep making the same claim: "We are obeying and helping to conclude an inevitable Law of Nature."

I think that we must counter this thinking with a renewal of both spiritual and physical sciences to include evolution of life and integration of all living creatures. We must end the subordination of life on this planet to the greed and ignorance of a few and the detriment of life itself."

Wolf finally exhaled deeply and Maria stepped up to him, took him into her arms and held him for a long time.

Chapter 59

Stefan returns from the snow

We talked late into the night. When the last word was spoken, we had made the decision and agreed, that we could not purchase property for a pilot project, but had to convince people, who live in the area we found to be suitable, to enter into a contract with us, to establish a collaborative community, a province, that will act as a model for Africans retaining influence and for granting indiginous people the right, to participate and to benefit from the merger of traditional life with contributions, Germany can make, as a supplier of education, medical services, infrastructure, and trade facilitation.

That decision altered the way we looked for suitable land.

We also resolved, that we would keep our intentions private for now.

This would give us more time and opportunity, to explore seemingly in accord with the new administration, and to maintain the continuation of their support.

When we brought Stefan off the mountain and placed him in the care of doctors at Dodoma hospital, we asked for permission to have him placed in one of the larger private rooms so we could hold meetings in his presence.

Ever since Stefan knew that we were expecting a baby, he was very attentive to me. I was amazed how he was able to endure pain in his feet, while refusing to take pain medications.

He asked to hear everyone's report, after sharing his experience on Kili, as we called the mountain affectionately. I will give you a summary of what our teammates found, while we were exploring Mount Kilimanjaro.

Maria took the all-terrain vehicle and together with a botanist and an interpreter, they went to visit plantations and did some exploring of 'undeveloped' land. She was very upset about the condition Africans were living in once they had been relocated by planters. She met people who were still living their traditional lifestyle in their original setting. She found a vast array of skills, building musical instruments, hunting gear like spears, bows and arrows and tools to carve, paint, weave and tanning animal skins and collecting feathers for adornment and ceremonial objects. She saw how this way of life was quickly disappearing with changes brought on by colonization and civilization.

Together with wolf she spent several days on an excursion to a river-crossing where the annual wildebeest migration takes place. The guides made camp high up on a riverbank. From here they had an unobstructed view on this epic event. Countless wildebeest were on the move and every conceivable predator was ready to jump on the opportunity to cull the weak and the young, gathering along the banks of the river and in the water: Crocodiles, ready to pull pray under water, lions taking advantage of the distraction caused by the flood of bodies pressing each other into a narrow passage that was shallow enough to provide a foothold. Included in this feast were clouds of mosquitoes. Hyenas were making sudden, very fast attacks and tried to steal even from lions as they worked on carrying their kill to safety, providing for their pride. There was a cloud of dust on either side of the river along the migration path. Vultures were sitting in nearby trees awaiting scraps of a kill to be left by lions fighting off competitors.

Wolf would sit quietly by the fire in the evening and write poetry for children, which he shared with Maria. They described the life of animals in the wild with a sense of humor that was endearing to Maria. These poems would later be a delight for their children and their children's friends.

Maria confided in me the heightened passion the two experienced, with the discovery of this amazing nature event and the presence of each other in an atmosphere of life at its most breathtaking and daring manifestation. Life of Nature in a play of forces far exceeding the wildest imagination in their power and beauty. Both outside the tent and inside, in the privacy of long delayed passion and a hunger for closeness, that could not be stopped any more than to halt the flood or wildebeest crossing a river.

Wolf reported on his visits to 'wild lands' as he called them. He was shocked about the expanse of the steppes and waterways in them. He witnessed a wildebeest migration and saw every kind of large animals. Giraffes, zebras, gazelles, lions, rhinos, water buffalo and crocodiles. He witnessed the arrival of countless flamingoes in a shallow lake. He was in awe about free roaming wildlife and his guides even lead him to a site where an elephant was giving birth while the herd was standing guard and fiercely fending off lions and hyenas. He saw species he knew only from zoos. He felt like a child in the face of such amazing nature. He followed Masai herders, who impressed him with their skill of working their herds in harmony with free roaming wildlife. He visited settlements and villages that were still more or less untouched by colonizers.

Helena returned from her visits to hospitals, schools, vocational training facilities and missions. She was impressed with the dedication, people brought dedicating their time and energy to these institutions even though some of them are still on the 'white man's mission to elevate the brutes.' Helena also mentioned, that she found there to be a disconnect of opinions from reality and that she was afraid that this might do more harm than good, because the arrogance of Europeans makes it impossible for them to see the real potential of the indigenous population of this place.

Herbert visited administration offices and workshops, where locomotives and ships were being assembled from parts, imported from Europe. He saw the garrison and was taken to conflict zones, where security forces were active. He developed a sense about what the combination of good intentions and military intrusion into this world had done to the indiginous population. He concluded, that there could be no future for a colony with this approach. He also reported on rumors, that suggested, that Germany and other countries were building up their armed forces towards war in every branch of the military and navy and that it was impossible to predict, what the official trigger would be.

"I am observing that this arms race will not prevent, but ignite war." Herbert said.

"China has a new government; the emperor Pu Yi was deposed and Sun Yat-sen is calling for elections. The Ching or Manchu dynasty has ended.

The Balkans are at a boiling point, the Balkan alliance is at war with the Turks and massive dislocation of civilians, fleeing from war theaters has taken place."

Herbert found that officers of the schutz-truppe were well informed about what was happening on the African Continent and around the world.

"Military intelligence," he said, "has an internal communications network, that is not burdened by political-, economic- or administrative mandates.

It operates separately from the official public news stream.

They are a separate fraternity of career soldiers, who enjoy their isolation from the Reich. This gives them a chance to experiment with different and new methods of warfare. Officers I talked to, seem to be constantly looking for opportunities to engage in conflict and to experiment with new methods of combat and people control, rather than seeing their task in providing security and preventing armed conflict. "There is no future in peace," I heard them say." A bitter burst of laughter followed.

Wolf and Maria had been waiting for a chance, to tell us about their expedition into the Rift Valley. Maria told me her story, after she had examined me and my pregnancy and the women in our party were sure, that my prenatal care was in good order.

Maria began with her arms spread out wide, like a cormorant on a rock, drying her wings.

"Wolf and I were preparing a journey into an area of the rift valley, known as Hadza-land or Wahadzabe, as it was called in Swahili. The promise- and our interest was, that no one knew anything about the inhabitants of this area: The Hadza tribe.

It started with a conversation Wolf had at the Dodoma Garrison with one of the German officers. I was hoping for a chance to explore some of this region, just with Wolf. I knew, that something had captured his attention and imagination.

Wolf was secretive about what he was working on. Finally, he told me about an acquaintance, he had made at the Garrison of Dodoma, while Herbert was off to inspect armories. Wolf met a young officer named Hans-Georg Lemke. Officer Lemke was here in his third year. He could hear Lemke's Stuttgart accent and Lemke recognized his to be also from Stuttgart. This discovery prompted Lemke, to invite Wolf to his quarters. Officer Lemke spoke about his education. He mentioned attending the Dillman Gymnasium in Stuttgart, the same technical and science high school, Wolf graduated from. This opened a flood of memories and created instant rapport between them.

Lemke told him about the reason, he had signed on with the schutz-truppe. He said:

"I was obsessed with the quest, to find out, what happened to my older brother Konrad- Friedrich. I owed this answer to my heartbroken parents and to my large family back home. Being here, would give me a chance, to search for my brother, who had gone missing. He had not returned from a solo expedition into the rift valley, several years earlier. He was known to be an experienced naturalist, who always did his research by himself, claiming, that the secret to his success as a researcher was being able to make himself invisible in the bush."

Chapter 60

Hadza

I began making inquiries with guides and traders in the region. I finally heard rumors about a German explorer, who had 'gone native.' I followed this trail.

I knew that Konrad Friedrich would only be found, if he wanted to be found.

I visited a group of Massai herders on the Serengeti plateau, who told me about a conflict with cattle thieves, who inhabited a region below the edge of the Plateau, at lake Eyassi. They told me, that these people do not understand, that you cannot simply hunt cattle on the Serengeti. The Massai reported to me, that they had come to an understanding with these hunters and that they had gone on their way peacefully.

I hired the man, who had done these negotiations, to guide me to this tribe.

He told me about a white man who was living among the Hudza.

This Massai herder was a talented, stealthy observer and tracker of wildlife.

He helped me find the camp of about thirty people, that included this white man.

He used his past acquaintance with this group, to gain access and to give word to the elders of this family and the white man.

My Massai guide told me:

"You can only find them with their permission. Otherwise, they will simply disappear."

It took a few days of negotiations. I needed to learn about what gifts to present, as they do not accumulate things, other than what they use, wear, or can carry. They do not build permanent houses, but live as their ancestors have lived since the beginning of time. They move their camps with the seasons, connecting to other families only to find a mate to live with. These families are not dominated by a leader, but live in mutual support of one another, peacefully from childhood to the end of life, avoiding confrontation, by giving each other room.

When we finally had permission to approach them. I saw a tall, slender white man in the middle of his family and two lighter colored children. There was no question in my mind: This is my brother.

After introductions and handing over my presents, I was invited to approach.

The minute he saw me, he greeted me in German.

"Gruess Gott", the tall European man said, as if we had just met at a street corner in Stuttgart, pretending it was nothing.

Knowing, that it was really him, came from the unmistakable sound of his voice and his unforgettable smile. We held out our hands, inviting an embrace, looking into each other's eyes. I was flooding with tears of joy.

A long conversation followed: News about the family back in Germany, my promise to search and to find him was prompted by our parent's and our sibling's heartbreak, of not knowing what had happened to him. I mentioned the good fortune of finding this Massai guide, who raised my hope to be allowed to visit him in his new life.

I was invited to share food with his group, and after filling his water container, my Massai guide said good-by and returned to the plateau of the Serengeti.

Now I was introduced to my brother's family and his young children and learned about his story:

Mt brother told me:

"I found myself in a parched steppe during the dry season, tracing and observing a cheetah mother and her seven cubs. After a couple of very hot days, I had run out of water. I became dehydrated. The water hole was contested by ferocious wildlife. Animals in need of a drink or hungry for a kill, approached. I did not intend to become a meal. I soon lost my balance and had to sit down.

Then I fainted.

When I woke up, I learned, that a group of men, who were hunting at that same water hole, found me while stalking their pray. They found me unconscious. They took me to their camp, where one of the younger women took me into her care.

She knew how to treat dehydration, giving me tiny amounts of salt from a nearby natron lake. She slowly nursed me back to health.

The harmony, quiet dignity, and thoughtful collaboration I observed and the ever more special attention I received from this young woman, made me fall in love with her.

I was soon in love with her entire family, the gentle way, they took care of each other in this four-generation family. I felt so comfortable with these people, was so in love with the girl and she with me, that I decided it was impossible for me to ever leave her.

The young woman asked me to stay. In her family's eyes, we were already married.

I learned the Hazda language. The tribe liked the fact, that I was very quiet and, like them, could make myself invisible in the bush. The young woman stayed with me and we became a family, had a son and a daughter and are now part of her extended family.

I learned to hunt the way they do. I learned about the tubers and berries the women gather and how to make a smokeless fire, as that was a man's job. They hunt only what they need to eat and to share. A favorite is wild honey they find in bee hives, they access both from inside and outside of the giant baobab trees.

Life with my new family was very similar to the way I had been doing my research in the wild by myself, without much luggage or noisy habits, with the stealth of a native hunter, the way they teach their children. Boys naturally learn how to make bows and arrows, shaping and smoothing them even with their teeth. They hunt with bows and arrows or use spears, they carry. Girls learn to find tubers with pointy sticks, to gather berries and to prepare meals, after the men start cooking fires and hand them the meat, they have carried home, to share.

My gift to the men was a small hatchet, with a very sharp blade on one side and a hammer opposite, together with a grinding stone to hone the blade or to make a spark to start a fire. With it, they can drive stakes into the ground or hammer pegs into the baobab trees as steps, both on the inside and on the outside, to gather slabs of honey comb to bring back to camp everything they had not eaten themselves on the way.

Hunting success is the measure, by which a man of the Hadza tribe is regarded. It goes along with the success of raising healthy children.

The Hadza have an egalitarian social order.

Coming from a strict patriarchal family in Wuerttemberg, I felt, that the conflict avoidance practiced here, was a good companion to their division of labor and their acquisition of skills from child's play to crafting bows and arrows, together with their generosity of sharing and caring for the youngest to the elders of the tribe.

There is time for jewelry making with beads and feather adornments on clothing, worn both by men and women.

I learned that they move their camp from time to time to new locations, following the seasons.

This contributes to their very good health. Hygiene is practiced with the same attention and care as the preparation of meals.

Immediate consumption of berries and seeds, right in the bush, where they are found and harvested, makes storage and preservation unnecessary.

Meat is the prized food For the Hadza.

Hides are tanned and used as blankets and ground cover and in the rainy season, to help keep water out of their improvised twig and straw huts.

Poisoned arrowheads are used for large game, like wildebeest or giraffes.

The men track the pray over long distances, until they are overcome by the poison.

Poisoned arrowheads are carefully wrapped, to avoid injuries and to keep the poisonous paste from drying out.

Contact with surrounding tribes is being avoided whenever possible and the fact, that the families do not own objects of value other than what they use daily and no permanent housing is ever built, makes it easy to avoid confrontations.

They respond to threats from intruding humans by disappearing in the landscape, until the threat is no longer there.

Slave hunters told me, that these poison arrows are more deadly to an intruder, trying to steal a person, than to a lion, elephant, or rhinoceros. Hadza elders told me:

"They have no chance to shoot us with their rifles, because we shoot them like baboons, before they see us."

That story makes them laugh endlessly, just as laughter and expressions of joy are very much part of their language and communication.

They sing and tell stories. They have no alcoholic beverages or stimulants, other than what is contained in leaves or tubers."

To be able to contact my brother occasionally, I made a green flag, which I can mount high up in a baobab tree, which he can see from a distance.

This is done on rare occasions only. I do not interfere with his life, never bring strangers with me without their permission. I approach him usually by himself.

This has made it possible for us to stay in touch. Our family in Germany now receives my regular reports."

Maria spoke with her dark eyes on the horizon:

"This visit was such an occasion. It was carefully orchestrated, with gifts and announcements, made ahead of time, permission requested and permission received with the assurance, that no uninvited persons would show up and that our transport vehicle would be left at a designated location, not to interfere with his tribe's way of life.

We rose a little after midnight and, having an experienced driver in Hans-Georg, we felt well guided.

We arrived at first light at our destination on a rise overlooking the rift valley, with bodies of water in front of us, the rift valley crossing the land diagonally and the Serengeti Plateau high up to our left.

In the distance to the south-east behind us, was Mount Kilimanjaro showing the silhouette of its twin peaks above a ring of white clouds. To the north-east, we saw Mount Kenia. Two enormous mountains, drawing a sharp silhouette against the eastern sky, that was now in its pre-dusk glow, reminiscent of our mornings at sea.

Almost all the rainbow colors became visible one after the other, too beautiful for words to describe.

All this was laid out before us as one feature emerged after another, all with the prospect of meeting one of the oldest tribes on Planet Earth, still alive, in their original habitat, in their un-altered way of life since time immemorial.

The first light from the East, revealed the silhouette of eastern Mountains and the purple and blue shading of the foothills and undulations of the landscape. The sun's rays soon began touching the edge of the Serengeti plateau, making it glow red and gold and revealing tans, greens and browns of rock ledges, lush vegetation and white mist in depressions and above lakes and riverbeds. Reflections on mirror flat waters were picking up the changing colors of the magnificent light of an East African morning overlooking Hadza-land.

This land had not changed hands in thousands of years.

Wolf was holding me. Both of us were trying not to breathe. Just to listen. Once I had to breathe again, I tried to find words, to describe how I felt, when I heard Wolf who stood behind me, whisper into my ear:

"This is God's creation and we were sent here to witness it."

"Utopia" is all I could say and I turned around and gave my Wolf the most passionate, deep kiss of my life. When he caught his breath again, he whispered:

"You have one gift, God has given to you: You can find Him everywhere you are.

The rest of us need temples, churches, altars, rituals, and meditation.

I want to be close to you. You shine the light of the divine onto those around you and you do not even know it."

With very little breath I answered:

"For me, God's existence is visible and tangible during moments like this.

I feel that here God's creation has been left undisturbed, since the twilight of time.

I am in shock and I feel blessed, that we were able to find it.

I feel, that we were sent here, to witness it and to feel it.

God can see into our hearts and reassure himself, that his creation is good."

"Let us eat the breakfast, Hans-Georg has prepared for us and then follow him, to meet his brother and the Hadza family he is living with." Whispered Wolf.

Like a magician, our guide had created a classical German breakfast without a smoky fire to give us away. We enjoyed this meal ad much as any meal we had ever eaten. We left our belongings in the vehicle and carried only water and our gifts when we headed down a narrow game trail. In the distance we could see the 'flagged' baobab tree and underneath it we saw a Giraffe, browsing on leaves in its reach. Without speaking another word, we approached the tree, watched the Giraffe move off, followed by a pride of five lions with a male, who's enormous mane was reflecting the early sun's rays, like a halo.

A slender, tall figure emerged from a hole in the wide stem of the baobab tree, holding several pieces of honey comb in his hands, passing a small piece to each of us in greeting, giving his younger brother a wide smile.

"Hallo Konrad," said Hans-Georg. Meet Maria and Wolf."

"Welcome to my world," he answered, beaming at the three of us, pleased to see that his request had been honored, not to bring porters with gear and stuff which would have caused his family to disappear and to stay in hiding.

"Let me take you to my tribe" he said, handing each of us a large chunk of honey comb.

"Give this to our elders when we arrive," he said.

We followed him along a narrow game trail, each of us carrying a satchel with our gifts.

It was quiet, except for the chirping of birds in nearby bushes and our breathing. We took in the aroma of ripening berries and the scent of damp earth and dew-covered vegetation. Konrad Friedrich spoke very softly.

"Our autumn camp is near where we find ripe berries to pick and eat and to bring home for our little children, our elders and those watching over them.

We do not know how old anyone is, since our language has only four numbers. Anything beyond four is described as many. I estimate, that the oldest person in our camp is nearly eighty years old. I can only measure time by stories about encounters with outside tribes like herders, slave hunters or planters, attempting to intrude here.

Shhh." He said: "Be quiet. Here they are."

We stepped into a clearing, where almost thirty people from toddlers to elders appeared to be in various stages of getting ready for this day's activities. Their curious eyes followed us to where our host's family was gathered, awaiting us.

After handing them our gifts and the honey combs, I noticed that the person, he introduced as his wife, was not able to get on her feet in greeting, but appeared to be in distress.

I gently pushed Konrad-Friedrich out of the way and said to him:

" Let me. I am a trained nurse and birthing assistant; I suspect your wife is in labor and she seems to be in serious trouble. Ask her to let me help, and send Hans-Georg back to the vehicle, to fetch my medical bag. In it are supplies I need for birthing assistance."

Our host told me, that his wife had consented, for me to go ahead and to examine her. A circle of elders, mothers and young children had formed around us.

"Find me a pile of dry grass and some hides to make a bed, fetch plenty of water, I told Konrad Friedrich. Hans-Georg, hurry and please bring me also towels and wash cloths. Time is of the essence. Be quick about it.

Konrad Friedrich sent his children to bring what I had asked for.

I looked at the patient and found, what looked like a stalled delivery of twins.

With a bar of soap, I had with me, and some water, I lathered up my hands and forearms and the examination began.

It turned out not to be twins, but a breached position, and I went to work on lubricating the fully dilated birth canal, with my narrow hand reaching in, to correct the baby's position and to make sure, there was no wrap of the naval chord around the infant's neck.

I instructed Konrad Friedrich to stay at the mother's head, to calm her and to breathe with her, out to relax, in to prepare for a push and out to relax again.

First Panting sounds in the distance, then footsteps, then my medical bag was in my hands.

It had arrived just in time, for the final push and for the first breath of a new member of the Hadza tribe.

There was a hushed sound of approval coming from the bystanders. I was holding a baby boy by his feet, head down and, after clearing his airway with my pointing finger, I slapped his behind. The impact made him gasp for air and he gave me a nice first cry.

The bystanders laughed, clapped, and did a little dance of joy.

I wiped the newborn down, swaddled him in a large towel and laid him on his exhausted mother's breast. There was a clucking sound from the bystanders, which I took for relief and applause.

Konrad Friedrich was shedding tears of joy.

The mother held her newborn with one arm and did not want to let go of my hand, which she had grasped as I placed the baby on her chest. The mother needed water.

The women wetted her lips, then held her up, so she could sip some water from a gourd they had brought for her.

Happiness was all around. Happy were the sounds as Konrad told us that we had been accepted in the circle of this family and his tribe.

I still had to finish the other tasks of after-birth and disinfection, tying up and bandaging the navel and swaddling the infant in another fresh, soft towel, which caused more sounds of approval from the women of the tribe.

I felt like praying and giving thanks for the two lives saved. Baby boy was now happily suckling his first meal.

Wolf was there, and in his very serious way, he placed two fingers on the baby's forehead, describing three crosses.

"In the name of the Father, the Son and the Holy Spirit: Welcome to our world."

He whispered." I heard him say these words. It was an act of his faith to bless the newborn.

We spent the following days immersed in the Hadza way of life. I went with the women and girls into the berries, Wolf accompanied young hunters at night for shooting small pray with bows and arrows and going after Gazelles with older hunters, using bows shooting poisoned arrows, as they approached a watering hole. During rest periods, boys and men were quietly whittling on sticks for arrows and bows, shaping bows with their teeth to be thinner at the ends and thicker in the middle, straightening arrows and splicing-in arrow heads, made from glazed, volcanic rocks, that they artfully chip to be very sharp and slender with grooves, to hold the sinew-ties for perfect alignment.

We saw boys practicing shooting targets, using bows and arrows they had crafted themselves. They would try to shoot baboons at night from the branches of trees. They eat them. Hunters took us to the lake, where they spear eels, fish, and waterfowl. The secret is patience and stealth, and very well-honed skills.

The Hadza live with one wife, Konrad Friedrich told me. Divorce is very rare, often initiated by the wife, if she remains childless. Young men often visit one of the other family camps to look for a mate. There are more than forty in the region in groups of about 30 members each, according to Konrad-Friedrich. A young couple will stay together, if they like each other, they are considered married. There is no gender related hierarchy. Hadza are an egalitarian society with adoration of the stars and no religion.

The men make fire, craft staffs for digging tubers, make axes and hammers out of stone for cutting open bee hives and for hammering pegs into trees to climb up, to reach the hives.

Men and boys do most of the hunting, while women prepare meals and dig for various tubers and gather seeds and berries, make clothing, give birth, and rear the young.

Boys work together in small groups practicing hunting skills and weapon-making. Many hunting trips are solitary events, especially for larger animals, which will be shot with poisoned arrows and later tracked, butchered, and transported in pieces back to camp, where they are roasted over the open fire and eaten right away.

Conflicts are rare and usually avoided or ended by the parties simply walking away from confrontations.

Hadza are friendly and disputes are caused sometimes by mating choices or when intruders from outside try to squeeze onto Hadza land. They confront only, if they cannot disappear in time. Rare are disputes with herders, when Hadza mistakenly hunt domesticated livestock, belonging to the Massai, thinking it was wild game.

We had asked Hans-Georg- and were given ten days, to spend with the Hadza.

Even without language, we were able to forge lasting friendships and tears flowed all around when we finally had to leave."

Joan sat back in her overstuffed armchair and closed her eyes. She was missing her Maria and her Stefan and her life, acutely. Tears welled up in her eyes. She was private with her emotions, a battle-hardened member of a traumatized generation. She closed her eyes again.

Gottfried looked at her. Thinking she had fallen asleep, he got up as quietly as he could, left the room to take a walk down to the dock, where he sat on a bench, looking at a sailing dinghy. In the little changing enclosure, he saw life vests and sails.

He thought of asking permission to use this boat, imagining all the scenes on the waters of the North Sea, the Atlantic, the Mediterranean, the Arabian sea, and the Indian Ocean.

He took a long walk along the shore. Deep in thought, gazing across the lake to the mountains standing erect, a mass of majestic limestone rock pushed high into the sky by forces from the African plate pressing Europe, buckling tectonic plates.

"This is our planet," he mused. "Earth does not need humans to survive. Humans need the planet in pristine condition and we must understand, that we are neither entitled to dominate one another, nor to dominate nature. We are just a speck of dust, granted permission to live on her for a short while.

We have not come far, despite two world wars and countless armed conflagrations in different parts of our planet. We have become more proficient at taking lives than at saving life. We are back in an arms race now, that has dominated the psyche of nations in a standoff of East against West.

We have a long way to go, before we can agree to grant each other the unalienable right to life that is our birthright and to also grant nature a legal right to life, with meaningful protections against uncontrolled use of poisons, pretending that the world population cannot be fed, unless all insects and pathogens are chemically destroyed."

These were Gottfried's thoughts while sitting by the lake.

Chapter 61

◆

To Life

The next time Joan invited Gottfried to the terrace for tea, the clear, dry, warm, early September had come over the land, days praised for their beauty and the rich aroma of late summer blossoms and ripening fruit and berries.

Joan told Gottfried, that she was coming to the end of her story. She began:

"As soon as Stefan was able to walk again, we took him to our headquarters, where I took care of him, with Maria and Helena assisting between excursions.

We had our own conference room next to our sleeping quarters.

I think he was enjoying being fussed over by me, Maria and Helena.

Stefan was our captain. He gathered information from our ventures into the territory.

Wolf and Herbert came to see him regularly and reported to him.

The air was now getting hot and damp, even at this distance from the coast.

Servants at the hospital had taken turns, fanning Stefan with palm branches, to keep him comfortable.

Our meetings now took place during cooler evening hours.

Stefan kept track of us. He was our communicator and acted as a link to the colonial administration.

I could see that he was beginning to worry about the future of our mission and I urged him on to make his concerns the topic of a meeting.

Together with Helena, Maria, Wolf and Herbert, Stefan, and myself, we agreed on an agenda for our next meeting:

Reality of the colony in comparison to the narrative of the administration to the nation.

Replacement of Baron von Rechenberg with a new governor.

Consequences for our project, and our conclusions about our findings.

State of the world in our view, after our journey.

State of the world as seen by military personnel.

These meetings were held in private, without colonial administrators present.

We set up our conference room the way we had done at the Waldeck Estate.

Helena was facilitator, Herbert the keeper of records and Maria, Wolf, Stefan, and I were completing the circle around the table.

Stefan looked and sounded very serious, when he started the meeting:

"We have not just arrived here in Africa. We have traveled the world, approaching Africa. We have observed the way things work in different places. It was not just a journey on- and around different continents, it was a journey that made us straddle time, touch on different eras of human existence and observations of ongoing change.

Changes in ourselves, for us to observe- and changes in the world around us, that we were being challenged, to understand.

We now must find our place in this world. We had the benefit of being led by a very unusual guide, Captain Paulus. He called to our attention things mankind has in common and things that divide us.

Our investigation did not just start there on board of Stella Maris. It began, when we met at Waldeck. When we decided to form a pilot group after sailing together. We did not just observe, what we saw with our own eyes, from different points of view. We also looked inside of ourselves and shared with each other, what we saw and felt in our hearts, once trust was established between us.

Life has prepared lessons for us. We must open our minds to the reality of things and to potential that life has laid out for us in plain sight.

Experience is our common entry gate. Together, we have encountered the entire range from saving life to taking life."

Helena looked at each of us and after thinking where to start, she began:

"We were sent to observe conditions in the colony of German East Africa.

We were asked to report and to make recommendations to the Governor Baron von Rechenberg and to his administrative team. A report that was intended to be shared with the colonial administration in Berlin and with the public at home.

Everything has changed: Von Rechenberg has been recalled and replacement has been sent, together with a new administrative team.

We have been informed, that our input is no longer needed.

We also learned, that no report will be sent to Berlin.

Rumors we have heard about an arms race, have been confirmed.

I was informed, that the nation's armed forces and navy are being increased in response to threats, the beginning of which we became aware of after we had left Morocco and were approaching Genoa. With this, I will hand the conversation back to Stefan."

Stefan got up from his chair. Leaning with the palms of both hands on the table, he began:

"I have completed one item on the list of things to do, while we are here:

The survey of Kilimanjaro is now complete. The results have been sent to Europe.

It did not all go as planned. I came back with frostbite to my toes. I needed surgery. This will make me ineligible for military service, so Joan and I will return to an estate my family owns at a lake at the foot of the Bavarian Alps.

Joan and I are expecting a child. Joan will be my nurse and I am very happy to tell you, that she will grace our kitchen and bakery with the culinary arts she has learned from the best chefs at Waldeck, on Stella Maris and from her own observations, wherever we sat down before a plate."

Stefan lowered himself onto his chair.

Helena pointed at Wolf and turned the floor over to him.

Wolf was unable to sit any longer. He stood up and slowly walked around the entire table, giving each of us one of his piercing glances straight into the eyes as though he wanted to reach deep into our soul. He began:

" Being part of a group of citizens on this assignment, has been an honor for me. Personally, it is a privilege to belong to such an outstanding team of observers and investigators. Have we accomplished out mission? I think the answer is yes.

We have achieved to raise more questions than what we found in answers.

What made this journey significant for me is the fact, that Maria and I fell in love with each other and that we have discovered, that we are soul mates, best friends, and partners for life.

The world will have to come to terms with changes, that are beginning to overwhelm the best minds, with conflicts of interest in economic activities, that are threatening our very connection to the foundation of our faith and the purpose of creation as we understand it. I will mention just one:

Monoculture may threaten human life on this planet. It may be efficient and economical, but ecologically it is a life-threatening disaster.

Why?

Monoculture is an industry that starts by removing people from the best land.

Then it commits habitat destruction.

There is no example for this type of efficiency in nature.

Monoculture creates deficiencies, the consequences of which are yet unknown.

It does not bode well for humans and for the resiliency of life on our planet

We have lost our ability to distinguish right from wrong, truth from lies and power from justice.

We have begun to delegate responsibility to a higher authority. Beyond humans.

We do this in houses of prayer, halls of government and boardrooms of corporations.

The order of our military with its division in ranks, from foot soldier to four-star general, is a demonstration of how we have seen no reason, to question the total subordination of ninety nine out of a hundred soldiers under one percent of individuals.

Thereby denying people their human rights and the dignity, that comes from the creator as a birthright.

Industry and business organizations both have achieved the subordination of humans, which defies the laws of nature, where only diversity can create resiliency.

I see a total breakdown of humanity in a conflict, that will soon draw in every existing individual.

Decisions, based upon false premises can achieve no good outcomes.

I believe, mankind will have to find ways to reconcile spirituality with reality in the way nature has demonstrated. Our claim of supremacy over creation and each other is threatening our very existence, because we deny being part of nature.

We cannot be accountable, while we act as though we were the creator himself."

Wolf sat down hard and tried to regain his breath. His eyes were piercing like lightning.

After he had regained his breath, he said more softly into total silence:

"There will be no peace on Earth, unless we get over ourselves and become part of creation, as we found to be true in the way some indiginous people have lived in this part of Africa since the dawn of time."

Helena now turned the word back over to Stefan.

He rose like Wolf and spoke, holding on to the back of his chair with both hands:

"I do not have much to add to Wolf's remarks. I have taken notes throughout this journey and my focus will be on the status of the world at this moment.

Our project was terminated, because it served a different mission, than "what these times require," as staff members of the new governor have phrased it.

We have observed and gathered information from our sources, that major powers around the world have begun to enter an arms race. It has not been made public.

Early on, there were negotiations about the building of war-ships.

Britain wanted Germany to limit the size of its fleet of battleships, in trade for the right to colonial expansion in other parts of Afrika.

The outcome? We have just finished building the first submarines. We promised to limit our fleet on top of the water, so we went under water. That is military strategic logic.

Traveling to Africa, we became aware of several wars, going on in the Mediterranean and in the Balkan states. The region felt like a powder keg about to explode.

The public at home seems unaware of the magnitude of this threat, even though the size of the standing armed forces has been substantially increased and taxes have been raised, to pay for military expansion.

The switch of governors and generals here in Africa, stands symbolic and has verified our observations. I am afraid, this trend is unstoppable. I like to use a metaphor for the explosion of industry, with consequences, few are prepared to face, or to understand:

The state is like the Titanic.

Politicians decide the destination, government steers it, people do all the tasks, so everyone is fed, has water, beds to sleep in and the ship has fuel and people to operate the boilers, that make the steam, that drives the propellers, that move the ship.

Countless people are on board: The citizens.

The ship of State, like the Titanic, is deemed unsinkable.

The Press said:

"ICEBERG SINKS TITANIC."

That is what the public is told.

Every mariner, who has followed these investigations, and the opinion of fellow mariners, knows, that the iceberg story, that prevails on the minds of the public, is pure fabrication and the truth is hidden from view.

This was to be the inaugural journey for a ship like no other and the prestige to complete construction of it on time, to begin the maiden voyage as scheduled, was at stake. The rumor, as it passes from ship to ship around the world is, that there was a fire in a coal storage compartment, still burning, as the ship began its Atlantic Crossing "on time," as scheduled.

Titanic, the unsinkable, left port, with an ongoing fire on board, inside one of the coal storage compartments, that would soon damage the integrity of the hull and sink the ship, even without a collision with an iceberg.

Iceberg warnings had been sent and received, and the speed of the ship was increased, despite the warnings. Time of arrival as scheduled, was worth the risk to owners and operators of the unsinkable ship.

The "ship of state" of the German East Africa corporation, went under, for multiple reasons. Taking property from the inhabitants started the fire.

The replacement of this organization by a protectorate, followed by colonial annexation, with nationally funded armed protection for investments, was supposed to make the colony a new, unsinkable ship. Reforms are like the warnings about icebergs. Our mission is part of the warning system. As it turns out, we are being dismissed. No one is willing to put out the fire. The sinking ship, being on fire, lead to increasing the speed of development, rather than putting out the fire, to keep it afloat.

We have seen, that the idea of a big, unsinkable 'ship of state,' a colony, as an expansion of our homeland, is conceived, and pursued, based on false premises, which is the fire in the belly of the hull, that will cause it to sink, no matter what the leadership decides. Countless lives will be lost in the disaster of its sinking, just like the Titanic.

We have observed the ways, different countries and city states have made different choices with vastly varying results. Trading with nations and communities around the world has proven to be profitable and beneficial to the people trading with- and residing in- these economically independent states, cities, and countries.

During my many hours, spent next to captain Paulus at the helm of Stella Maris,

I learned, that countries exist, that did not look to send armies to colonize the world, but concentrated instead on creating facilities for shipping at home and trading posts in various parts of the world.

Genoa, Venice, Hamburg, and Bremerhaven, which are city States, have developed and favored trade for the benefit of all participants.

To me, the best example is what the Dutch royal family has decided to do:

They built dams and canals in Amsterdam and Rotterdam, giving their country some of the best harbors in the world for trade, which has attracted scholars, artists, craftsmen, shipbuilders, and visitors.

Holland was persistently one of the most liberal countries on Earth.

My conclusion must therefore be, that colonization, as it is being practiced now, is doomed to fail, because it comes with a fire burning inside, that cannot be extinguished by force of arms. It was built on the false premise, that there are still parts of the world that are available, or uninhabited, just because they are not known to us, or because they have not been surveyed and registered by conquerors or annexed to other people's motherlands.

To me, the best assessment is, to trade with-, instead of raiding places, to cultivate relationships, rather than to dominate or trade in humans, turning the entire world in front of our own door into privately owned merchandise, including its inhabitants.

We can see our mission as a success, because we now understand this fact, even though we have no control over the fate of the world at this moment in time.

Personally, I think that we are entering an era of survival of the smartest, not the fittest."

Helena turned the floor over to Herbert.

He too stood up. He said:

"Our mission has been recalled.

Our assignment has been cancelled.

I say, let us celebrate potential and communication. Let us find our individual areas of engagement and thank our good fortune, that we did not sink the ship on which we first met.

We might be able, in the future, to support those, who are willing to embrace human rights and the right of nature herself. Because those are the champions of hope for mankind.

As Stefan has experienced on Mount Kilimanjaro, inside the ice-cold crevasse:

Dying is easy. It feels sweet, warm, and fuzzy until the light simply turns off.

Living is hard. It requires the willingness to fight, to endure, to persist and to love passionately. The reward is, when someone, - and nature love us back.

The inalienable right to life is worth spreading, and fighting for. It is the hard way.

It will be a hard and treacherous road to travel.

All human activity will need to be measured to one standard: To do no harm to life.

I raise my glass of water and I say:

To life!"

We all took our water goblets and gave cheers to life and to the success if our mission.

In the days following this meeting, we were busy collecting and packing our belongings, securing our notes and papers for our return to Europe.

The instability of the eastern Mediterranean prompted a redirection of steamers, going between Dar Es Salaam and Bremen, to round south Africa, refuel in Nigeria, stop at the Canary Islands, make landfall in Lisboa in Portugal, before returning to Bordeaux, Amsterdam and finally to Bremerhaven.

Chapter 62

$\Diamond$

Home

We were welcomed home in floods of happy tears by our families.

We spent a couple of days in Bremen with them, before reporting to the department of foreign and colonial affairs at Belin for debriefing.

The mood in the country was that of high alert and anticipation, which we were trying to ignore as best we could.

We had the task ahead of ourselves, to process a vast amount of information, observations, and experience, we had accumulated under the guidance and care of our captain Paulus."

Joan was happy about having shared so much of her youth with someone who would carry the ideas of her pilot group into the future.

She prepared a feast, that showed to Gottfried that she had not forgotten the way Paulus would celebrate endings and beginnings.

Gottfried told Joan that he was inspired by all that he had learned from her story.

He told her that he had made a resolution for his future life.

He explained:

"Other people can play music as well as I do and we will always recognize the fact, that music is proof of a common language, that crosses borders and can inspire collaboration, to create harmony and sound, to touch everyone's heart.

What I think I must do, is to find out, if it is not possible to feed mankind without poisoning the planet or each other in the process.

I want to study farming without poison, in harmony with Nature, find the best teachers and coaches to show me how it is done.

I will qualify myself to be a master organic farmer and to share my knowledge with future decision makers, who presently believe, that milk comes from a bottle or a cardboard box, that bread comes from a plastic wrapper and that meat comes from a butcher.

I think, that only if decision makers have a good understanding of how life works, or even fall in love with life, are they qualified, to write policy and regulations about industry, land use, nutrition, and sustainable agriculture.

I will show them, that they must integrate Humans into nature and grant humans and nature both a full bundle of rights and protection, as dignity and sustainability of life demands."

Joan took Gottfried into a long embrace and said:

"Maria would be proud of you. You are continuing the path, she was unable to finish, because she was overwhelmed by the tragedy of her time. She gave all of herself to her community and to her family, until there was nothing left to give.

She was a beacon of light, a compass, and an anchor to everyone who knew

her and who had the good fortune to be inspired by her humanity.

She was a Mensch."

When Joan said good bye to Gottfried at the end of his season at the spa, she kissed him on both cheeks and said: "You have my blessing, my child."

EPILOGUE

The world was overrun by the horrors of World War One. Wolf and Herbert served in the same artillery unit, that was sent towards France against the allied forces, where they experienced the famous unauthorized Christmas Cease Fire, during which soldiers from both sides left their trenches, to sing Christmas carols together and to exchange good wishes in the name of the new born holy Child, his mother Mary, and his father Joseph.

The following day, the bombardment commenced and Wolf witnessed an explosion, that took the life of his great friend Herbert with a direct hit. Helena fell ill and died of a broken heart.

Wolf decided then, that if he survived the war, he would become a founding member and priest in a Christian church, that was neither Protestant nor Catholic, but would take an entirely new approach to Christianity and spirituality. He and his wife Maria took a parish ministry in this new Christian community, raised a family and were adored and considered to be saints by their community. Maria died of pneumonia, right after the Nazis came to power. Wolf survived attacks by National Socialists, who closed his church, burnt his books in the village square and threatened to come for his family, if he were to tell anyone about the raid on his parish sanctuary.

Stefan and Joan retreated to a family estate, where Gottfried found Joan, who had been Stefan's life support and where they raised a beautiful family.

Stefan became a mountaineering and skiing instructor for the Alpine society.

To Joan and Stefan, family was everything, even though the hardships of two world wars left them traumatized and brokenhearted.

They never gave up on their quest for justice and their fight for a livable planet.

Gottfried, inspired by Joan's passion for a livable planet and nature's rights, changed careers, completed a farming and agriculture education, became a master farmer, conducted week long seminars on organic farms for farming students and students from universities, together with apprentices, journeymen. They relieved the host families of all chores for the week so they could attend lectures. Harvested ingredients, cooked and served all the meals built new friendships and grew a new understanding about the possibility of creating a sustainable world. These seminars were a life changing experience for all the participants.

Gottfried never gave up on his vision that eventually, mankind will agree on making the choice to live in harmony with life and nature and with quality of life that affords people the choice to stay with their own families and communities, rather than to become refugees of wars, climate collapse or economic disasters.

Realizing that to die by their own weapons or be killed by a poisoned, depleted, unlivable planet with toxic water is a very poor business model in which money is deemed speech in a hijacked democracy. Money will make very poor nutrition, even if it has zero calories.

REACTIONARY FORCES

by Christian Vogel:

"Reactionary forces have succeeded to dominate society with special interests.

This despite the fact, that only the free individual can lead mankind into the future.

The individual human is the fundamental force, bearing the potential of a free society.

It is this knowledge, that stood in complete contradiction to the epochal phenomena of rapid industrialization during the latter half of the nineteenth Century.

Progressive- and reactionary forces of our social organism became engaged in a tug of war, creating a sphere of compromise, heating and chilling sentiment and passion, an intellectual schizophrenia that has failed to shed light into the future.

Society, half progressive, half regressive, gave one another the honor of mutual recognition and respect in their joint inquest only to succeed in the murder of individual freedom and liberty, giving birth to a monster:

An instrument of violent power, inhumanely structured, that subordinates and forces the very substance of humanity into its service, to transform it into a phantom in its own image.

We now have a society, unwilling and unable to reach up to achieve the true human potential as the beginning and end of all social existence and endeavor, to be cultivated and validated.

Instead, society is trapped in pursuit of monetary gain, legal manipulation, and certain death through unfettered technology, industrialization, and automation.

Life and the essence of community are solely the human being, that understands itself in its core, through freedom and the recognition of self.

That is why empowerment against the endangerment of humanity rests with the inner enhancement and nurturing of the individual.

It requires to develop the power of new ears for new music and new organs for our human existence.

We must take up this armor and never put it down."

Christian Vogel was a merchant marine cadet who traveled around the world only to find physical abuse, suffered at the hands of fellow sailors and a system of total dehumanizing subordination of the individual under a strict hierarchy of rank, which forced him to jump ship twice, once in Japan, where he was returned to the same ship, now subject to life threatening abuse, to finally save his own life by jumping into shark infested waters of the Indian Ocean at Durban, South Africa, where he ended up being jailed. From there he was finally returned to Europe on a retired steamer with the help of the German foreign service. His epic journey gives him authority to make comments about the purpose of the human existence.

He is Gottfried's younger brother.

www.ingramcontent.com/pod-product-compliance
Lightning Source LLC
Chambersburg PA
CBHW051130120626
46547CB00012B/737